AF445424

AMERICAN DREAMS

The story of the

CYPRUS FULBRIGHT COMMISSION

AMERICAN DREAMS
  The Story of the Cyprus Fulbright Commission

Keith E. Peterson © 2024

Armida Books is a founding member of the Cyprus Publishers Association, member of the Independent Publishers Guild (UK), and a member of the Independent Book Publishers Association (USA)
www.armidabooks.com | **Great Literature. One Book At A Time**

Cover | Photo by Joshua Hoehne on Unsplash
Cover design by Armida Books | Cover symbolically captures the impact of the Cyprus Fulbright Commission's work over 52 years. The rows of mortar boards represent the thousands of Cypriots who were educated in America because of the Commission's resources and efforts.

Images | List of credits/sources on page 290

Summary | "American Dreams: The Story of the Cyprus Fulbright Commission," tells the story of the 52-year run of an independent bicommunal educational institution founded in the hopes that it would help keep Cyprus within the circle of liberal democracies post-independence.

Through the lens of the Commission's work, it is also a history of American involvement in the island, where strategic interests, Cold War politics, and the idealistic vision of Senator J. William Fulbright came together to form one of the most unique such Commissions in the world.

It is also, in its own way, a history of the island and its people over the past 60-plus years and their efforts to reconcile their very different visions of how Greek and Turkish Cypriots might move forward together into the future.

The Cyprus Fulbright Commission was unique because of its bicommunal nature, where Greek and Turkish Cypriots worked and benefitted together; because a conversation between a Senator and an Ambassador led to a multi-million-dollar scholarship program that made the Commission – on a per capita basis – one of the largest in the world; and because the Commission poured millions of dollars into the quest for peace through a program of conflict resolution training.

The conflict resolution work did not always find a positive reception. The Commission was accused of "brainwashing" a population of Cypriots or committing treasonous acts in trying to teach Greek and Turkish Cypriots to find common ground.

A trio of Greek Cypriot Executive Directors and a group of committed Greek, Turkish, and American Board members kept the Commission focused on its mission. Their perseverance reflected Senator Fulbright's belief that education is a slow moving but powerful force.

Author Keith Peterson, a former diplomat, and Commission Board Chairman, draws on his extensive experience in Cyprus to capture the enduring legacy of the Fulbright Commission's commitment to educational exchange and diplomacy.

[1. EDUCATION / Reference 2. EDUCATION / Organizations & Institutions 3. EDUCATION / Social Aspects 4. EDUCATION / History 5. HISTORY / United States / 20th Century 6. HISTORY / World / Modern 7. REFERENCE / Research]

1st edition: April 2024

ISBN-13 (paperback) | 978-9925-601-47-9

AMERICAN DREAMS

The story of the

CYPRUS FULBRIGHT COMMISSION

KEITH E. PETERSON

ARMIDA

For Collin

&

For Renos, Daniel and Anna

Table of Contents

AUTHOR'S NOTE

In April 1989, I was informed that my position as Assistant Cultural Affairs Officer-Center Director in Tunis, Tunisia was to be eliminated by across-the-board budget cuts imposed by the U.S. Congress under what was known as Gramm-Rudman-Hollings. My boss at the American Embassy stuck his head in my office and said simply: "You have to leave so you need to find a job."

Within weeks, that job materialized as a posting as the Assistant Public Affairs Officer at the U.S. Embassy in Nicosia, Cyprus. In short order, I arrived in the divided capital of that Mediterranean nation. Within nine months, rolling budget cuts would have me on the move again, but my relationship with Cyprus was far from over.

During my nine-month posting in 1989-90 I became involved with a Fulbright scholarship program that was large in scope and represented one of the only functioning bicommunal institutions on the island. I had the privilege of sitting on the Board and selection panels for both Fulbright and Cyprus American Scholarship Program (CASP) grants and was deeply impressed by the quality of the Greek Cypriot and Turkish Cypriot students and their strong desire to study in the United States.

Twenty-one years later, I returned to Cyprus as the Public Affairs Officer and, as such, the Chairman of the Board of that Fulbright Commission. The Commission's program was still disproportionately large given the population of Cyprus, but the eventual elimination of the Economic Support Funds from the U.S. Agency for International Development (USAID) that had sustained the program and made it so unique was already ordained.

So, over the next three years, it was my duty to orchestrate the dismantlement of the Commission, piece by piece, and leave in place a small program that at this writing brings a handful of American scholars and students to Cyprus, but no longer grants undergraduate or graduate scholarships to Cypriots.

The Binational Commission that began in January 1962 quietly closed its doors in 2014, shortly after my departure from Cyprus – my last overseas posting in the Foreign Service over 29 years.

Prior to my departure, I sat with former staff members and agreed that someone needed to write a history of the Cyprus Fulbright Commission. With my retirement looming, I decided that I should be that person. I sometimes think of it as my penance. It was a great honor to serve my country as a Foreign Service Officer, but I am not alone in recognizing that my country, and more specifically my government, can – at times – be penny wise and pound foolish.

As the story of the Commission will illustrate, the scholarship programs administered by the Cyprus Fulbright Commission and other Commissions throughout the world largely paid for themselves in ways that were both tangible and intangible.

The quality of a nation and its people can often be measured by its generosity. Let there be no mistake, the tens of millions of dollars given to Cyprus over five decades for the education of its people was an incredibly generous gift, one that was not always appreciated as such by the Cypriots. Yet, America most certainly profited, too, and so presiding over the shuttering of the Commission was a painful and frustrating exercise.

As with any human institution, the story of the Commission is a story of people – people who kept the Commission going, sometimes under difficult circumstances; people whose vision made the Commission so unique; and people who took advantage of the resources provided to do extraordinary things. I trust those who read this account of the Commission's history will come to understand just how very special it was and how much it will be missed.

PREFACE

In September 1945, the junior Democratic Senator from the State of Arkansas rose in the well of the United States Senate and proposed a modest bill entitled simply "A bill to amend the Surplus Property Act of 1944 to designate the Department of State as the disposal agency for surplus property outside the United States, its Territories and possessions, and for other purposes."[1]

Senator J. William Fulbright, elected to the Senate the previous year and the former president of the University of Arkansas, explained in his brief remarks that he sought to create a program through which the credits obtained from the sale of the substantial surplus military goods abroad at the end of World War II would be used for the promotion of international good will through the exchange of students and scholars in the fields of education, culture and science.[2]

The President of the Senate said "without objection" and the bill was referred to committee. In May 1946, President Harry Truman signed the bill and a program of international scholarly exchange was born that would forever take the name of its creator.

Fulbright – like so many others – had been appalled by the carnage of World War II and, with the Cold War gathering force, he believed Americans could no longer shelter behind two oceans and had to engage with the world if there was to be long-term peace.

Nearly 6,000 miles to the east, on the island of Cyprus, the question of long-term peace was stirring. It was a British colony and an important military outpost in the Eastern Mediterranean, but its population of Greek Cypriots, Turkish Cypriots, Armenians, Maronites and Latins was thinking about its long-term future and the anti-colonial movement that eventually dissolved the British Empire would soon wash over Cyprus.

Over the decades that followed, the idea of scholarly exchange as a tool to promote peaceful relations would find one of its most astonishing incarnations in Cyprus with the founding, in 1962, of a Fulbright Commission of modest means and goals. That it became one of the largest, most elaborate, and unique Fulbright programs in the world is the subject of this book.

***

J. William Fulbright came from an upper middle class family in Fayetteville, Arkansas. He attended the University of Arkansas, won a Rhodes scholarship to Oxford, and ultimately obtained a law degree from George Washington University. After teaching law for several years at the University of Arkansas, he became, in 1939, the youngest university president in the country. Two years later, political opponents forced him from that position.

At that point, history would intervene. The bombing of Pearl Harbor plunged the nation into war and Fulbright found himself at a crossroads. He wanted to enlist in the military but his age – 37 – and his bad knees from a lifetime of athletics meant there would be no combat role for him and only a desk job. As such, his friends and family convinced him to run for a vacant seat in Congress from Arkansas's third district.

Despite having no previous political experience nor a political machine to back him, he bested his rivals and headed to Congress in January 1943. After less than a full term in the House, Fulbright set his sights on a Senate seat occupied by the widow of the late Senator Thaddeus Caraway. Hattie Caraway, the first woman ever elected to the U.S. Senate, was known as "Silent Hattie" because she rarely said – or did – anything in her role as a Senator.[3] Using a network of University of Arkansas graduates, Fulbright won that seat, launching a Senate career that would last 29 years.

Fulbright had been shaped by his studies at Oxford in history and extensive travel in Europe and, in an astonishingly short period of time after his arrival in Washington, became a national spokesman on matters of foreign affairs and a staunch advocate for a Wilsonian internationalist perspective.

Fulbright was certainly not awed by his more senior House and Senate colleagues. Many were small town lawyers and isolationists who believed that America should stay out of the affairs of other nations. However, Fulbright – shocked by the devastation of World War II, frightened by the power of atomic weapons, and deeply concerned by the aggressiveness of the Soviet Union – believed that the United States must engage with the world.

A conversation with a friend from Arkansas, a lawyer named Bernal Seamster, who had attended the San Francisco conference that created the United Nations, helped Fulbright crystalize an idea for a program that would finance the exchange of students and scholars like the Rhodes Scholarship that had sent him to Oxford. Ideally, it would send Americans abroad to learn more about the world and bring foreign students and scholars to America to learn more about the country that would emerge from World War II as the leader of the liberal democracies.

The question was how do you pay for it? The answer was the disposal of hundreds of millions of dollars of surplus military equipment that had been sent abroad under the Lend-Lease program.

Fulbright moved his bill and several amendments through the Senate and House by drawing as little attention to them as he possibly could and using old fashioned horse trading to overcome the initial opposition of one powerful House committee chairman. He was wise to do so. "Young man," said Senator Kenneth McKellar of Tennessee to Fulbright after the bill had been passed and signed by the President, "that's a very dangerous piece of legislation...You're going to take our young boys and girls over there and expose them to all those foreign 'isms.'"[4]

Others in Congress believed that the program might be used by communist nations to infiltrate the United States and the program was endangered during the period of anti-communist hysteria stoked by Wisconsin Senator Joseph McCarthy.

However, as it grew it gained more and more supporters and defenders that helped protect it. As Fulbright advanced in seniority, ultimately becoming the Chairman of the powerful Senate Foreign Relations Committee, his political opponents found that one way to attack Fulbright was to attack his scholarship program. Sometimes this took the form of funding cuts, but ultimately the program survived and prospered.

In creating the program, Fulbright called for an independent ten-person Board of Foreign Scholarships to oversee the program and protect it from political meddling. Overseas, bi-national commissions were established to insure that the best and the brightest were selected to participate in the program.

The first bi-national commission was established in the United Kingdom and a grant of $20 million funded a program that included the U.K. and its colonies. It was

Senator J. William Fulbright

through this mechanism and the U.K. commission's "colonial committee" that Cyprus received its first Fulbright grant, which was given, in 1958, to Arthur Hubert Stanley "Peter" Megaw, an architectural historian and archaeologist who spent many years in Cyprus. The grant allowed him to travel to Dumbarton Oaks to do research.

Various bills in Congress modified the program through the years until 1961 when the passage of the Fulbright-Hays Act rationalized the various piecemeal changes. Fulbright-Hays was part of larger foreign affairs changes that included the Peace Corps and foreign aid proposed and passed during the first year of the administration of President John F. Kennedy.

The next year, in 1962, the Fulbright program officially came to Cyprus. To understand how and why one must first understand the political environment in Cyprus, American interests, and the specific challenges posed by the mix of Cypriot and Cold War politics. To try to do this, we turn to "a little history."

A LITTLE HISTORY

Relating the history of Cyprus, particularly recent history, is an undertaking fraught with peril. Greek Cypriots and Turkish Cypriots each have their own narratives as illustrated by remarks made by Turkish Cypriot Mustafa Akinci. He was speaking at an event at the University of Cyprus in the summer of 2014 entitled "The Cyprus Problem: 40 Years On."

Akinci, a mild-mannered man, smiled at his audience, who were primarily Greek Cypriots, and noted that from his perspective the title should have been "The Cyprus Problem: 50 Years On...or perhaps 55 years."[1] No one should be surprised that the two communities cannot agree as to when the Cyprus Problem began, for they agree on little else.

From 2015 to 2020, Akinci was the elected leader of the Turkish Cypriot polity in the northern third of the island that is unrecognized except by Turkey. Greek Cypriot sensitivity to anything that implies recognition of that polity means that such suggestions are invariably met with swift and vehement denunciation.

The history of the island since World War II has been punctuated by the struggle for independence from Britain and the subsequent struggle among Greek Cypriots and Turkish Cypriots and their respective motherlands over who would control its 3,600 square miles.

It is important to understand the history of the island and, more specifically the involvement of the United States and its interests in Cyprus, if one is to understand the environment in which the Cyprus Fulbright Commission operated for its 52 years.

***

The island of Cyprus lies in the eastern Mediterranean basin, 47 miles (75km) south of the Turkish coast, roughly 67 miles from the Syrian and Lebanese coasts, 235 miles north of Egypt, 175 miles from the closest Greek island in the Dodecanese and 500 miles from the Greek mainland. This geography has had a determinative impact on the island's long history.

The island is roughly 150 miles from east to west and 100 miles from north to south. Approximately 100 of those square miles are the sover-

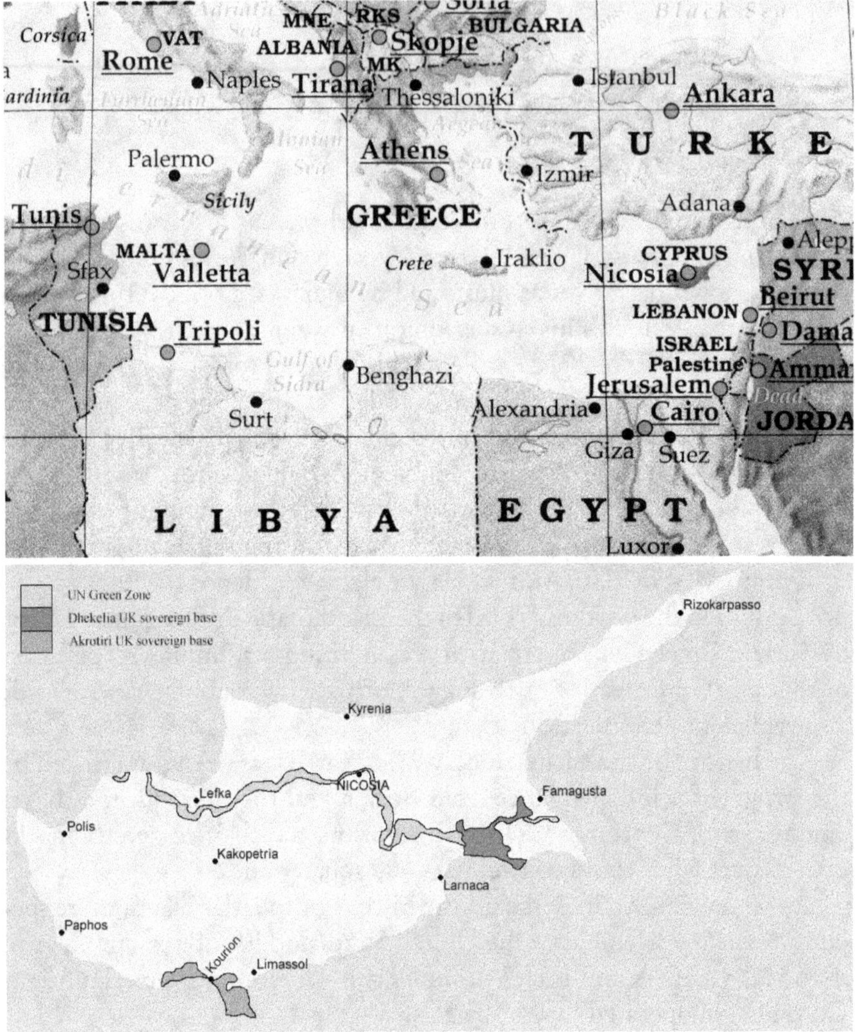

The Eastern Mediterranean region and Cyprus after 1974 showing the UN-patrolled Buffer Zone and the sovereign British base areas.

eign territory of the former colonial ruler the United Kingdom and are divided between two military bases along the southern coast of the island, Dhekelia and Akrotiri. In the 1960 London-Zurich agreements that granted Cyprus its independence, the United Kingdom insisted on maintaining these sovereign base areas, something the United States supported for its own reasons. Their presence remains contentious to this day.

There has been human activity on the island for some 12,000 years. And while there were periods of self-rule in antiquity, "Cyprus has had one absentee landlord after another: first Egypt, then Greece, which colonized the island, then Rome. It has been occupied successively by Richard the Lionhearted, the Templars, the Franks, the House of Lusignan, the Venetians, and the Turks (Ottomans). In 1878, the British acquired it from Turkey in exchange for help in defending the Turks against Russia, and the island was declared a British Crown colony in 1925."[2]

The 300 years of Ottoman rule that began in 1571 when the walled city of Famagusta fell to the forces under Lala Mustafa Pasha changed the ethnic character of Cyprus. One result of Ottoman rule that carried forward was the increased power of the Greek Orthodox Church and the Archbishop, who was given the power to own land and to oversee the taxation of the island. In essence, the Archbishop was not only the head of the church but became the political leader of the Greek Cypriots or ethnarch as well.

A second consequence of the Ottoman conquest of large swaths of territory occupied by ethnic Greeks was a concept known as the Great Idea (μεγάλη ιδέα), which set forth the hope that all ethnic Greeks could someday be reunified under a single political entity, a new Byzantium. The idea animated Greek foreign policy for a century, including the Greek revolt against the Ottomans in 1897, but even after Greece's defeat in the Greco-Turkish War (1919-22), the flame never died.

At the Paris Peace Conference in 1946, Greece's diplomats accomplished what its army could not in securing sovereignty over the Dodecanese, bringing the motherland that much closer to Cyprus. Post-World War II, this would lead, in the Greek Cypriot community, to the idea of *enosis* (ἐνωσις) or union with the motherland of Greece as the struggle against colonial rule unfolded, an idea that Greek Prime Minister Alexandros Papagos looked upon with favor.

Turkish Cypriots had no desire to live under Greek rule and as a result they embraced the idea of *taksim* or partition in response. Taksim, in this case, meant that a portion of Cyprus would become a province of Turkey. Thus, in addition to being divided by both language and religion, the two main ethnic groups were divided over their very different visions of how the island should be governed in the future. These differences stoked a strong sense of nationalism in both communities, accentuating their Greek and Turkish identities and diminishing any sense of Cypriotness.

As the post-World War II anti-colonial movement gathered force, Britain was determined to hold on to Cyprus for its value as a military outpost, especially when its position in the region was severely weakened by the Suez Crisis of 1956-57. By that time, the National Organization of Cypriot Fighters (Εθνική Οργάνωσις Κυπρίων Αγωνιστών), or EOKA, had been founded by military leader George Grivas with the express purpose of achieving enosis. It had begun attacks on British installations, which resulted in a security crackdown. The British exacerbated the ethnic divisions by creating an auxiliary police force composed entirely of Turkish Cypriots to help combat EOKA.

In reaction, Turkish Cypriots founded, in November 1957, the Turkish Resistance Organization (Turk Mukavemet Teskilati), or TMT. Turkish leader Adnan Menderes had argued, in the 1950s, that Cyprus was part of Anatolia and believed the island important to Turkish security. He argued that "Cyprus is Turkish," but the reality of the demographics of the island saw that assertion evolve into "partition or death." The TMT was led by Rauf Denktash and Riza Vuruskan and had as its aim the protection of Turkish Cypriots and, ultimately, achieving taksim or partition of the island. Both Greece and Turkey smuggled arms to the island and nationalist media in both countries stoked the eventual conflict.

EOKA launched more than one thousand attacks, the vast majority against the British military, but there were also increasing attacks against Turkish Cypriots, the kind of communal violence that had previously been rare. There was also collateral damage. In June 1956, American CIA officer William Pierce Boeteler, 26, was killed in the bombing of a restaurant in the walled old city of Nicosia often frequented by the British. He would not be the last American casualty in the conflict.[3]

On the left, Archbishop Makarios III of Cyprus, and on the right, Rauf Denktash.

While Britain regarded the EOKA fighters as terrorists, Prime Minister Harold Macmillan was predisposed toward finding a way to give the Cypriots more power over their affairs. Uppermost in his mind was the preservation of the British bases and communications/listening facilities on Cyprus that were "so necessary both for the protection of British interests in the Middle East and for the support of the right flank of NATO."[4]

However, Macmillan despaired that there seemed to be no acceptable solution to the problem and regarded partition as a failure.[5] Britain was working with both Greece and Turkey to try to find a solution, but struck one roadblock after another. Britain had, in March 1956, exiled Archbishop Makarios to the Seychelles because it was believed, given his close ties to EOKA, that he was supporting terrorist activities. Makarios was not only the head of the church but was seen as the political leader of the Greek Cypriots as well. His exile, in various locations, would last until March 1, 1959 when he would return to Cyprus and receive a rapturous reception.

His return was possible because in late 1958, the Greek and Turkish Foreign Ministers approached Macmillan. The Ministers proposed to pursue an agreement "under which the United Kingdom would hold the bases in full sovereignty and the two communities would enjoy a measure of autonomy in an independent Cyprus." That agreement was concluded and finally signed July 1, 1960. On August 16, 1960 the Union Jack was lowered at Government House in the Cypriot capital of Nicosia and Archbishop Makarios was invested as the first President of an independent Cyprus.[6]

This over-simplifies the often-tortuous nature of the negotiations. In the end, the London-Zurich agreements allowed Britain to retain its bases and facilities. At the time of independence, about 77 percent of the population of just over 573,000 were Greek Cypriots and about 18 percent Turkish Cypriots. The agreements called for the President to be a Greek Cypriot and the Vice President a Turkish Cypriot. Seventy percent of the positions in the parliament would be reserved for Greek Cypriots and 30 percent for Turkish Cypriots. Similar provisions were made for civil service positions and in the modest security force the ratio was 60/40. It was hoped the larger percentage would give the Turkish Cypriots a greater stake in the arrangement.

The two communities retained autonomy in areas such as religion and education and would elect their own communal chambers. Britain, Greece and Turkey became "guarantor powers" that could intervene if the constitutional order was threatened. There were veto power and other checks to prevent the majority Greek Cypriots from curbing the rights of Turkish Cypriots. Neither enosis nor taksim would be permitted.

To paraphrase Massimo d'Azeglio, a host of actors had created Cyprus, but at that point the challenge was to make Cypriots. Ultimately, the Fulbright Commission would attempt to make a contribution to that process.

The structure of the accords functioned uneasily for just over three years. The majority of Greek Cypriots still favored enosis. The majority of Turkish Cypriots still favored taksim. In both communities their respective motherlands – Greece and Turkey – maintained a strong hand.

In late 1963, President Makarios proposed 13 constitutional amendments, arguing they were needed to make government more functional. They eliminated some protections, such as veto power, for the Turkish Cypriots and when Makarios moved to implement them unilaterally, the Turkish Cypriots boycotted the government.

Tensions simmered and in December 1963 violence broke out between the two communities. Hundreds were killed and Turkish Cypriots either retreated to or were forced into defensible enclaves. British forces initially controlled the violence, but within a few months, the United Nations created a peacekeeping force – UNFICYP – to keep order on the island. It remains the longest continuous peacekeeping operation under UN auspices. The situation on the island remained unresolved, with flare-ups of varying intensity, for the next decade. Attempts by the international community to find a workable solution were unsuccessful.

The conflict came to a head in the summer of 1974 when the military junta in Athens engineered a coup against President Makarios. Makarios's contacts with communist countries and his demand that Greek officers leave the island precipitated the decision in Athens to launch the coup. Those Greek officers, backed by the pro-enosis militia EOKA B, led the coup. Makarios survived and escaped through one of the British bases, and the pro-enosis militiaman Nikos Sampson was installed as president. That triggered events that soon spun out of control.

Turkey, invoking its rights as a guarantor power, invaded five days later on July 20th when the U.K. indicated that it would not intervene. It established a protective enclave on the northern coast of Cyprus including the small city of Kyrenia (Girne) as well as a corridor to the Turkish Cypriot enclave in Nicosia. Though a ceasefire was secured after three days, fighting killed hundreds and hundreds more disappeared. The international community, principally under the leadership of the United Kingdom, tried to broker a deal but on August 14, Turkey renewed its attacks and this time over a four-day period captured the northern 37 percent of the island including Morphou, Famagusta, the Karpas, and the agriculturally rich Mesaoria Plain.   The two phases of the Turkish operation caused Cypriots in both communities to flee to areas under the control of their respective communities – 175,000 Greek Cypriots and 50,000 Turkish Cypriots were displaced.[7]

President Makarios returned to Cyprus and served until his death in 1977.   Rauf Denktash established himself as the leader of the Turkish Cypriots. UNFICYP's mandate was amended to police the buffer zone or Green Line between the two parts of the island.   Tens of thousands of Turkish troops remained and solidified their positions.   The junta in Athens, already fragmented in the aftermath of the 1973 Polytechnic uprising, fell and civilian government was restored.   Greece saw Cyprus as a catastrophe and its influence on the island would wane.   Turkey and Turkish Cypriots called the Turkish military intervention a "peace operation," and Turkey would continue to exert strong influence via the presence of its troops and its financial and political support for the Turkish Cypriots.

In the aftermath, Greece withdrew from NATO and the number of American military installations in Greece was reduced.   Greece would not return to NATO for six years.   The U.S. Congress placed an embargo on military assistance to Turkey that would last four years as well as a ban on military sales to Cyprus that would last until December 2019.

The lines drawn by the violence of 1974 remain unchanged today.   For nearly 30 years after those events there was scant contact between the two communities, though they shared the same island.   International efforts, primarily under the auspices of the UN, continued to try to solve the conflict because of the danger of two NATO members – Greece and Turkey – coming to blows over the issue.   In 1977, Makarios and Denktash agreed to a four-point plan known as the "high-level agreements," that called for a federal solution – ultimately, a bi-zonal, bicommunal federation with a single international identity that would have a small federal government, but most of the power invested in two "states," – one Greek and one Turkish.

There were occasional incidents along the Green Line during this period.   However, the most divisive act occurred in 1983 when the Turkish Cypriots declared the portion of Cyprus under their control as the Turkish Republic of Northern Cyprus. This drew almost universal condemnation.   Only Turkey recognized the TRNC and UN resolutions condemned the declaration.   Under the leadership of Denktash, the Turkish Cypriots negotiated but never came close to agreeing to a settlement, earning Denktash the nickname Mr. No. In addition, the character of the North was changed by the influx of tens of thousands of ethnic Turks from Anatolia, known as settlers, who tended to be more conservative than the largely secular Turkish Cypriots. However, for most of this period, Greek Cypriots were under the leadership of a series of presidents who had their own red lines that they would not cross.

What changed this dynamic was the formation and ultimate enlargement of the European Union. The Republic of Cyprus had already established a customs union with the EU and applied for EU membership in July 1990. There was hope that the carrot of EU membership might induce Turkish Cypriots to be more flexible at the negotiating table, particularly since Turkey harbored ambitions to join the EU. In 1994, however, the EU made it clear that Cyprus would be included in the next round of enlargement whether or not a solution was reached. In June 1999, UN Security Council Resolution 1250 requested that the UN Secretary General invite the leaders of the two communities to engage in talks. After initial meetings, there was little progress but the effort was renewed in 2001.

In this period, the Greek Cypriot and Turkish Cypriot communities negotiated what became known as the Annan Plan, named after UN Secretary General Kofi Annan. On the Greek Cypriot side, they included the more moderate Glafkos Clerides and the more hardline Tassos Papadopoulos and on the Turkish Cypriot side, Denktash and the more moderate Mehmet Ali Talat, though even under Talat Denktash remained a primary negotiator. However, by early 2004 there were still fundamental disagreements. On February 4, 2004, after having discussed matters with U.S. President George W. Bush, Annan sent a letter to both sides in which he invited them to New York on February 10, 2004. In his letter, Annan proposed that talks resume with the aim of finalizing the plan by March 31st, and holding a referendum on April 21st. He also reserved for himself the task of completing the text of the plan if necessary:

"It is clearly desirable that the text should emerge completed from the negotiations...," wrote Annan. "However, should that not happen, I would, by 31 March, make any indispensable suggestions to complete the text. Naturally I would only do this with the greatest of reluctance..."[7] In the end, Annan was compelled to complete the plan.

The referendum was held on April 24, 2004. If approved, it would have created a bicommunal, bi-zonal federation with a single international identity. However, in simultaneous referenda in the two communities, the Turkish Cypriots approved the plan by 65 percent, while the Greek Cypriots overwhelmingly rejected the plan by 72 percent. That, however, did not stop the Republic of Cyprus's accession to the EU, which took place six days later on May 1st. While all of Cyprus was technically now part of the EU, the aquis communautaire, or body of EU laws, was deemed suspended in the 37 percent of the island under Turkish control.

In general, the international community expressed its disappointment with the vote by the Greek Cypriots and there were calls to end the isolation of the Turkish Cypriots. However, as this is written, the two communities are no closer to a settlement than they were in 2004.

One very significant change that occurred during the Annan Plan negotiations was the decision by Turkish Cypriot leaders to open the crossing between the two communities in April 2003. Despite President Papadopoulos' admonition that Greek Cypriots should not cross into what was regarded as occupied territory, thousands queued to cross. Predictions of violence were proved wrong. Poignant stories of Greek Cypriots returning to homes they had not seen in 27 years only to be welcomed by the Turkish Cypriot occupants were related in the media in both communities. Since that opening, several more crossings have been opened, but contact between the two communities – while possible – remains limited more by language and choice than by physical or political barriers.

This is a brief history of the island that leaves out a great deal. For example, in recent years Cyprus, which was seen as a "one-issue" country by the international community, became a three-issue country. The second issue was the discovery of natural gas and oil in the exclusive economic zone of the Republic of Cyprus off the southern coast near Israel's Leviathan Field. That raised the question whether the Turkish Cypriots had any claim to those resources or if the most efficient way to get the gas to market was a pipeline running through northern Cyprus and Turkey. The third was the economic crisis that struck the Republic's two largest banks in 2012-13 requiring an international bailout.

What it portrays are three phases of Cypriot history since independence in 1960: An uneasy attempt to find a way for the two communities to govern the island together, which resulted in tension and violence and estrangement; a post-1974 reality that lasted nearly 30 years with the two communities existing quite separately with little or no contact between the two; and finally the post-Annan Plan vote period which continues to this day with periodic attempts to bridge the remaining gaps, but each community largely going its own way.

The communities continue to have very different views on the fundamental root of the problem. For Turkish Cypriots, the problem is inter-communal. The events of 1963 onward convinced many that the two communities could not live together. Indeed, Turkish Cypriot grievances preceded independence from Britain and were only exacerbated by the structure of the London-Zurich Accords. For Greek Cypriots, the root of the problem is simply international aggression – the invasion by a foreign power (Turkey) and the occupation of the northern 37 percent of the island and that the solution to the problem runs through Ankara. This history, with one or two brief exceptions, does not touch upon the role of the United States in Cyprus, its interests and actions, and its own attempts to solve the conflict between the two communities. That is the subject of the next chapter, which describes how Cold War concerns, strategic interests, and domestic politics drew America into the middle of the conflict that divided the island.

CYPRUS AND AMERICA

Even in the era of jet travel, many Cypriots speak about America as a place that is far away, even though the journey is shorter in duration than a bus ride across the island just a couple generations ago when the route traversed uncertain roads and the driver stopped at nearly every village.

In many ways, that speaks to the insularity of an island culture, but also to the strength of the Cypriot family. Mothers, faced with the prospect of their children going abroad to study, wanted them to stay close by.

Like Cyprus's own history, the story of American involvement in Cyprus can be divided into eras before and after independence. Primarily, however, the story of America's involvement in Cyprus is driven by larger forces – the "special relationship" with Great Britain, America's anti-colonial policies, the Truman Doctrine that saw America take a greater stake in the region post-World War II, the efforts to hold together NATO, American domestic politics, but, most importantly, the Cold War and the confrontation with the former Soviet Union and international communism writ large.

On occasion, Cyprus was buffeted and bruised by these larger forces and that influenced how Cypriots, particularly the majority Greek Cypriots, felt about America. And sometimes these feelings spilled over in ways that created significant challenges and costs for the American Embassy, the Fulbright Commission and their leadership.

***

The United States would name its first consul to Cyprus in the early 1830s, Marino de Mattey. He served largely as a commercial agent, a job that was not necessarily that easy. In writing to his superior, the American Chargé d'Affaires in Constantinople David Porter in 1833, de Mattey said: "I have found it impossible to fulfill entirely the wishes of your excellency concerning the exports and imports of this place, not being able to find, in the customs house, any register that could give me the least light on the subject."[1]

However, some American consuls cast a larger shadow than others.

Luigi Palma di Cesnola, born in Turin, an immigrant to America and a Medal of Honor recipient during the American Civil War, arrived in Cyprus in 1865. Over the next 11 years, he dug up, bought, stole, and plundered some 35,000 archaeological treasures. As Cesnola said himself about one of his finds: "I captured rather than discovered" the stone treasures at Golgos.[2]

Theoretically, Cesnola was banned as the American Consul from shipping his collection from Cyprus, but apparently did so wearing his hat as the Russian Consul, with some additional help from the Turkish Governor of Cyprus.[3]

Ultimately, he sold his collection to the newly established Metropolitan Museum of Art in New York after which he was offered the position as its first director, a position he held for a quarter of a century until his death in 1904. The treasures remain in the museum's collection to this day – the Cesnola Collection – with the best arrayed in four rooms on the upper level.

He would not be the last American diplomat to leave the island with a significant collection of Cypriot antiquities. In the future, however, the Cyprus Fulbright Commission would make a more positive contribution to Cypriot archaeology.

Despite the posting of consular/commercial agents, economic interactions between America and Cyprus were few in the first century after they arrived with one major exception. On Boxing Day 1912, a nervous, chain-smoking mining engineer and prospector named Charles Godfrey Gunther sailed into the harbor in Famagusta in search of ancient mines that, perchance, might once again yield valuable ore.[4]

Colonel Seeley Mudd and Philip Wiseman, who had worked as managers for various mining companies but sought to establish their own firm, backed Gunther's quest. Gunther found many ancient slag dumps in Cyprus that indicated previous mining activity, and by April 1914 he had secured permission to mine. The good news was that the electrical revolution was driving up the demand for copper; the bad news was that the world was on the brink of war.

Ultimately, Gunther focused on the areas around Mavrovouni and Skouriotissa near Morphou Bay and began operations. Through a war, an economic depression, fires, labor unrest, storms, accidents, malaria and influenza, and then a second world war they persisted. Mudd ceded control of the Cyprus Mines Corporation (CMC) to his son Harvey. And when the senior Mudd passed away in 1926, his son wrote to a friend: "Our venture in Cyprus absorbed his interest and even though the enterprise was beset with difficulties and disappointments, it never ceased to appeal to him and held a kind of romantic charm."[5]

The Corporation grew, but was not consistently profitable. They built housing and facilities for workers originally known as the "Sixty Houses" and then built more. By 1937 the workforce had increased to 5,720 men and women.[6] At one point, the Corporation was responsible for about 20 percent of the island's gross domestic product and was a significant source of foreign exchange. A Russian doctor hired by CMC named Dr. Paul Smitten became somewhat of a local legend when he led a public health campaign that greatly reduced the incidence of malaria on the island.[7] Post-World War II, production soared and then in the 1960s the mines began to reach exhaustion.

CMC also played a role in American efforts to strengthen the right-wing labor organization, the Cyprus Confederation of Workers (SEK), to act as a counterweight to the left-wing/communist labor union PEO. The Embassy convinced Archbishop Makarios to use his influence to make SEK the official union of the company shortly after independence.[8] Ultimately, however, the events of July-August 1974, which split the mines from CMC's transport facilities on the bay, brought an abrupt end to the company's operations in Cyprus.

There would not be that level of private American investment until October 2008 when Noble Energy of Houston, Texas obtained the rights to drill for natural gas and oil in Block 12 of Cyprus's exclusive economic zone. However, the American government would ultimately find many reasons to invest in the island and its people.

The United States established its first true consulate in Cyprus on April 13, 1948 with the arrival of William J. Porter in Nicosia. However, America had already been in negotiations with both its British partners and the local government of Cyprus to waive certain laws that would allow it to establish a Foreign Broadcast Information Branch on the island.[9]

FBIB, which became FBIS (Service) and, since 2005, The Open Source Center, is an unclassified branch of the CIA. It was being compelled to move its Mediterranean operations from Cairo. The branch would monitor and translate radio and TV broadcasts and other material from throughout the region, particularly the Middle East.

The U.S. purchased land for the construction of the station at Karavas near Kyrenia, as was noted in the Cypriot media, which suggested that about 65 American personnel would work at the station.[10] That station would operate until 1974 when the Turkish invasion forced its evacuation. With the permission of the Government of Cyprus's Council of

Ministers, FBIS would re-establish itself in Nicosia, where it operates to this day near the University of Nicosia.

However, more important to the United States was the more clandestine work that they had begun in concert with the British during the Second World War and formally established in 1946, and that was the collection of signals intelligence. In addition, the U.S. wanted to establish a relay station that forwarded all official communications from the Middle East.

GCHQ, the British signal intelligence service, set up shop in Cyprus on the British base near Ayios Nikolaos (Ἅγιος Νικόλαος) in June 1947, transferring personnel and equipment from Palestine.[11] The forerunner of America's National Security Agency engaged in close cooperation with the Cyprus operation almost from the beginning. Cyprus's geographic location as well as the atmospheric conditions made it ideal. Ultimately, U.S.-British global cooperation expanded to include Canada, Australia, and New Zealand in what became known as the Five Eyes.

America's first Ambassador, Fraser Wilkins, revealed in later years how extensive American participation was at the time of independence. "The Embassy itself was only about 35 people," explained Wilkins. "The 'radio station' was, say, 500. And if you count all the dependents, we had 2,000 Americans on the island."[12] Later, there would also be equipment at Cape Greco linked to NATO's early warning system. Ambassador William Crawford, who was previously the Deputy Chief of Mission in Cyprus, estimated that when he first came to Cyprus in 1968 that there were "more than 1,000 American personnel from five different agencies" on the island.[13]

All this made Cyprus very valuable for America in the Cold War years and as the negotiations over independence moved forward in fits and starts the U.S. insisted that the preservation of access to these facili-

America's first Ambassador to Cyprus, Fraser Wilkins.

ties be set forth in the London-Zurich Agreement and not be left to the whims of a new Cypriot government. That said, the U.S. anticipated that Archbishop Makarios would ask for a quid pro quo and they were not disappointed.

"There is no question that the U.S. facilities will be welcome," the Archbishop told American Consul Taylor Belcher during a meeting in October 1959, "but you know we will be poor, so you will have to pay us something."[14]

U.S. policy toward Cyprus in the run-up to independence was largely an arms-length affair. They saw it as a British problem, though concerns about NATO unity were ever-present. As President Eisenhower wrote to Greece's King Paul I in September 1958, "The United States is gravely disturbed by the imminent dangers posed by the failure to reach a mutually satisfactory settlement of the Cyprus dispute. We have considerable sympathy and understanding for the difficult position in which Greece finds itself. I know you understand that since we are not a direct party to the controversy and are a friend of all concerned, we face real limitations on our ability to intervene in this matter."[15]

U.S. Ambassadors in Athens and Ankara were routinely asked to try to nudge those two governments toward a settlement and to show reasonableness, reminding them of the importance of NATO. In turn, Greek and Turkish leaders tried to enlist the U.S. to take their sides and to involve itself more deeply in the dispute. Both brandished the communist threat to make their points. Meanwhile, the U.S. pushed the U.K. to allow Makarios to return to the island from his enforced exile in the Seychelles and kept open a backchannel to him, even as violence escalated. In September 1958, American Vice Consul John Wentworth was shot multiple times by an EOKA gunman, but survived his wounds.

It did not mean that the U.S. did not, internally, kick around a few ideas to solve the problem, not all of them viable. In June 1958, President Eisenhower and Secretary of State John Foster Dulles, who saw the world in black and white terms – you were either with the U.S. or with the Soviets – had the following exchange during a phone conversation:

"Pres. asked about Cyprus. Sec. said all we have is that there are big demonstrations going on in Athens largely anti-American.

Pres. said he did not understand Greeks getting mad at us. Sec. said everywhere in the world everyone thinks we can fix everything. They don't realize we don't run the whole world. Pres. said how do we do anything with the Turks or Greeks. Turkey is thinly populated—couldn't we get Turks out (of Cyprus) and in better position elsewhere? Sec. said we would never get them out of there. Pres. said there were only 5,000 Turks in Cyprus. Sec. said (after checking with an aide) there were 160,000– about 20 percent of the total population. Pres. said that knocks out any resettlement. Pres. said he guessed all we can do is pray."[16]

Ultimately, of course, prayers were answered by the London-Zurich accords, though the Greek and Turkish majorities on the island still prayed for enosis or taksim. In anticipating an independent Cyprus, the Eisenhower administration, in its final year, began to formulate American policy toward the new nation. The policy objectives were clear enough: A politically stable country able to resist communist subversion; a cooperative relationship among Greece, Turkey and the U.K.; the continued availability of the military bases and the unhampered use of the communications facilities; economic development; free democratic institutions; and a pro-Western orientation.[17]

That much was clear, but the devil, as they say, was in the details. How would the U.S. government support that policy? The National Security Council Report laid out 20 actions often beginning with the words "encourage, discourage, look with favor, urge, discreetly encourage, and avoid," as in "avoid any U.S. action that would suggest partiality between Greek and Turkish communities."[18]

The largest sticking point was military aid. The U.S. believed the guarantor powers had primary responsibility for aid and that any U.S. contribution toward aid in general should be modest. Archbishop Makarios had something else in mind. In his first meeting with the American Consul he explained he sought £20 million from the U.K and $20 million ($175 million in 2020 dollars) from the U.S., plus U.S. military aid for Cyprus's new security force. Turkish Cypriot Vice President Fazil Kutchuk echoed that request. Makarios made clear this was his first request, but it would not be his last. American Consul Belcher told Washington that were the U.S. not prepared to provide aid Cypriots would view it as a "dereliction of duty."[19]

What Eisenhower had in mind was some modest aid such as grain because of a drought that had stricken the island. He was opposed to military aid because he feared the weapons could be turned on the British. Though CIA Director Allen Dulles thought the prospects of a stable Cyprus post-independence were good, he warned that Cypriots were a violent people and that a hard-core communist element existed on the island.[20] However, Eisenhower's time in office would soon end and decisions could be left for the next administration. When independence was finally achieved, Fraser Wilkins was nominated, confirmed, and on the ground in Cyprus as America's first Ambassador within a month, surely a diplomatic record.

When John F. Kennedy took office in January 1961, he chose to keep Wilkins, a career officer, on as Ambassador and in the summer of that year the Kennedy administration decided that it could not depend on the guarantor powers to provide Cyprus with aid nor insure that the objectives set forth by the National Security Council could be met without increased American leadership in Cyprus.

Wilkins noted that he soon needed to copy all his cable traffic to the State Department to the White House because of the President's high level of interest.[21]

It helped that neither Makarios nor Wilkins was bashful about asking Washington for aid, and within a short time 50,000 tons of wheat and barley were on their way to Cyprus under the PL480 program and the International Cooperation Agency (the forerunner of the U.S. Agency for International Development) was starting to work with Cyprus. (Early aid efforts will be discussed more fully in the next chapter.) In the summer of 1962, Archbishop Makarios was invited to the White House and shortly afterward Vice President Lyndon Johnson visited Cyprus. Kennedy Administration officials boasted that U.S. efforts had increased American prestige in Cyprus and strengthened America's ability to secure its interests on the island, particularly the communications facilities.[22]

However, there were darkening clouds. The increased U.S. attention caused a frenzy of speculation in the Cypriot media about levels of U.S. aid that frightened Embassy officials because it created expectations that could not possibly be met. During Johnson's visit he was handed an eight–page document by Turkish Cypriot leaders detailing a long list of grievances against the Greek Cypriots.[23] Soon, Makarios would begin his efforts to amend the constitution and, ultimately, by the end of 1963, President Kennedy was dead, Cyprus was reaching the boiling point, and the U.S. feared being drawn into the dispute, particularly after Cyprus exploded into violence in December.

Lyndon Johnson was barely a month into his presidency when that violence erupted with hundreds killed. In January, the British approached the U.S. and said they could no longer shoulder the burden of trying to keep peace on the island and insisted on U.S. involvement.[24] The threat of a Turkish intervention was ever-present and when troops began to assemble in early June 1964, Johnson sent a "brutal" message to Turkish Prime Minister Ismet Inonu that Undersecretary of State George Ball characterized as the diplomatic equivalent of "an atomic bomb." It stopped the pending Turkish invasion of Cyprus in its tracks but would negatively influence Turkish-American relations for more than a generation.[25]

Over the next several years, U.S. involvement deepened as it watched Makarios buy weapons from the Soviets after Western powers refused. Although the UN had the primary role in trying to broker a settlement, the U.S. sent former Secretary of State Dean Acheson to Geneva to "consult" and he tried to formulate a plan acceptable to all, but ultimately gave up despite a high level of diplomatic intensity that dragged on for many months. At this point, the U.S. largely backed off. As Acting Secretary of State George Ball told Cypriot Foreign Minister Spyros Kyprianou and Ambassador Zenon Rossides:

"The treaties are still on the books. No one denies that they are not very workable. When this is the case, the only thing to do is to get together and talk. We told Turkey that we have no solution. Furthermore, a United States solution would not be useful. Because of the power and size of the United States, even if we made a proposal it would be taken as an attempt to coerce the parties concerned; so we refuse to make such a proposal. ... [Mr. Acheson's] effort did not work and is now academic. At present, there is nothing we can contribute by choosing a solution. On the contrary, we would be doing a disservice. ... The United States by the nature of things is not directly concerned with any particular solution. We do not support enosis, nor do we condemn it. We do not support federation, nor do we condemn it. We want only to have peace and stability in the area."[26]

The U.S. also made it clear to both Greece and to Archbishop Makarios, that it would not use force against Turkey, a NATO ally, to stop it from exercising its rights under the Treaty of Guarantee. However, two years later, in 1967, future Secretary of State Cyrus Vance flew to the region on just hours' notice and succeeded in negotiating an agreement that, in Vance's words, allowed Greece and Turkey to "save face and climb down from the limbs that they had gotten themselves on."[27] Vance was able to accomplish the accord despite the fact that the U.S. had little leverage with Makarios. The U.S. did not provide military aid that could be withheld while it needed Makarios's favor to maintain its communications facilities. Still, America once again stepped up its diplomatic engagement to try to keep a lid on the conflict.

During Nixon's first term, Cyprus simmered. General Grivas secretly returned to the island to lead pro-enosis forces and in September 1973 the CIA warned that U.S. efforts as a mediator had lost their effectiveness and that a "violent eruption was possible at any time."[28] Eight months later, an interdepartmental study stated that Cyprus faced several potential scenarios including a Greek putsch against Makarios.[29] The report also noted U.S. interests had diminished because the U.S. communications facilities were being civilianized and "much reduced," that the U.S. had no aid relationship with Cyprus, but that it still regarded the British bases as strategically important. They would eventually serve as a base for the U2 flights – Operation Olive Harvest – that would monitor the Sinai Peninsula and the Egyptian-Israeli Peace negotiated by President Carter.

As events started to unfold in the first half of 1974, particularly Makarios's increasingly difficult relationship with the junta in Athens, Washington was roiled by the Watergate scandal and President Nixon became the lamest of ducks. It left Henry Kissinger, who was both Secretary of State and National Security Advisor, in command of American foreign policy.

At 3:00 a.m. in Washington on July 15, 1974 the State Department's Cyprus desk officer Thomas Boyatt was awakened by the Operations Center and was told "you better get in here. There's fighting in Nicosia and it does not look good." Boyatt explained what happened next:

"When I got to the Operations Center they put two pieces of paper in front of me. On the left hand side was the Daily Intelligence Summary, which is done by the entire intelligence community for the President, Vice President, Secretary of State, and the highest officers. And its lead item said 'we have been assured by General Ioannides [leader of the Greek junta] that Greece will not move its forces against Makarios.' To the right was a cable from our Embassy in Nicosia describing the fighting between Cypriots loyal to Makarios and Cypriots and Greeks trying to overthrow him. The Presidential Palace was in flames and the Cypriot force had been decimated. We don't know where Archbishop Makarios is and presume he is dead. A government has been installed headed by [EOKA gunman and pro-enosis militant]Nikos Sampson."[30]

Whole forests have been leveled to print the books and articles about what happened in the lead-up to that morning and its aftermath and it is beyond the scope of this book to litigate the events of that summer. However, many, many Greek Cypriots and Greeks, particularly on the left side of the political spectrum, believed then and still believe now that there was a conspiracy between the junta in Athens, the CIA, which had a relationship with members of the junta going back to the 1940s, and Secretary Kissinger to get rid of "the troublesome priest."[31] Or, at least, that Kissinger could have acted to stop Turkey as Lyndon Johnson and Cyrus Vance had done in the past. And while Kissinger sent Under Secretary for Political Affairs Joe Sisco to the region to try shuttle diplomacy and the

U.S. voted for UN Security Council Resolution 353 condemning Turkey's actions, neither the U.S. nor Britain, as a guarantor power, stopped Turkey from launching the second wave that split the island.

Writing in 2011, Dr. James Ker-Lindsay, Professor of international relations, found "recent research conducted by independent scholars with access to extensive British and American archives has painted a very different story (from the conspiracy theories). The sheer enormity of the archives makes it difficult to believe that the papers could have all been uniformly doctored to present a false picture of events. Rather than a conspiracy, they detail a complex picture of misunderstandings, misinterpretations, and political upheaval...Although many Greek Cypriots like to view Kissinger as an 'evil genius' masterminding the invasion, the evidence suggests that he was rather ill-informed about events on the island. His primary concern was to prevent a war between Greece and Turkey. Moreover, the archives show that in the early months of 1974 the Nixon administration on the whole believed that Greece would not overthrow Makarios and that Turkey would not invade even if Greece ousted him."[32]

Ambassador James Williams, who was a political officer in Cyprus in 1974 and later a Special Cyprus Coordinator, recalled that "in the 1990s there was a conference held by the World Bank and Kissinger was there and Boyatt was in the audience and asked a question that did not have anything to do with Cyprus and had something to do with the NATO alliance. But before Kissinger answered he made a remark that was as close to an apology as you might get and it was something to the effect of 'I remember you writing a memo and it was very prescient and it did not get the attention that it deserved.'"[33]

In addition, Kissinger was concerned that the Soviets would see an opportunity to meddle and wanted them kept out of the crisis. For example, when the Soviets suggested all foreign forces leave Cyprus, they also meant Britain, its bases, and the communications facilities with an aim toward weakening NATO.

But perception is often reality and the aftermath of July-August 1974 was both grave and tragic. On August 19, the day after Turkey halted its operations, a demonstration outside the American Embassy in Nicosia turned deadly when snipers fired into the Embassy, killing Ambassador Rodger Davies and local administrative assistant Antoinette Varnavas. Because of the violence, ambulances would not come to the Embassy so Cyprus's President Glafcos Clerides rushed to the Embassy in his car and took Davies to a nearby clinic where he was pronounced dead with a bullet wound to his heart.[34]

Public Affairs Officer David Grimland wrote about the Ambassador: "Rodger Davies was perhaps the finest diplomat it has ever been my pleasure to work with. He had arrived in Cyprus a couple of months earlier with his two children, Dana, 20, and John, 15, having lost his wife to cancer in the previous year. As a very senior diplomat, he could have gotten a much more prestigious ambassadorship, but his choice was this professionally quiet assignment in a little Mediterranean backwater. He hoped this would give him and his children the opportunity to recover from the trauma of his wife's suffering and death. Instead, he found himself at the epicenter of a political and military maelstrom that required that he order his own children, along with the families of his American staff, out of the danger zone to our designated safe haven in Beirut."[35]

As noted in the previous chapter, there was a cascade of repercussions. In America, the Congress intervened, cutting off military aid to Turkey and, at the urging of the Greek lobby, allocated millions for relief of the displaced (which will be covered in Chapter Six). Almost from the moment the Turkish operation ended, British Prime Minister Callahan attempted to launch talks. Kissinger suggested to President Gerald Ford that the administration should let Britain take the lead and that the U.S. could take a more active role later. But, over the final 18 months of the Ford administration there was almost constant contact between Greek, Turkish and Cypriot leaders and Kissinger and his envoys. However, with each passing month the division hardened into place.

In the coming decades, the arrival of a new American President would provoke speculation if not hope that a new American effort would help bring a solution to the problem. This was true of President Carter, who hugely disappointed the Greek Cypriots and Athens when he supported and then succeeded in lifting the arms embargo on Turkey. With increased pressure from the Congress, both the White House and the State Department felt compelled to demonstrate seriousness of purpose by designating special envoys dedicated to the Cyprus problem. In the case of the Carter administration, the President sent one of the architects of the Truman Doctrine, Clark Clifford, and the State Department sent Counselor Matthew Nimitz.

In February 1977, Archbishop Makarios and Rauf Denktash achieved a breakthrough under UN auspices by agreeing to the four-point "High Level Agreements." Using those as a base, Nimitz – working with Britain and Canada – formulated what became known as the ABC Plan in 1978. As set forth, it had 12 points and created a framework for the creation of a bicommunal federation. Seeing it as a roadmap to partition, the Greek

Cypriots immediately rejected the plan, as did Athens, Ankara, and the Turkish Cypriots.   However, that basic framework remained at the heart of future efforts, including the Annan Plan 25 years later.

Writing 13 years after the rejection of the plan, Nimitz said:

"To those familiar with the intricacies, the Cyprus problem appears solvable. After all, the island is small and prosperous; its people are educated and responsive to a democratic political process; the two metropolitan powers – Greece and Turkey – are at peace and are nominal allies. The issues that divide the two sides are negotiable – legalistic concepts to be settled in devising a constitutional structure and territorial issues to be settled in determining the border between two federal zones. If the Cyprus problem were presented to 100 world experts on constitutional and political systems, there would be 100 proposed solutions – all of which would be reasonable and any one of which would have a fair chance of working. However, if we were to actually perform that experiment, based on past experience, I would guess that neither the Greek nor the Turkish Cypriots would be willing wholeheartedly to accept any of the proffered solutions."[36]

Indeed, there was no shortage of diplomatic creativity by the Americans with the UN acting as the fulcrum of ongoing efforts. From the beginning of the post-1974 efforts, diplomats tried to create so-called confidence-building measures (CBMs), such as re-opening the Nicosia airport under UN auspices or allowing the return of Greek Cypriots to the resort city of Varosha on the southern edge of Famagusta, which remains a ghost city to this day.[37] None of these things happened.

U.S. Ambassador Richard Boucher (1993-96) described his own efforts: "I had a Deputy Chief of Mission named Caroline Huggins who had been [in Cyprus] a while and as far as I was concerned knew everything about the place. In my own naiveté, I would go into her office and say 'I've got it...why don't we try blah, blah, blah' and she would smile at me sweetly and say we tried that in 1973 and it did not work. And three-four weeks later I would walk in and say 'why don't we try blah, blah, blah?" and she would say, 'oh yes, we tried that in 1984.' I did this about five or six times. The deal was not the problem. I had the deal written on a three-by-five card that I carried with me. It was wanting to do the deal that was the problem."[38]

In the wake of the events of 1974, the Greek lobby in America came into its own and pushed the Congress, which pushed each successive administration. Soon, smaller Greek Cypriot and Turkish and Turkish Cypriot lobbies would learn their way around the House and Senate office buildings. The State Department's creation of the Special Cyprus Coordinator in 1981 was one response to Congressional pressure and Presidents would name their own envoys such as Richard Holbrooke and high-powered attorneys such as Dick Beattie and Al Moses.

It is telling that Holbrooke, who wrote about the Balkans, "not since Vietnam have I seen a problem that is so difficult and compelling," but still plunged in to try to solve it. Yet he decided to give Cyprus a wide berth.

The State Department's coordinators came and went. Reggie Bartholomew, with a reputation for bluntness and a breaker of diplomatic crockery, quickly judged the conflict unsolvable and moved on. Christian Chapman came to the same conclusion. Richard Haass testified that it was up to the Cypriots to work it out, but that the U.S. would be there to help. The Reagan administration and Congress dangled the promise of $250 million ($675 million in 2020 dollars) in aid to facilitate a settlement, if the two communities could agree.

James Wilkinson lamented that doing nothing or trying to coerce a solution were both unrealistic and concluded that a forceful U.S. initiative would not be successful. Nelson Ledsky came in 1989 and thought there were those in the Department who wanted to abolish the coordinator position, but that Congressional pressure kept it alive. He worked on a plan called "The Set of Ideas" that saw some agreement, but not on the thorniest of issues. The efforts of the coordinators were something that an administration could point to in reports required by the Congress every two months on what was being done to solve the Cyprus problem.[39]

Former Ambassador to Cyprus Robert Lamb spent less than a year in the position and then James Williams, who served part of the time in tandem with White House envoy Dick Beattie, came on board. That caused Senator Claiborne Pell to inquire at one hearing if the American Ambassador to Cyprus and all these envoys wouldn't start tripping over one another. Williams thought it was a good question. Carey Cavanaugh served briefly in an acting capacity but played a role in the U.S. efforts to convince the Government of Cyprus to stop delivery of a Soviet S-300 air defense system in 1997 that had provoked Turkish threats. With some heavy diplomatic lifting from Washington and America's Embassy in Athens the Greek Cypriots, loath to succumb to Turkish pressure, swapped the system for other military equipment with Greece.

The final two coordinators, Thomas Miller and Thomas Weston, came on board as an initiative by the G-8 evolved into UNSCR 1205 and, ultimately, the Annan Plan. This effort was also tied to the EU candidacy of Turkey, for as long as Cyprus remained unresolved Turkish entry into the EU would be virtually impossible and the U.S. supported Turkish accession.

America's role was largely to assist in the drafting of five versions of the Annan Plan and to push the parties toward agreement, not only on the substance of the plan, but to even allow the parallel referenda to take place. Weston believed there were still U.S. interests at play – Greek-Turkish relations, the domestic pressure from the Greek lobby, and, more idealistically, the American role as a permanent member of the UN Security Council, although the atmosphere at the UN was "poisonous" at that time because of America's invasion of Iraq in the wake of 9/11.[40]

On the ground in Nicosia, the American Embassy was busy trying to improve the atmosphere surrounding the creation of the Annan Plan and to use USAID funds to inform Cypriots about what was in it, but were seen as firmly on the pro-side, earning the enmity of the Papadopolous government. "It was a crazy 24 months," said Ambassador Michael Klosson. "I was pretty outspoken and newspapers connected to the government were writing stories that I would be kicked out. We pushed back after the referendum. We held our head high. We felt we had done the right thing."

"The referendum ended the way it did and that was that," said Klosson. "[After the referendum] we shifted our priorities to trafficking in persons, which was a problem in both communities. We moved the needle significantly and helped some women get out of some bad situations."[41]

In the wake of the Annan Plan vote, the UN pulled back saying that it would re-engage when leaders of the two communities indicated a willingness to talk. This happened in 2008 after the election of Demetris Christofias, the first President of Cyprus from the leftist/communist AKEL Party. In America, the position of Special Cyprus Coordinator was not filled as the global war on terror kept the American focus elsewhere.

However, America did briefly boost the amount of aid that it was sending to Cyprus with the stated purpose of strengthening the Turkish Cypriot economy and helping to reduce the economic disparities between the two communities, an issue that was raised during the debate over the Annan Plan. This provoked furious protests from Greek Cypriot officials and set in motion the conditions that would eventually end the stream of aid that had begun at the end of 1974.

The last major effort by the American government to try to create some forward movement between the two sides came in 2014 when the two Cypriot sides and Turkey asked the United States to take the lead in brokering the resumption of talks. The successful negotiation of the

Cypriot leaders' "Joint Statement of February 11," brokered by Ambassador John Koenig, was followed in May by the visit of Vice President Joe Biden, the highest level American visit to the island in more than 50 years. Biden arrived with the hopes of coming to agreement on a series of confidence building measures. That effort largely failed even before Biden touched down in Cyprus.[42]

Despite the fact that neither the Greek Cypriot leader Nicos Anastasiades nor the Turkish Cypriot leader Dervish Eroglu were regarded as particularly "pro-solution," Biden's visit was designed to push the process forward modestly by coming to agreement over some of the same confidence building measures that had been discussed for 40 years – the Nicosia Airport, Varosha, etc. Those negotiations reached a dead end 10 days before Biden arrived. What were left were some minor CBMs, the opening of a new checkpoint or two.

There was a second part to Biden's visit that was also doomed to failure and that was a discussion about the role that Cyprus and Israel might play jointly in the supply of hydrocarbons to Europe, even though the combined quantities of natural gas and oil from their fields were not large enough to make a significant impact.

As Ambassador Koenig pointed out, the combination of geopolitics and hydrocarbons will always find an eager audience in Washington, but the evolving discussion was fraught with complexities that made it largely unworkable. "The ideas Biden came with eventually died, but it took several stakes through the heart to kill it," said Koenig.[43]

Five months after the Biden visit, as the U.S. government's fiscal year came to an end, the USAID money that had started in the wake of the events of 1974 quietly stopped, the bicommunal Fulbright Commission closed its doors, and a much more modest Fulbright program set up shop in the Public Affairs Section of the American Embassy – all long-time symbols of American involvement with the island.

If one were to count American aid using inflation-adjusted dollars, it certainly surpassed more than $1.5 billion from 1960 onward and that does not count the rent paid to the Government of Cyprus for the American FBIS and communications facilities on the island, nor various other Embassy-sponsored training programs, nor the money spent by the large contingent of Americans on the island through the years.

American involvement in the island and region had been particularly robust between independence in 1960 and the events of 1974, but that involvement would begin to wane post-1974 as the realization set in that only Cypriots could, at the end of the day, solve the "Cyprus Problem."

Yet the steady stream of aid money, though no more than a "rounding error" in the U.S. federal budget, resulted not just in houses and schools for refugees and a host of other projects carried out via the UNDP, but in the education and training of thousands of Cypriots, something that was barely on the radar of American or Cypriot leaders. Their focus was on the larger geopolitical issues.

For an accountant named Renos Kamenos and, soon, his bride Stella, that lack of high-level attention was absolutely fine.

RENOS AND STELLA

"That's the kind of man that was needed to run Fulbright in Cyprus!"

As Michael Sarris cast his mind back to 1967, when a Fulbright scholarship sent him to America's heartland and Wayne State University in Detroit to pursue a master's and Ph.D. in economics, he remembered the impression that Renos Kamenos made on him.

"He put Fulbright on the map. He was socially active. He was accessible and people would go to see him," remembered Sarris, Cyprus's former Finance Minister. "You had to have the right man there. His legacy speaks for itself."[1]

Sarris, in the fifth class of Fulbright scholars from Cyprus, would find himself in the midst of America's industrial heartland dominated by the major automakers and in a city roiled by the social protests of the 1960s. A department chairman, who had come from the University of Chicago where Nobel laureate Milton Friedman's ideas held sway, was his mentor. Sarris learned many lessons that informed his work at Cyprus's Central Bank, the Bank of Cyprus, and then the World Bank.

One of those lessons was a willingness to take risks, which is what the Board of Foreign Scholarships did when it decided to place a new Fulbright Commission in Cyprus in January 1962.

The passage of the Fulbright-Hays Act by Congress in September 1961 fixed a number of problems that had stunted the growth of the Fulbright program, such as more secure funding and exempting grantees from American taxes. As 1962 dawned, there were 44 Fulbright programs in the world headed by bi-national commissions. Twenty-nine were in Europe and Asia, while the State Department – organizationally – still regarded Cyprus as part of the Middle East, a view that would not change for another decade when it would be moved to the European Bureau. Most commissions had been established based on America's military presence and the availability of surplus military hardware. Now, the Board was anxious to expand the number of commissions to other countries.

Cyprus was an unlikely candidate for a bi-national commission. There were no four-year universities on the island, which made the exchange of scholars virtually impossible. It was largely agrarian with 70 percent of the population engaged in agriculture. It was certainly the smallest nation to have a commission, with the exception of Iceland (which, in 1962, had three universities, including one established in 1106). And its historical ties to the United Kingdom meant that ambitious Cypriot students would look there first if Greece or Turkey did not suit. Rarely would Cypriots look across the Atlantic.

However, the aforementioned larger forces were at work. Just six weeks after President Kennedy was inaugurated, Cyprus's Ambassador to the United States, Zenon Rossides, met with Secretary of State Dean Rusk to discuss possible aid.[2] The Secretary assured the Ambassador that these efforts were well-advanced and that they looked forward to the arrival of the UN-sponsored Thorp Report on the Cypriot economy authored by economist Willard Thorp, one of the architects of the Marshall Plan. However, America was doing its own evaluation and in August 1961, President Kennedy wrote to Rusk:

> *"Having read the Department's status report on the Cyprus situation, I am concerned over its gloomy tone. The inadequacies of the Makarios government, as contrasted with the discipline, energy, and able leadership of the local Communist Party (AKEL), are most worrisome. Perhaps we need some preventive medicine here to forestall further deterioration of this situation. Shouldn't we at a minimum push the UK, Greece, and Turkey to take a more forthcoming approach? Moreover, in view of their limited resources, we should carefully review our own policy of relying on these guarantor powers to shoulder the principal share of the Western burden. Since Cyprus' real estate and strategic location are of considerable importance to us and to our allies, I would be grateful if the Department of State would advise me on what measures would best ensure our holding on to it, including whatever use of U.S. resources may be required."[3]*

In addition to this push from Washington, there was also the pull from the American Embassy in Nicosia and Ambassador Wilkins, who aggressively requested a variety of resources. By September, President Kennedy had approved a State Department plan for Cyprus that included America "playing a major role in the economic development of Cyprus."[4] He asked the International Cooperation Administration (ICA) to urgently get to work. Later that year, the ICA was folded into the new U.S. Agency for International Development (USAID) created by Kennedy's executive order to make U.S. aid efforts a true foreign policy tool.

As noted, U.S. aid to Cyprus post-independence began with 40,000 tons of wheat and 10,000 tons of barley, as Cyprus was in the midst of a four-year drought. The grain was sold in Cyprus and the proceeds were used to finance a program to build roads and schools –but also, initially, they helped to fund the new Commission. In September 1961, a technical cooperation agreement was signed and the first two consultants arrived in short order to help with the establishment of the Cyprus Development Bank. The U.S. worked with CARE to provide milk and meals to 85,000 Cypriot school children. In addition, a substantial Peace Corps program brought dozens of volunteers to the island.

The U.S. was certainly not alone in these efforts. Britain's aid was still substantial – not to mention the economic stimulus provided by the bases and their personnel. The other guarantors also provided aid, as did numerous countries and organizations such as the International Bank for Reconstruction and Development.

However, the USAID mission began to grow, starting with three officers and expanding, by 1964, to a staff of more than 35. In addition to the monetary aid and consultants, ICA/USAID had, in the 1950s, begun sending Cypriots to the United States for training in the fields of agriculture, education, labor relations, policing, and finance.

There were several goals here: to expose future Cypriot leaders to Western ideas and methods with the hope that they would look favorably on the United States; to counter the significant influence of communism on the island; to bring the Greek and Turkish communities closer together or at least to keep them from becoming further estranged; to demonstrate America's interest in the well-being of their country.[5] Ultimately, USAID created a program to send 10 to 12 Cypriots a year to the American University in Beirut (AUB) for academic studies in finance, agriculture and public health.

There was also a study done to see if an American university could be established on Cyprus. USAID documents suggest that idea turned into a "saga" and that there was the thought that perhaps a branch university could be established with Claremont Colleges in California.[6] That made some sense. One of the five highly selective colleges in that consortium was Harvey Mudd College, supported by the owner of the Cyprus Mines Corporation. AUB was also approached about establishing a branch in Cyprus, but the university president wrote that it was beyond their means.[7]   It is not clear whether any effort would have succeeded. Constantine Spyridakis, the Education Minister for the first decade of the Republic, thought the establishment of a university was "premature." He feared that creating an intellectual center in Cyprus would undermine the traditional links with Athens and that a university with anything other than Greek as the language of instruction would be ethnically "catastrophic."[8]

The Embassy was also in negotiations with the Makarios government over rent for the American communications facilities on the island and the possibility of establishing a Voice of America transmitter. Meanwhile, the United States Information Service opened an American library on Homer Avenue near the Cyprus Museum, a place where future grantees would get a first taste of America by browsing magazines, academic journals and books and attending lectures.[9]   It appeared that America would contribute far more than the $20 million President Makarios requested – until it didn't.

The deal for the VOA transmitter fell through because Makarios asked for double what other countries received for similar rights and the transmitter was placed in Rhodes. As for many of the economic development projects the U.S. was prepared to finance, they, too, failed to launch. As Ambassador Wilkins recalled bitterly: "At one point we had as much as $40 million a year [$335 million in 2020 dollars] for US-AID assistance," explained Wilkins. "Makarios blew the whole thing by dragging his feet on the details of projects. Cyprus received the PL480 [grain], but they never got any of the substantial assistance that would have been available."[10]

Another factor was convincing investors that the island would be free from turmoil, as then USAID Director in Cyprus Joseph Toner explained to the Cyprus News Agency.[11]   Toner made the point that on a per capita basis, the USAID mission in Cyprus was one of the largest in the world, but he also provoked commentary when he bluntly asserted that U.S. aid efforts were there, first and foremost, to serve American interests. Yet, by 1966, USAID started to withdraw from the island and completed that withdrawal in the spring of 1969, with the exception of the AUB grants. The Embassy's Economic Officer and the Commission administered these grants, with most of the work falling on the shoulders of the Commission, without compensation. Some on the Fulbright Commission Board expressed the opinion that that situation should not stand.

So, the establishment of a bi-national Fulbright Commission was almost lost amid all the other U.S. Government activity.

On Thursday, January 18, 1962, Cyprus's Foreign Minister Spyros Kyprianou and Ambassador Wilkins signed a five-page agreement creating the Commission for Educational Exchange between the United States of America and Cyprus. The agreement stated:

"The Government of Cyprus and the Government of the United States of America, desiring to promote further mutual understanding between the peoples of Cyprus and the United States of America by a wider exchange of knowledge and professional talents through educational activities, have agreed that there shall be established a Commission to be known as the Commission for Educational Exchange between the United States of America and Cyprus, which shall be recognized by the Government of Cyprus and the Government of the United States of America as an organization created and established to facilitate the administration of an educational program to be financed by funds held or available for expenditure by the United States for such purposes."[12]

The Commission, the 45th in the world, was to be established in Nicosia and have a Board of eight members – four Americans and four Cypriots. The American Ambassador or Chief of Mission would be designated the "Honorary Chairman" and could break any ties in voting. At least two American board members would be American Foreign Service Officers assigned to the Embassy. One would be the Chairman of the Board of the Commission and one would be the treasurer. The Government of Cyprus would appoint the Cypriot members annually. There was an understanding that three would be Greek Cypriots and one a Turkish Cypriot. The agreement also called for the hiring of an executive director and other staff to run the day-to-day operations of the programs.[13]

Just over six weeks later, on March 5, the newly constituted Board held its first meeting. By that time, they were already five months deep into the U.S. Government's fiscal year and deadlines were looming for students to apply to American universities for the fall 1962 term. The Commission had to get busy.

Cultural Affairs Officer Daryl Dayton, from the U.S. Embassy in Athens, came to Cyprus to help launch the Commission. Greece had one of the oldest Fulbright Commissions, established in 1948, and a new Executive Director for Cyprus – American James F. Warner – came from Athens, where he had spent the previous year as a Fulbright scholar. Warner, who spoke Greek, stayed just over two years until the summer of 1964, when he was appointed Executive Director of Greece's Fulbright Commission.

With the departure of Warner, the Commission had two consecutive acting Directors who were also the Cultural Affairs Officers at the Embassy – first Jack Goodwin and then Herbert Berthold. The hiring of Americans for the position was expensive. It was a problem that the Board of Foreign Scholarships wrestled with everywhere.

A three-person staff was also hired in the first months of the Commission. Renos Kamenos was hired as the fiscal officer, Nitsa Tavanaris as his secretary, and Constantinos Ioannou as the part-time driver/messenger/custodian. By 1967, Kamenos was named Assistant Executive Director and a year later, with Berthold's early departure from the island, Kamenos was named Executive Director with Ambassador Taylor Belcher's blessing. The granting of the title only recognized what was by then the day-to-day reality.

"The American officers listened to Renos," observed Daniel Hadjittofi, who would eventually succeed Kamenos. "He had a way of speaking and explaining things that earned their trust."

Kamenos came to the position with a background in accounting – but more importantly in the culture of Cyprus – he came from a large and prominent family. He seemed to know everyone or, at least, everyone involved with running the country. He worked hard – in a Mediterranean sort of way. Former staff members describe him as someone who was at his desk when they arrived and was still there when they departed for the day. He was demanding, a perfectionist, a chain smoker, with a deep and commanding voice. He spoke deliberately, giving him more gravitas. It was clearly his office.

"Yes, a lot of people knew our family," noted Kamenos's youngest brother, Dr. Andreas Kamenos. "I was not surprised when Renos took the position with the Commission. He thought education was important. Fulbright was respected in Cyprus, and he would do anything to help someone. He was kind and professional and, yes, he had a strong personality."[14]

Two years before Kamenos formally assumed the directorship, his secretary took temporary leave for medical treatment in London. The Labor Office sent 18-year-old Stella Yiasemidou, who had graduated from a French convent school at 16 and had taken the Pitman office management course in London. Upon her return to Cyprus, there were no offers of work so she went to the Labor Office where she was told there was nothing except a temporary position that would last but 15 days. "I was bored and said that would be fine," recalled Stella, today Stella Zavallis.[15]

Initially, the Commission worked out of the American Center on Homer Avenue, but when Stella arrived for an interview in January 1966 it had moved to an office at 21 Diagorou Street. "It was a house behind another house and there was a long hallway with boxes. I had no idea what kind of work this was. I thought it might be an import-export company."[16] She was hired and when the 15 days ended and Tavanaris did not return, Stella stayed – for 41 years.

Soon after she arrived, however, Kamenos began to court Stella, a surprise given the significant gap in their ages. "I was 18 and not interested in marriage but I got to know Renos as a person. He was very kind in heart and very special in his manners. He could be a difficult person to work for but he came to value my point of view. He was also very persistent so things went pretty fast," said Stella.[17] They married in July 1967.

The program they were running was modest, but busy. The Commission was given a budget of $100,000 ($850,000 in 2020 dollars), although there was some confusion. Washington wanted that money to last through the end of the next fiscal year as well, but the Cyprus program spent its funds quickly and Washington had to supplement the program in the following year. From that point on, the annual budget would be approximately $100,000 most of the first decade.

They managed to get six students to the U.S. in the fall of 1962, all Greek Cypriots – Aristides Costeas, a science teacher who received an as-

Renos Kamenos, the first Cypriot Executive Director of the Cyprus Fulbright Commission, courted and married his administrative assistant Stella Yiasemidou, who remained at the Commission more than 40 years.

sistantship at Columbia University; Tasoula Sparilla, a math teacher who did graduate work at the University of Washington; Kyriacos Orphanides, who went as an undergraduate to study science at New York University; Christos Ktorides, an undergraduate majoring in electronics at Carroll College in Wisconsin; Theodoulos Kattamis, who received an assistantship at UC Berkeley; Stelios Phiniotis, who received an additional scholarship from Cornell University to study industrial and labor relations.[18]

The graduate students received full grants, but the undergraduates received only travel grants, essentially a plane ticket to the United States and one to return home. The Commission relied on the Institute of International Education (IIE) – helped by the Fulbright imprimatur – to place the students and to negotiate a package of financial aid. Some of the students were from a stratum of Cypriot society that could afford to pay for study in the U.S., particularly since tuition costs were still comparatively modest.

However, not all had the necessary finances. When Sophocles Michaelides left as an undergraduate for Wake Forest University in the fall of 1966 he knew the amount his family could pay would not stretch far enough. "I did not know Wake Forest at all but because of the limited means of my family I had a limited choice, but it turned out to be a wonderful thing," said Michaelides. "Everyone wants to go to Oxford or Cambridge and spend a lot of money but that was not an option for me."[19]

The Dean of Michaelides's department recognized his financial situation and found him a job grading mathematics papers and exams. And he had a host family that looked after him. Serendipitously, both the husband and wife in that family had gone to Cornell. Years before, Michaelides had seen pictures of the leafy Cornell campus with its Second Empire and Romanesque architecture and had fallen in love. So, when he finished his undergraduate degree at Wake Forest, he headed to the Ivy League and Cornell to complete his master's and Ph.D. degrees in four years. He then taught for a year at Eastern Michigan University, but he never planned to stay in America.

"That is not how I was brought up," said Michaelides. He returned to Cyprus a year after the events of 1974. His father's business in the citrus industry had collapsed and Michaelides went to work for the Central Bank, where he rose to be its Senior Director in 2006 at a time when the bank was adjusting to the new EU rules.

"I had gotten a fantastic and broad education in economics, political science and mathematics," explained Michaelides. "Degrees in, say, England can be so narrow. I can't say everyone in Cyprus valued American degrees, especially if they came from the left of the political spectrum, but I was stubborn."[20]

The fact that the Commission chose to award grants to undergraduates made it unique in the world, and this exception did not please Washington. But the Government of Cyprus and the Embassy argued strenuously that since there were no four-year universities on the island, grants to undergraduates were valuable and necessary. Walter Douglas, who was Board Chairman from 1999 to 2002, remembered the pressure from Washington to end the undergraduate scholarships: "but, the Cypriots were pretty dug in, so we just decided that this is what we were going to do." This argument with Washington would continue for decades. There was also the matter of establishing the selection panels, which would include Board members and outsiders. These had to be seen as absolutely fair. Cyprus was a small place and it was not unusual for people to believe that someone might be putting a thumb on the scale. A cryptic note in the early Board notes slaps the hands of some unnamed American officers at the Embassy who might have tried to promise the awarding of a scholarship to a Cypriot contact's child.[21]

From top to bottom: Sophocles Michaelides, Kenan Atakol and Michael Sarris were all early Fulbright grantees. All earned their Ph.D.s and became (respectively) the Director of Cyprus's Central Bank, the Foreign Minister of the Turkish Republic of Northern Cyprus, and the Finance Minister of the Republic of Cyprus.

As far as travel grants were concerned, not all liked them. They felt they cheapened the Fulbright brand. However, it was a simple trade-off. Bigger grants meant fewer grants, given the limitations of the budget, and if it was just a handful of grants there was no need for a bi-national Commission.

Dr. Socrates Pantelides felt the travel grant was a gamble worth taking. He came from a village outside of Limassol, where his father was a shoemaker. There was not a lot of money. He received a scholarship offer from Northern Illinois University, west of Chicago, but the offer said the grant was for just one year and not renewable. Kamenos told him not to worry about it; that "they all say that." As it turned out, NIU meant it. Pantelides scrambled, obtained a tuition and fee waiver, but needed room and board. At the last moment, he secured a position as a resident assistant and, ultimately, a part-time job at the university and made it all work. With a large number of existing credits, he finished his undergraduate degree in physics in two years and accepted a fellowship at the University of Illinois where he studied for his Ph.D. He was ultimately recruited by another University of Illinois graduate, Walter Harrison, to come on board at IBM, where Pantelides spent 20 years. The job offer, an American wife, and a time when rules were more flexible allowed him to get around the J-1 visa requirement that he return to Cyprus for at least two years. "It was the glory years of IBM. We had amazing resources. We could do anything we wanted. We were judged on the basis of basic physics that we produced and published in the best journals. It was an amazing time." However, as Pantelides noted, IBM misjudged the personal computer revolution and he departed just as mighty IBM downsized. Again he landed on his feet at Vanderbilt University, where he is the Distinguished Professor of Physics and Engineering. "The scholarship was my fairy godmother. I am grateful to the Fulbright program. If I had not got that scholarship I don't know what would have happened."[22]

In the second year, the Commission was able to award 20 grants, and five went to Turkish Cypriots. Over the years, an unwritten rule evolved at the Commission that it would strive to keep the ratio of grants four-to-one, reflecting the distribution of the population. It did not always happen. The enclaving, the low number of Turkish Cypriots at English language schools in Cyprus, the discouragement from Turkish Cypriot authorities over the issue of military service – all these factors conspired to keep the number of Turkish Cypriot applicants low in the early years. Indeed, the Commission decided it would not offer grants to any Turkish Cypriot males for three years (1965-67), until these issues were finally worked out with Turkish Cypriot authorities.

One of the first Turkish Cypriots to receive a Fulbright for graduate study in the U.S. was Kenan Atakol, who departed early in 1964 for the University of New Mexico to study engineering and hydrology. His departure was anything but joyous. In the days after violence broke out on December 21, 1963, he married his bride Gönen and then retreated with her and 40 others to shelter deep in the Turkish quarter of Nicosia at the home of his in-laws. Three weeks later, a British armored car took them to the airport for their own protection. They would not come back to Cyprus for eight years, warned by their families that it would not be safe to return.[23]

In those eight years Atakol completed his master's and then his Ph.D. degree at the University of Virginia. Afterward, he taught for a number of years at Penn State University, and formed a life-long bond with his two host families. His daughters were American-born, but he always intended to return to Cyprus. In 1974, shortly after the division of the island, he was appointed the Turkish Cypriot Minister of Energy and Natural Resources and, ultimately, Foreign Minister. In those roles he was an early advocate for piping water from Turkey and he pushed every American Ambassador to provide more money for scholarships.

One of the principal arguments for a Commission in Cyprus was that it was necessary to counteract the efforts of the Soviet Union and Eastern Bloc countries that were not only offering scholarships to the children of AKEL members, but going after top students as well. Telemachos Mouschovias remembers that the pitch could be persuasive.

"AKEL was pursuing many of the best students and offering full scholarships to Moscow University," recalled Mouschovias, who received a Fulbright as an undergraduate to study physics. "I was just about to depart for Yale in the summer of 1964, when a senior AKEL official offered a full scholarship and also offered to take care of my parents while I was gone."[24] Given the fact that his father had been blinded in a work accident and his family was in dire financial straits, the offer was tempting.

"My family always wanted me to think for myself and I had long been attracted to the American system of education," said Mouschovias. "In addition, Yale had offered a full scholarship and IIE had offered a supplement on top of that, which allowed me to help my family."[25]

Mouschovias was pulled back to Cyprus to do military service by his unyielding government, but was able to return to America to earn his Ph.D. at University of California-Berkeley, do a post-doctorate at

Princeton, and then land in the physics department of the University of Illinois where he has remained since. He briefly entertained the idea of accepting a position at a university in Crete in the 1980s, but stayed at Illinois as part of a team that won a $44 million ($115 million in 2020 dollars) National Science Foundation grant to develop a super computer in the 1980s.

Of course, all Fulbright grants came with the requirement under a J-1 visa that recipients return to their home countries for a minimum of two years. The idea of the Fulbright program was not to take the best and brightest and keep them in America, but to have them return and make a contribution to their respective countries. The RoC wanted Fulbrighters to return to the island and to stay even longer than the two required years, and tried hard to enforce that policy. That said, there was a process to receive a waiver because life happens, including those students who not only gained an education in America, but found love as well and married an American. The acquisition of an American spouse would not automatically lead to a waiver, but more often than not it was a major factor in deciding to seek a waiver.

Given his achievements and academic interests, returning to Cyprus was not a viable option, and Mouschovias did marry an American. "I was not going to return to teach high school physics." However, Mouschovias was involved in some of the early discussions about establishing a university in Cyprus when Andreas Philippou was Minister of Education, but when Philippou departed that role ended.

In its first decade, the Commission awarded 150 grants, both graduate and undergraduate – 121 to Greek Cypriots and 29 to Turkish Cypriots; 128 to males and 22 to females. Engineering (20), physics (15), economics (14), administration (11), education and agriculture (10 each) received more than half the grants, but grants were given in some 30 different disciplines. Still, by 1971-72 there were only 189 Cypriots studying in the U.S., more than half as a result of Fulbright grants from the Commission.[26]

These were the Fulbright recipients, but did not account for the 12 to 15 USAID grants the Commission helped administer annually for the American University of Beirut, nor teacher development grants that sent Cypriot educators to the U.S. for shorter, non-degree courses, nor the handful of grants given each year for the Cleveland International Programs for courses in social work and youth leadership.

Then there were also some small programs that did not fit the traditional Fulbright mold, but fit in the Cyprus context while also supporting

American institutions. These included tuition grants to the American Academy in Larnaca, a Presbyterian mission school founded in 1908 that offered American-style education, as well as the American Academy for Girls in Nicosia. The Commission also began, in 1966, a relationship with the American Farm School in Thessaloniki, another school founded (1904) by an American missionary that provided a high school education with an emphasis on agricultural subjects.

In the first year of the Farm School program, the Commission awarded six grants of approximately $1000 each. Things did not go completely smoothly. On June 27, 1967, one of the boys, Ioannis Kyriacou, ran away from the school and was not located for four months. He returned safely to Cyprus in the company of his father on November 2.[27]

There was also, briefly, an attempt to create a teacher exchange program where Cypriot teachers would spend a year teaching in the U.S. while an American counterpart would come to Cyprus. They would not only swap jobs, but homes as well; but the turmoil of the 1960s in Cyprus as well as financial issues never allowed that program to take off. For example, in 1967 American teachers on the island along with the dependents of American officers at the Embassy were evacuated to Beirut, which was still considered the nearest safe zone for evacuations.

The Commission believed it was attracting some of the best and brightest in Cyprus. Even in the first year when Fulbright was little known on the island, there were 193 applicants for the six grants awarded. Many were eliminated in the first wave of tests, particularly the TOEFL or English language test. To receive a visa to study in the United States one either had to have a passing score on the TOEFL or be enrolled in a preparatory English course. In the years that followed, the number of applicants grew to between 200 and 300 annually. Both Michaelides and Mouchovias remembered that they inquired about scholarships to study in Britain, but that none were on offer, which created an opening for the Commission and the idea of study in America. Of the 150 grantees in the first decade, 19 were accepted at Ivy League schools and several others were accepted at top schools such as MIT, the University of California at Berkeley, and Vanderbilt.

Like Michaelides, who had never heard of Wake Forest, most of the students who came to the Commission knew about Harvard, Yale and Princeton, but few other schools. There was no Internet. It was the job of the Commission to convince them that not everyone was going to be accepted at those schools and that America had many fine universities that would meet their educational needs. Indeed, the vast majority of the

Cypriot students who went to the U.S. prospered, but not all, and that worried the Commission.

In 1967, the Commission had to cope with its first true tragedy when Stavroula Georgiades of Paralimni was killed in an auto accident near a small town 135 kilometers southeast of Seattle, Washington. Georgiades had been given an undergraduate Fulbright grant in 1964 to study languages at the University of Washington. A large delegation from the Commission and Embassy headed by Ambassador Belcher attended the funeral, but the Commission found itself in the middle of the disputes between the American insurers and the Georgiades family, with all the cultural misunderstandings that would attend. It was a tragic and uncomfortable situation.

Then, early in 1968, the Commission received word that former grantee Christodoulos Mouzakis had hung himself at the University of Wisconsin.[28] Mouzakis had received an undergraduate grant to study economics at Wisconsin in 1963, had graduated and stayed there to earn his master's degree, but then came the news of his death. Unlike the death of Georgiades, which had been discussed in depth by the Board, the news concerning Mouzakis was closely held and not discussed. "It was a very sensitive situation," remembered Zavallis. Because Mouzakis was no longer a Commission grantee, IIE was no longer contacting him and checking on his well-being, which it did for all grantees.

Soon after, another Cypriot grantee experienced psychological issues and returned to Cyprus with an attending psychiatrist and this, along with a handful of other so-called fall-outs – students withdrawing from their programs – set off alarm bells in Washington. The chairman of the Commission Board, Public Affairs Officer Robert Benedict, was asked to prepare a report.[29] Still, the number of "fall-outs" was only four, and most of them had spent many years in the U.S. before deciding to withdraw. There were also several Cypriot high school students who had gone to the United States for a year under the American Field Service (AFS) auspices, but had trouble adjusting to life in America. It was not unusual. The AFS program, which was run in its first years by the Embassy's Public Affairs Section and not the Commission, had – from time to time – students who had trouble adjusting, were overcome by homesickness, or just did not get along with their host families. The numbers were small, but cumulatively, these problems worried some in Washington.

During the spring of 1969, the Commission and the Board discussed the idea of perhaps having grantees undergo some sort of psychological evaluation before heading to the U.S. The Commission requested copies of the "physician samples" used for screening students at Columbia University.[30] Asking the students who had already been notified of their grants to sit for a psychological evaluation made the Board members uncomfortable. Nor were they comfortable with involving a psychologist in the selection process for future grantees. In the end, Washington and the Commission agreed that they would just try to be mindful of possible issues identified in the application forms and letters of recommendation.[31]

The selection panels were largely made up of the Board members, but might also include outsiders, particularly visiting American Fulbright scholars who were pressed into service to not only help evaluate the applicants, but also to offer counseling to those interested in study in the U.S.

Despite the lack of universities on the island, the RoC was anxious to have American academics come as consultants, particularly in the field of education. In its first year, the Commission did very well. Dr. Harry Meyering arrived to conduct a survey of Turkish Cypriot schools; Dr. Anthony Stampolis researched a report entitled "The Social Economic Development of Cyprus," which became recommended reading for military attachés at the Embassy; Dr. Irving Brown taught speech and drama at the Pedagogical Academy; and Dr. Stanley Sahlstrom worked on curriculum development and teaching methods.

A second group of academics arrived in the fall of 1963 in the fields of educational administration, English teaching and vocational education, but were evacuated and reassigned after the violence of December 1963. The unsettled situation, with one or two exceptions, stopped the recruiting of Fulbright scholars for long-term (one or two semesters) assignments until 1970. What the Commission was able to do was attract Fulbright scholars from other countries in the region to come for a few days or perhaps a few weeks under Fulbright's Inter-country Lecture Program. Here the Commission, working in conjunction with the Embassy's Public Affairs Section, did very well, bringing in 10 to 12 scholars a year.

If it wasn't Cyprus's unsettled political situation providing the impediment, it was American politics.

In 1965, Senator Fulbright began to turn against President Lyndon Johnson, first over Johnson's decision to deploy troops to the Dominican Republic and then over the growing American involvement in Vietnam. A furious Johnson retaliated by forcing massive cuts to the Fulbright program budget, aided and abetted by Representative John J. Rooney (D-NY), Chairman of the House subcommittee that oversaw the Department of State's budget. Rooney, a staunch anti-communist and defender of the war in Vietnam, was skeptical of educational exchange programs in general and inflicted a brutal 43 percent cut on the Fulbright budget for fiscal year 1969 (which began on October 1, 1968). It was decided that the programs for American scholars, rather than foreign students, would take the brunt of the cuts.[32]

For the Commission in Cyprus, the cuts were devastating, reducing the budget from approximately $100,000 annually to $57,826. The Commission had, almost from its inception, tried to find other sources of revenue but Cypriot laws made that difficult. It was not until 1970 that tax laws were changed to allow donations to the Commission to be treated as charitable donations. There were small donations from Coca-Cola and an oil company, and then in 1969 the Cyprus Mines Corporation agreed to fund a scholarship in engineering with a $6000 contribution. Also, with a bit of coaxing from the Embassy, the RoC made its first contribution with 1,000 Cypriot pounds, which would gradually increase to CP2,000. At a luncheon to mark the 10th anniversary of the Commission, Ambassador David Popper noted that the Commission was able to do a great deal with a small amount of money and that it constantly pushed Washington to increase the budget. In response, Foreign Minister Spyros Kyprianou praised the Commission and its impact on Cyprus and noted that in the following year Cyprus would increase its contribution from CP1500 to CP2000.[33] It was small steps for a small program.

In many countries, the hosts were making substantial contributions to their bi-national commissions, so the drastic cuts by the American government were seen as a breach of trust.[34] That, and the departure of Johnson from the White House in January 1969, allowed the reversal of the cuts over the next several years. As the budget was restored, so was a modicum of political stability in Cyprus and American scholars began to arrive again for long-term stays.

The Fulbright program's visiting scholars were supplemented by a new relationship with the State University of New York (SUNY) at Albany. In February 1969, Dr. James Heaphey arrived in Cyprus to give a lecture and to discuss the creation of an institute of Cypriot studies at SUNY Albany. That institute was founded shortly afterward and a special grant from the Department of State followed. Professor Richard Nunez was the first academic to come to Cyprus. SUNY Albany also announced that it would provide two grants to allow Cypriots to come to Albany to undertake a master's degree in public administration. Ambassador Popper asked the Commission to handle the selection process. At this point, the Commission's resources were limited, but they offered to support the fledgling Cyprus Institute with a handful of travel grants beginning in the spring of 1970 with archaeologist Dr. John Overbeck. Even this program was not free from tragedy. In April 1970, Dr. Paul Lapp, also an archaeologist, arrived from SUNY Albany to begin a new excavation at Idalion and five days later he drowned while swimming in the waters off Cyprus. He was 39.

Even with the lack of American scholars arriving in the mid-1960s, the Commission was still busy. Applicants for Fulbright grants exceeded 300 most years and by 1970, the Commission was handling more than 2,500 inquiries a year about study in the U.S.[35] Throughout the 1960s the staff still numbered only three, with Hambis Koutalianos replacing Constantinos Ioannou in October 1965. Koutalianos would become a fixture at the Commission and stay for 35 years. In the fall of 1967, the Board called for the Commission to hire an additional program assistant to help carry the load, but the sudden budget cuts forced by Washington politics delayed those efforts. In the early 1970s, a series of program assistants were hired; first Neophytos Tsioutis, who stayed a month, and then Photini Sofroniou and former Fulbright grantee Charalambos Hadjipolycarpou, who stayed the longest at 20 months. At that point Kamenos shifted his thinking and decided to hire another former grantee, Necla Oktay, the first Turkish Cypriot at the Commission. "Renos thought that hiring a Turkish Cypriot would help bring the communities together," remembered Zavallis.[36] As Zavallis earlier observed, Kamenos was not an easy person to work for given his demanding nature. His successor concurred. "I would not have lasted six months if not for the encouragement of the Public Affairs Officer Dan Howard," recalled Hadjittofi, who originally came to the Commission as Kamenos's deputy. Oktay was succeeded by Nicos Nicolaou, who left some months later after the invasion and the division of the island.

By fiscal year 1971, the budget had been restored to $115,000 and the Commission was able to attract American scholars for long-term stays. Jack Balswick came from the University of Georgia to research the Cypriot social services and the Cypriot family, working at the Ministry of Labor. "The Ministry of Labor was very cooperative and I mainly worked with social workers," recalled Balswick. "I found them strongly oriented toward serving their clients, but these were Greek Cypriots serving Greek Cypriots. My feeling was that Cyprus was Greece and that the Turkish Cypriots were part of another country."[37] Professor Donald Reeb came from SUNY Albany and had most of his grant paid for by the RoC. Over the course of nine months, Reeb, under the auspices of the Ministry of Finance, did his best to visit and conduct interviews studying economic activity in 600 largely Greek Cypriot villages, beginning in December 1972. It was the kind of study that might have been carried out by a Cypriot professor from a Cypriot university, had one existed. Instead, Cyprus had the use of a Fulbright scholar to undertake a somewhat rare study of a developing nation's grassroots economy.

Reeb was aided by his escort and translator, Costakis Apostolides, who, a few years later, would be granted a Fulbright to earn his master's degree in economics at Boston University. "Renos and Stella took very good care of us. All the details of our stay were arranged and Renos always made sure that I had my picture taken with the Minister or other high official," said Reeb. Reeb found that being a Fulbrighter in Cyprus had some cachet. "It was sometimes embarrassing," he explained. "My wife and daughters and I went to stay a night in a little inn in the Troodos and they would not let us pay because I was a Fulbrighter."[38]

The Fulbright program was always meant to be a two-way street. Americans were supposed to learn just as much about Cyprus as Cypriots were supposed to learn about American methods and thinking. Many of the scholars brought their children. Dr. Balswick ambitiously tried starting his two children in the Cypriot schools but found they could not absorb the Greek quickly enough. Kerri Ballantyne, whose father, Dr. Robert Ballantyne of Duke University came to advise on vocational education, remembers vividly the impact the experience had on them. "I was 12 when we came to Cyprus with my brother and two sisters. I went to the English School and remember being very behind in some subjects but they named me games captain and I liked that," recalled Ballantyne. "Dad had a kind of charisma and people opened up to him. He could even talk his way through checkpoints." There were also reminders that the world could be a serious place. "I made friends with the daughter of the Israeli Ambassador and she would come to my house for a sleep-over. I did not know it at the time, but when she came Israeli security guards would be posted around our apartment building. It made my Dad nervous, but I was 12 and don't remember ever being worried."[39] The Ballantynes left in the spring of 1974, just before things got very serious.

In the early 1970s, as the dip in the budget was reversed and the country seemed to find some stability, the Commission stepped up its activity with more scholars/consultants. It also was able to grant more scholarships after giving just 11 in 1969, coming back up in the range of 18 a year. In early 1974, the Commission moved its offices to a second floor flat on Severis Avenue in Nicosia. However, in the early 1970s, the United States was going through an economic recession provoked by the Arab oil embargo, and the amount of financial aid offered by American universities fell. There was also pressure from the Board of Foreign Scholarships to adopt policies that would conform to a vision that it had set forth in a report on educational exchange in the 1970s. In the case of Cyprus, this would once again mean an effort to reduce, if not eliminate, undergraduate scholarships.

Public Affairs Officer and Board Chairman Robert Wozniak held a special meeting of the Board at his house in December 1973 to discuss a "new direction" for the program that included a greater emphasis on graduate scholarships.[40] By putting more money into graduate grants overall, the number of grants were reduced. But the Board pushed back, particularly Turkish Cypriot Board member Mustafa Raif, who argued that some undergraduate travel grants had to continue.

However, for a year or two the Commission succumbed to Washington's pressure and in its 1976 Program Plan, which was adopted in June of 1975, it was noted that: "the Commission has tried to implement the relevant portions of the 'Educational Exchange in the Seventies' in its program goals. One result has been the replacement of the popular undergraduate scholarship competitions with a strictly graduate degree program. This has met with a certain amount of displeasure, but the more practical contributions of graduate degree holders are generally accepted and the government is committed to granting generous leave status to successful civil service applicants."[41] That decision would not stand for long.

One of those who received an undergraduate grant in 1973 for study in the U.S. in the fall of 1974 was Michael Tringides, who had been accepted at Yale to study math and physics. He was just finishing his military service when the coup and subsequent invasion occurred. "Of course I fought, but those who had places in universities were released a bit early," explained Tringides, today a professor of physics at Iowa State University. "Renos and Stella managed to arrange everything. As the airport had been destroyed, I took a boat from Cyprus to Athens, where everything was in chaos. I flew in a 747 from Athens to New York, the first time I had ever been in a plane. Then there was the short flight to New Haven. I came three or four weeks late, but I soon found that I was kind of a celebrity. Everyone wanted to ask me about Cyprus."[42]

Tringides, from Famagusta, might have found himself opposite Sarper Ince, who had also received an undergraduate grant in 1972, also to study physics, in this case at Hamilton College, a small liberal arts college in upstate New York. Ince and a friend who was studying in the U.K. made a pact that they would stay in America and the U.K., respectively, in the summer of 1973 to work and save money and then, in the summer of 1974, meet in the U.K. and travel together to Cyprus to see their families. "We arrived in early July and everything was normal," recalled Ince. "The Greek Cypriots at the airport were smiling and there was no sign that within a few days there would be a coup and a few days after that I would be in the ditches fighting. We were trapped in the old city of Famagusta and you had to fight."[43] When the Turkish military arrived, Ince was released from his duties and the Commission arranged for him to take a ferry to Mersin, Turkey and then back to America, just a week late. "I was the first generation in my family to go beyond elementary school, but it was the age of the moon landings and I wanted to study in America and be on the cutting edge of technology. I wanted to aim high," said Ince, who would receive a second grant to earn a master's at the University of Michigan. ("Michigan had great football teams in those years and my son learned the fight song," said Ince laughing.) He would return to Cyprus and teach science for many years at Türk Maarif Koleji, the main English-language school for Turkish Cypriots in Nicosia.

Renos and Stella were just as stunned as everyone else by events in the summer of 1974. "We were in the Troodos Mountains when the coup occurred," recalled Zavallis. "People believed that because we were connected to the American Embassy we knew something was going to happen, but we did not. Renos hated the summer heat and wanted get to the mountains as much as he could. I think it was a week before we returned to the office and there were bullet holes in some of the shutters as we were near the presidential palace."[44] When they returned, there were 13 grantees to get off of Cyprus and to America. Most made it, although a few were compelled to delay their studies until the second semester. The Board praised Renos and Stella for their skill and perseverance in pulling together the last-minute travel arrangements. However, what was clear was that the work of the Commission was now going to be changed by events.

For Sheila Austrian, who had recently arrived as the new Assistant Public Affairs Officer, life was going to be very different from what she had imagined. Austrian had come to Cyprus several years earlier with her husband, Mike, who was the Turkish-speaking political officer in the Embassy. She also wanted a diplomatic career, but archaic State Department rules said that a woman could not become or remain a Foreign Service Officer if she was married. In 1972, spurred by the women's movement in America, that rule finally changed and Austrian took and passed the Foreign Service exam to become one of the first married women to enter the Service. She went to Washington to train and then returned to Cyprus but found her duties very different from what she had anticipated. "I spent most of our final months in Cyprus trying to recover the personal effects of American citizens who had been evacuated from the island and could not return to their properties," explained Austrian.[45]

Shortly after they arrived in Cyprus, Austrian was asked to counsel a young Greek Cypriot girl who had been awarded a Fulbright for undergraduate study. "She was academically gifted but shy," recalled Austrian "and it came down to a choice between Columbia and Swarthmore," one of the so-called Seven Sisters, a collection of women-only colleges. The girl, Rea Yiordamlis, was pressured by her father to choose Columbia "because he wanted her to go to a university and not a college," explained Austrian. This was a distinction that the Commission often had to explain to Cypriot grantees. In the end, they convinced her father that Swarthmore, a small, liberal arts college in Pennsylvania, was the better fit.

"I actually don't remember that at all," said Yiordamlis, "but I was 17. I just thought that America suited my personality. My father knew Mr. Kamenos and while there were not a lot of women applying for Fulbrights, I thought that I would try. Going to Swarthmore was an extraordinary experience and shaped who I am today."[46] Yiordamlis returned to Cyprus with a degree in sociology and thought she would become a social worker, but in the wake of the war with tens of thousands of refugees, the Ministry of Foreign Affairs was looking for people with her skills and the Ministry, like the American State Department, had recently decided to bring women into the diplomatic service. "I joined in 1976 and was posted to Greece as a consul." She returned to Cyprus and stayed for a time with her young children and then was posted to India and, ultimately to Madrid as Cyprus's first woman ambassador. She then held a second ambassadorship in Latin America before holding a variety of Ministry posts in Cyprus including Political Director and Permanent Secretary. Yiordamlis, who studied in America in the midst of the Vietnam era, thought her American experience prepared her well. "I see myself as open-minded and someone who can reach compromises, which is important in diplomacy. I think my American education gave me the ability to think through different situations."

Washington asks all Fulbright programs around the world to keep track of alumni, particularly if they advance to positions of leadership or have significant achievements in their respective societies. After its first dozen years, the Commission staff in Cyprus had no idea that some of their grantees would go on to become ministers, ambassadors, or leading academics or whether they would even return to Cyprus or find ways to remain in the United States to continue their academic or professional careers. What they did know, because their grantees told them so, was that the Fulbright experience had fundamentally changed their lives and that life in Cyprus, after the summer of 1974, would not be the same again. That meant there needed to be a strong hand on the rudder to keep the program pointed in the right direction.

THE BOARD

Though the bullets had stopped flying six weeks earlier, Nicosia, in October 1974, still very much felt like a city at war.

The capital's airport was now in a no man's land controlled by the UN, its terminal largely destroyed and a bullet-riddled passenger plane was left abandoned beside a runway. The Ledra Palace, once the city's most elegant hotel, showed the scars of fierce fighting; soon it would billet those UN forces.

Heavily armed troops patrolled the divided city on both sides and a secant sliced through the circle of the Venetian Walls of the Old City, where the fighting had stopped. The space between the two sides, sometimes only meters wide, would be called the Green Zone, a bucolic designation that belied the violence that had occurred there.

Tens of thousands of refugees huddled in tent encampments that grew day by day on the edges of the city wherever vacant land could be found. There were communal showers set up in the middle and tents radiating out from that central point. The main shopping street in the Old City of Nicosia – Ledra Street – still functioned, but the barriers made traffic chaotic.

It was in this atmosphere that the Board of the Fulbright Commission met on October 3, 1974 in the Nicosia suburb of Strovolos at the home of Public Affairs Officer and Board Chairman David Grimland. The meeting, the Board's 99th since March 1962, was attended by the newly arrived Ambassador William Crawford, the former Deputy Chief of Mission, who had been hastily recalled to Cyprus after the murder of Ambassador Davies.

Also attending were Cypriot Board members Panayiotis Persianis of the Ministry of Education, Dr. Charis Menelaou of the Ministry of Finance, and Americans Ann Bass, a musician and resident of Cyprus who was poised to leave the island, and the Rev. Kenneth Ziebell, who headed the Near East Ecumenical Committee for Palestinian Refugees. Absent were Jay Grahame, the Economic Officer at the Embassy, Nicosia Mayor Lellos Demetriades, who was off the island, and Esat Hilmi from the Turkish Office of Education, who would not attend another Board meeting in person until December 1977. Also attending was Executive Director Renos Kamenos.

Ambassador Crawford gave the group a pep talk about the valuable work of the Commission and the contribution it had made to Cyprus, but the uncertainty of the moment hung over every word.[1] The division of the island would not stand, would it? There were words of praise for Kamenos, who had worked out the logistics of getting most of the grantees off the island and to their universities in the U.S., despite the lack of a functioning commercial airport. Two months later, at the end-of-year meeting reserved for the approval of the annual program plan, there was a growing determination that, despite the difficulties, the Commission had to continue its efforts to "provide unbiased and open exchange opportunities for *all* Cypriots."[2] The Commission's bicommunal character had to be preserved.

By 1974, nearly 40 individuals – 28 Americans and 11 Cypriots – had served on the Commission's Board. The Americans, particularly those at the Embassy, came and went in more or less regular cycles. By the time the Commission held its last Board meeting on April 11, 2014 – its 253rd – that number would swell to 177 individuals who had volunteered or, more often than not, been appointed to serve and offer guidance to the Commission.

At the beginning of each year, the American Embassy would send a diplomatic note to the Government of Cyprus with the names of the four American Board members. The Government of Cyprus would send its note with the names of the Cypriot members, including the Turkish Cypriot members. The Turkish Cypriots pretended that they presented the names of their Board members to the Commission directly and the Greek Cypriot Government of Cyprus pretended that it had some control over the selection of the Turkish Cypriot members.

Only once, in early 2008, did the Greek Cypriot government object to the appointment of a Turkish Cypriot to the Board, Dr. Erbil Akbil. The objection centered around Dr. Erbil's previous position as the Minister of Education and Culture in the Turkish Cypriot administration. Even though he had left that position to take up a teaching position at Eastern Mediterranean University, the Greek Cypriots still objected. Dr. Akbil was due to replace Mehmet Tahiroglu, who over his long tenure on the Board had been a unifying force. Dr. Akbil, according to Executive Director Daniel Hadjittofi, met "the criteria [for a position on the Board] in terms of personality and intentions," but the Greek Cypriot authorities would not budge and Dr. Cem Tanova was appointed in his place, but not without a great deal of anger from Turkish Cypriot officials.[3] It made little sense since every Turkish Cypriot Board member was an official from the Education Ministry, but the Greek Cypriots judged Dr. Akbil to be too "political."

Sometimes, because of bureaucratic inertia or to show its displeasure, the Cypriot government would delay naming Board members. In 2010 and 2011, the first Board meetings of the year did not occur until June because President Demetris Christofias, from the socialist/communist AKEL Party, who had studied in the Soviet Union, would not name Board members until pushed by the American Embassy. The feeling was that he would be happy if the American Commission ceased to exist. He would get his wish soon enough.

Much of the work of the Board was pro forma – approving a program plan each year and monitoring the implementation of the program. American scholars/consultants would report on their work to the Board and there would be reports on all the students in America and their progress. The Executive Director had a great deal of power to shape the agenda and the discussion, and many of the decisions were worked out with Board members before each meeting. As Daniel Hadjittofi, Kamenos's successor, said in 2016: "If I had Lellos [Demetriades] and [Dr. Chrysostomos] Sofianos behind me I could be certain of the Board's support."[4] However, his first stop would always be a consultation with the American Chairman. "I did nothing major without asking them first," said Hadjittofi.

Kamenos and Hadjittofi had a free hand to hire staff, once a position had been created and approved – up to a point. The Board made sure that personnel policies, which followed the American Embassy model, were up to date. And the Board approved the hiring of an outside accounting firm to audit the Commission's books, which was actually a requirement set by Washington. The Board also approved the panels that would conduct the interviews of the students and that included an unwritten rule that scholarships would be awarded at a ratio of four Greek Cypriots to one Turkish Cypriot, reflecting the population. The panels would always be comprised of two Greek Cypriots, two Americans, one Turkish Cypriot and the Executive Director acting as the Chairman of the panel. If it came down to a choice between two students, each with excellent credentials – as it often did – that unwritten rule would be in the back of everyone's mind and, more often than not, it would be decisive. Dr. Huseyin Yaratan, who was a primary Board member for the Turkish Cypriots in the early 1990s, felt that the ratio was not fair, given how much poorer the Turkish Cypriots were compared to the Greek Cypriots, "but we wanted the scholarships, so we kept our mouths shut."[5] Some Board members were able to carry out their duties on the selection panels with no outside pressure. Others faced constant pressure from anxious parents at selection time, which could include phone calls in the middle of the night.

At the very first Board meeting on March 5, 1962, three of the American Board members were from the Embassy: Deputy Chief of Mission Douglas Heck in the chair, USAID Comptroller Charles White as treasurer, and Cultural Affairs Officer Kristine Konold. The fourth American was Thomas Edgar, the head of the American Academy in Larnaca. The four Cypriots were Frixos Vrachas, the Principal of the Greek Pedagogical Academy; Michalakis Maratheftis, an instructor at the Academy; Mustafa Raif, the Deputy Director of the Turkish Education Office; and Mikis Sparsis, a senior industrialist at the Ministry of Labor and, coincidently, Kamenos's brother-in-law.

The decision to place the Deputy Chief of Mission (DCM) in the Chair was an indication of the importance of the Commission in the Embassy's eyes. However, it would not be long before the chairmanship fell to the Embassy's Public Affairs Officers (PAOs) and stayed that way. PAOs were different from Embassy political or economic officers, first because they worked for a separate federal agency – the United States Information Agency (USIA) or Service (USIS) as it was known overseas. USIA oversaw the Fulbright program and PAOs reported directly to the Ambassador and not indirectly through the DCM. In addition, they

On the left, Mikis Sparsis, and on the right, Mustafa Raif.

managed program budgets that included numerous exchange opportunities
and larger staffs, making them a more
natural fit to oversee the Commission's
finances and people.[6]

However, the Board notes suggest
that among the Americans it was Konold, the only woman on the Board,
who brought more ideas and energy to
the table. Konold had an interesting
back-story. A would-be actress from
Washington, D.C., she moved to New
York City in 1942 shortly after America entered World War II. She found
a day job in the Office of War Information and took acting classes at night,
but longed to be in London, closer to
the actual war. She got that chance in
1943, and throughout the duration of
the war and afterward she rose to positions of increased responsibility doing
information work. After the war, she
found her way into America's diplomatic service where she carved out a
career that included Cyprus, Greece,
Iran and India.[7]

Yet, it was Sparsis who was key. He
was on the cusp of being named the
Director General of the Ministry of
Labor, and was on the Board to make
sure that the programs and grants that
were funded conformed to Cyprus's
developmental needs as set forth by the
Planning Commission. It was an ambitious list that included scholars/consul-

Lellos Demetriades (top) and Dr. Chrysostomos Sofianos (cetner) were a driving force on
the Board, while Mehmet Tahiroglu (bottom)
was a unifying force during his long tenure.

tants in trade unions, secondary education, agricultural education, and technical and vocational education. The government's list also included a drama teacher, a specialist in youth leadership, and an English teacher. In presenting these priorities, he did so with the perspective of someone who had been educated in the U.S.

"My father was in the British Army in World War II and in 1947 he went to the States and earned a B.A. from Geneva College in Pennsylvania and then a master's in industrial relations from Columbia University. He returned to Cyprus in 1955 and joined the civil service," wrote his son Nicolas. "I am sure that his involvement with Fulbright was a result of his connection to the States."[8]

"He was an outstanding professional in his field," remembered Stella Zavallis. "He introduced the Republic's social insurance scheme that is in effect to this day."[9]

In the fall of 1962, Maratheftis departed for England for studies and the government was asked to appoint a new member. Thus, in early 1963, another strong voice was added to the Board with the naming of Lellos Demetriades, at that time practicing law. "Makarios asked me to serve on the Board," explained Demetriades.[10] He would serve for 41 years, the longest of any member.

Demetriades, or Lellos – as he was known to everyone – began his university studies in Greece, but wanted to practice law. Given the system of English law that prevailed in Cyprus, he left for England, sharing a flat with Tassos Papadopoulos and Spyros Kyprianou, and was admitted to the bar there. He returned to Cyprus and joined the youth wing of EOKA, using his skills to defend and free young Cypriots arrested by the British. More than 50 years later, he would still grow emotional over a single boy whose defiance made it impossible to save him from the gallows.

He was, by his own admission, an unusual politician. He did not belong to any party and, unlike the majority of Greek Cypriots, did not support enosis and was often attacked as being "anti-Greek." He would be elected to the House of Representatives and then, in 1971, he was elected mayor of Nicosia, a position he would hold for 30 years. In the late 1970s he had a serious problem to solve: Nicosia might have been divided above ground, but its aging sewer and water system was very much interconnected below ground. As a result, he began a series of meetings with his Turkish Cypriot counterpart Mustafa Akinci to find the solution. That willingness to work together as well as millions of USAID dollars led to a repaired system and the Nicosia Master Plan, one of the first tangible efforts to get Greek Cypriots and Turkish Cypriots to work together after

1974. Demetriades's son Achilleas noted that when he was given a grant in the mid-1980s for graduate studies in international law in the U.S. it was not a big deal for him to meet Turkish Cypriots at the orientation session "when Akinci was at your house for dinner all the time."[11] Those meetings presented a danger for both Demetriades and Akinci because there were many on both sides that viewed such contacts as treasonous.

"My father went to the U.S. on a study tour for parliamentarians arranged by the Embassy and it made an impression," said Achilleas, who now heads the law firm his father founded. "I think he saw the Fulbright program as something that was committed to bringing the two communities together and I think he believed that and that is why he served. We have to live with one another, so it is better to live in peace."[12]

"He was a larger-than-life character," noted Ambassador John Koenig, who served on the Board with Demetriades in the mid-1990s when he was a political officer. "He would argue with the other Board members and raise his voice at times – though not often – because he could be very impatient. I remember walking with him in Nicosia and doors would pop open and people would offer him a coffee or a sweet. He was just a very large personality."[13]

Dr. Judith Baroody, who became Board Chairman in 1996, remembers that she was at times startled by Demetriades's negotiating strategy. "He would make maximalist demands and get red in the face, but then he would compromise and eventually get to the place he actually wanted to get. Baroody's successor, Walter Douglas, remembered Demetriades a bit differently. "Lellos always worked for harmony. I thought he was a good figure. He had a good political sense. He was funny and charming."

The Turkish Cypriots on the Board faced their own dangers. Raif had studied English in Britain, but in the late 1950s was awarded a grant from the ICA to attend a six-month course in educational administration at the University of Wisconsin. He was asked to serve on the Board and was happy to do it, but after the violence of December 1963 he decided not to attend another Board meeting until March 1968. Nevertheless, he collected applications and sat on interview panels that were held at the National Library, which was located in an area controlled by the Turkish Cypriots.

"If you were a Turkish Cypriot going to an area controlled by Greek Cypriots you could be picked up off the street and just shot," explained Raif. "I had friends who were grabbed and never seen again."[14] Eventually, an American officer in a car with diplomatic plates would come to fetch Raif and take him to the meetings and home again for his protection and, after that, he had almost perfect attendance until he stepped down from the Board in early 1974.

His successor and colleague, Hilmi, had his own hiatus after 1974, which lasted until late 1978, though in that period there were only seven Board meetings. In 1975, the Board began to hold its meetings in the ballroom of the Ledra Palace Hotel, now in the Buffer Zone, with the grudging cooperation of the UN. It was a forbidding place, with sandbags blocking most of the light from the windows and dust and debris still littering the floor. The Board chose this venue hoping that both Greek Cypriots and Turkish Cypriots could attend together, reaffirming that despite the extended absence of the Turkish Cypriot member, the Commission would continue to maintain a "non-political attitude" in order to provide unbiased and open exchange opportunities for all Cypriots.[15] Eventually, Hilmi returned, though in the interim the Commission ran ads in Turkish Cypriot newspapers instructing Turkish Cypriot applicants to take their applications to Hilmi's office.

While Turkish Cypriots had withdrawn from the government in 1963 and the events of 1974 divided the island, there was never any question that they would withdraw from the Fulbright Commission Board. Because it was founded before December 1963, Denktash did not object to Turkish Cypriot participation. "People were happy to get the scholarships because it was hard to get to the United States," said Raif, who said he consulted with Denktash only a handful of times.[16] Hilmi, who had studied at the University of Georgia on a Rotary Scholarship in the mid-1950s, noted that he never spoke to Denktash about any Fulbright matters during his four years on the Board.[17]

The Commission used another conduit to keep communication and documents moving between the two communities, and that was through Dogan Yavuz. Yavuz, who had attended the American Academy in Larnaca, came to work at the American Consulate in 1959 at the age of 19, subsequently remaining at the Embassy for decades. He was given an Embassy jeep with diplomatic plates that allowed him to move between the two communities, in part because there were 30 to 40 American citizens who remained in the Karpas region (in the Turkish-controlled North) after 1974 who had to receive their Social Security checks. Yavuz supported the Commission in several ways. He collected student applications and took them to the Commission. "I would read them and it was obvious who the strongest students were and I would make a ranked list," explained Yavuz. "I had a very good relationship with Renos. He was fair and I liked him and the Board liked him."[18] He would also proctor the various exams – TOEFL, SAT, ACT and GRE – for Turkish Cypriots. A third role was to go to the Turkish Cypriot Ministry of Foreign Affairs or to Denktash himself and make sure that the American scholars who would consult on the Turkish side would be allowed to cross. Most of the time it worked, though with some haggling. Sometimes the crossing would be completely shut down to make a political point. Conditions could shift from day to day.

After the December 1974 meeting, the Board would not meet again for seven months. At that time they agreed they had to reorient the program and over the next several meetings they sought to adapt their work to the conditions on the ground in Cyprus, where more than one-third of the population was internally displaced. After briefly halting the undergraduate program they reinstated it, noting that the prestige of the Commission had been damaged when those grants stopped. They wanted to bring in scholars – particularly psychologists and sociologists – to work with the refugees and advise the government. Washington was convinced that with the new mandate for UNFICYP there was enough stability in Cyprus to allow an American scholar to come for an extended period of time. Dr. Ronald Jackson, the Acting Director of Research at the Massachusetts Advisory Council on Education, arrived on September 10, 1975 with his wife and two children to work with the Institute of Education.[19] By 1977, the Commission was bringing in scholars/consultants to work on both sides of the Green Line, most in the field of education.

What was happening was that the Commission and the Board were forging a distinct identity. It would be decidedly non-political. It would most certainly cooperate with the Planning Commission, but would not be bound by its priorities. It would be fiercely bicommunal, understanding that the moment it stopped being bicommunal the Commission would collapse. Even though the Cypriots on the Board believed that the Americans held the upper hand since the American Ambassador could break any ties, that never happened, and each community – Greek and Turkish – had the chance to form "alliances" with the Americans on the Board. With few exceptions, the Board operated consensually.[20]

The Board received praise from the Board of Foreign Scholarships for the relationship it had fostered with SUNY Albany, and now it was ready to help create something new.[21] That opportunity would come in June 1977, when the Board voted in principle to provide a grant that would pay the salary of a director of a new American-affiliated archaeological research institute.[22] Demetriades was a particularly strong voice in pushing the Commission to support this venture. The story of the Cyprus

American Archaeological Research Institute and the Commission's role will be covered in the next chapter.

At the same meeting, the Board noted with interest that there had been discussions within the government regarding the establishment of a university in Cyprus. The Board members agreed that they wanted the Commission to be involved in some way. However, more ambition required more resources, and many of the Board discussions through these years were about finding more money. The Commission had the verbal support of the Cyprus government, such as a speech by Foreign Minister Spyros Kyprianou that praised the Commission's work. However, it also wanted the RoC to start contributing funds, which it would do in 1968 with a modest donation of CP1,000 ($18,500 in 2020 dollars).[23] That sum inched up gradually to CP2,000 but given the unsettled nature of the country throughout the 1970s, that is where it remained. In wealthier countries, particularly in Europe, it was not unusual that the contribution from the host government would eventually exceed the contribution by the United States. The Board in Nicosia did not expect that, but it continued to push, often enlisting the Ambassador to lobby for them.

The Board discussed ideas that ranged from approaching every company in Cyprus with an American connection to holding fund-raising dinners with distinguished speakers. Their list of targets was a who's who of Greek Cyprus's wealthiest businessmen – George Paraskevaides, Solon Triantafylides, Evagoras Lanitis, Nicos Karantokis, Kalis Lefkarites, Nicos Shacolas, Constantinos Lordos, George Galatariotis, and former Fulbright grantee Minister Andreas Aloneftis. The effort was largely unsuccessful, and generated only token contributions. Why give money to an American institution? The Americans surely did not need Cypriot money. At least, that was the general attitude. Of course, the Commission could not seek money from the Turkish Cypriots. They were poorer, to be sure, but Greek Cypriots would have most certainly shut down the Commission if one cent had come from an entity that they deemed illegitimate. What they did not know then was that in 1981, a vast amount of money would transform the Commission via the Cyprus American Scholarship Program or CASP. That story will be told in Chapter Six, but its impact on the Board was profound.

First, the Cypriot representation changed. In 1986, the RoC began to regularly appoint the Directors General of the Ministries of Foreign Affairs and Education and, in later years, the Permanent Secretaries. These were busy people and while there were only four or five Board meetings in a year, many of these officials failed to attend a single meeting, particularly those from the Ministry of Foreign Affairs. Demetriades took a dim view of the new Board members. "I thought their arrival was a bad thing," said Demetriades. "It made things much more political."[24] To solve that problem, the Board agreed that alternate Board members would be appointed and, ultimately, both the primary and alternate Board members would attend and vote, expanding the Board to 16 members, although there was never a meeting when all 16 attended.

Demetriades would be the last to choose an alternate for himself, which occurred in November 1989 with the arrival of Dr. Chrysostomos Sofianos, who served for 14 years. Sofianos, a passionate man given to high-minded speeches, was American educated with a Ph.D. from Ohio State. He publicly opposed the junta in Athens and was only able to return safely to Cyprus once Makarios returned at the end of 1974, and appointed him Minister of Education. His political career had its ups and downs, but during his time on the Board he was serving in the Office of President Clerides and provided an important voice and source of information.

"I let it be known I wanted to serve on the Board," said Sofianos. "I thought it was a way of giving back. When I served on the Board some of my opponents spread the rumor that I was in the CIA, and there were many who thought of the Commission as something radical, but the scholarships were making a substantial contribution to the maturation of our society. It was not just the degrees, but the attitudes students brought back...to think about the things in front of you, to use logic, reason, to argue, to have respect, to express an opinion without oppression."[25]

No one worked harder than Sofianos in trying to raise funds for the Commission. He wrote hundreds of letters and made countless phone calls. "To be honest, it was the hardest thing I ever did. But they knew me and listened to me and I was able to convince the government to give more," he explained.[26]

In the (Turkish Cypriot) North, Board appointments could also be seen as political. Dr. Cem Tanova, who became an alternate Board member in 2008, noted that the primary Board members would change depending whether parties on the left or the right were in power. "There was a feeling among the nationalists and nationalist media that the Fulbright Commission was a tool of influence to try to brainwash our youth," remembered Tanova. "Of course, the people who received the scholarships took the grants and it changed their lives. It changed my life."

Tanova was a 1989 Cyprus American Scholarship Program (CASP) grantee who learned the true meaning of winter by attending Northern Michigan University (NMU). His future wife Seda, who received a CASP in 1990 and studied in Rochester, New York, would get used to snow as well. "A Turkish Cypriot had gone to NMU because of family connections and then others followed," explained Tanova. Yet other than social gatherings organized by the Commission for alumni, Tanova had not worked with Greek Cypriots until he served on the Board and there were certain things about the way the Commission operated that surprised him.

"The Greek Cypriot government would write letters to all kinds of people telling them not to have any relations with what they referred to the 'so-called universities' in the Turkish Cypriot North because they were illegitimate," said Tanova, who was at Eastern Mediterranean University, which is a *state* university in the North. "And yet the Commission was giving grants to students and faculty from these universities as well as our Ministry of Education and other parts of the government. I did not detect any influence from the Embassy and I felt as though we (the Board) were completely in the driver's seat."[27]

Gunfer Erkman, who served twice as a Board member in the 2000s as the primary member, also noted there were times when politics at least tried to intrude. "When the UBP (Ulusal Birlik Partisi or National Unity Party, the party founded by Rauf Denktash) was in charge, they gave instructions and I did not like it."[28] Erkman had received a Fulbright for a one-year program at the University of Oregon and knew the value of the grants.

Dr. Chris Schabel, an American, who began teaching at the new University of Cyprus in 1995, joined the Board in 2001 and even his appointment had a political element. "As usual, everything is a conspiracy. [Board Chairman] Walter [Douglas] invited me to lunch in 2001 and I had sponsored a couple of Fulbright scholars. Walter said they really wanted to have someone from the University of Cyprus on the Board, but the Government of Cyprus would not play ball," explained Schabel. "They didn't want any academics on the Board because they did not trust academics – even then. So, they were not going to appoint anyone from the University of Cyprus and this was before all the other universities on the island had been created and so the University of Cyprus was the only game in town. Thus, I was the only choice because I was the only American...and pretty much one of the only foreigners on the faculty. He did not need to convince me...he just asked if I wanted to do it and I said all right. It was not all that difficult. I happened to think at that time that it was a great way to create bonds between Cyprus and the U.S. and promote democracy and freethinking."[29]

Through the years there were just a handful of Board members who served for more than a decade. Demetriades served for 41 years. Resident American Betsy Tornaritis served the second longest at 19 years (1979-98) followed by the long-time Turkish Cypriot alternate Dr. Mehmet Tahiroglu from Eastern Mediterranean University who served 16 years (1991-2007) to be replaced by Tanova. Dr. Sofianos served 14 years. Original members Sparsis and Raif each served 11 years, as did Niyazi Alioglu (1979-90). Long-time resident Americans Nancy Scudder (1999-2013), Dr. Chris Schabel (2001-14), and Claire Georghiou (2000-2014) also found a home on the Board. Georghiou, a senior faculty member at the European University, described it this way:

"One of the things that kept me working on the Board is that we worked by consensus," explained Georghiou. "There might have been times when we were pushed to make a decision very quickly, but there was a feeling that things were discussed and Demetriades and Sofianos always took the Turkish Cypriot viewpoint into account. I was comfortable with what we were doing at the time."[30]

"You might have been called an alternate but that did not matter. You were expected to be at the meetings and you had voting rights," noted Georghiou. "You were expected to be prepared and the Turkish Cypriots always had the opportunity to express themselves. I never felt that they were somehow being controlled. We operated under the radar and that is the way that it was supposed to be because of the pressure you might get so that is the way I wanted it to be. We were shielded from the Cyprus conflict once we walked through the door. People were very pleasant and social with each other."[31]

There was another key aspect that motivated Georghiou to remain on the Board for so many years. "I sat on the selection panels and these were extremely impressive kids," said Georghiou. "The staff did their homework and provided us with the information that was not on the paper with their grades and test scores. I always felt we were working in the correct way."[32]

Through the two decades of the 1980s and 1990s, the Commission and the Board would ride a wave of funding of more than $100 million (more than $200 million in 2020 dollars) that gave it a power and prestige in Cyprus that protected it politically, even when it engaged in forward-leaning programs that some Cypriot leaders would call gross interference in Cypriot affairs or even "brainwashing." Only in the final years of the Commission would the Cyprus conflict pierce the shield of political neutrality of the Board and spark a series of events that would eventually lead to the closing of the Commission.

Before then, however, the Commission had enjoyed many golden years and it used those years to have a profound impact on Cyprus.

CAARI
The Cyprus American Archaeological Research Institute

In February 1931, Horace H.F. Jayne, director of the University of Pennsylvania Museum in Philadelphia, sent a message to the former director of the American School of Classical Studies in Athens, Bert Hodge Hill, asking if he would undertake excavations in Cyprus on behalf of the museum.[1]

Hill had never been to Cyprus, but accepted. The purpose was to build up the museum's "classical" collection. Hill assembled a team and focused on the village of Lapithos on the north coast and its vast Early and Middle Bronze Age necropolis, Vrysi tou Barba (Βρύση του Μπάρμπα). After three months, and with winter approaching, the excavation closed down. The team would not return, instead turning its attention to Kourion in 1934.[2]

With the exception of a narrowly focused article in 1940, the results of the excavation and its artifacts were never catalogued or studied – until a young Ph.D. student at the University of Pennsylvania named Ellen Herscher came upon the dusty crates from the excavation in the basement of the museum 40 years later.

Dr. Ellen Herscher.

In the early 1970s, American archaeologists were just starting to work in Cyprus in earnest but there was all this material at the Penn Museum and it was difficult for graduate students to get access to such artifacts, so Herscher went to Professor Rodney Young, known for his excavation of the city of Gordion, the capital of the ancient Phrygians (in present day Turkey), and pressed him to allow her to work on the Early

Bronze Age and Cyprus. "Professor Young had a low opinion of Cyprus and because I was female, he allowed me to do it," remembered Herscher. "If it had been a male with an academic career in front of him, Young would never have allowed it."[3]

A Swedish team was excavating in Cyprus and so Herscher spent a year at the university in Göteborg, which enabled her to go to Cyprus and work on its excavation. There she met Vassos Karageorghis, the head of the Department of Antiquities. Karageorghis wanted Herscher to stay in Cyprus and so he spoke to Deputy Chief of Mission William Crawford, who was a collector of archaeological artifacts, particularly from the enclaved areas in Cyprus controlled by Turkish Cypriot militias and, thus, off limits to Karageorghis's department. This is where the Fulbright Commission became involved.

It had been largely impossible to bring American Ph.D. students to Cyprus under the Fulbright Commission's auspices because there were no universities where the necessary affiliations could be created. However, with a little creativity from Renos Kamenos, Crawford, and Karageorghis, Herscher was able to affiliate with Cyprus's Department of Antiquities and she received a Fulbright in 1972, which allowed her to settle in and work on her research. She was the Commission's very first American Ph.D. student.

"It was a golden age and a wonderful time to be an archaeologist in Cyprus," said Herscher. "Cyprus was still a very traditional society and I can remember what the harbor at Kyrenia was like. And, if you wanted, you could go to the Nicosia Airport and jump on a plane and be in Beirut in 30 minutes and find some wonderful restaurants. Life was very simple and Renos was wonderful. He was a very typical laidback Cypriot man. Of course, I found the Cypriot women were much busier."[4]

However, in the summer of 1974, that idyllic simplicity would come to a sudden end. Herscher was working at an excavation at Morphou Bay directed by James R. Carpenter from Kent State University who had brought 20 of his students. Stuart and Helena ("Laina") Swiny were staff members. When they heard about the coup against Makarios they were certain that an invasion would follow. They were ultimately convoyed to the British base at Akrotiri by the U.N. "Laina was five months pregnant and there were armed men all along the route and you had no idea who they were. It was all very nerve-wracking," recalled Herscher.[5] They were all told that they had to leave the island. Herscher did not want to go, and neither did the Swinys, but they were not really given a choice by U.S. officials.

"I had a small apartment near the Paphos Gate, kind of the low-rent district, and all my research, books and dissertation were there. I assumed they were all lost," said Herscher. "But Sheila Austrian at the Embassy got in there and they packed everything up and shipped it back to me in America and everything was there, except for some of my nightgowns and nicer clothes. I assume some of the soldiers who went through the building had girlfriends."[6]

Herscher eventually finished her dissertation in 1978, and in 1990 she received a second Fulbright grant to return to Cyprus, but by then, however, she would be affiliated with the Cyprus American Archaeological Research Institute and was one of a steady stream of American scholars who were coming to Cyprus to work on archaeological and anthropological projects and their advanced degrees under CAARI's umbrella.

Karageorghis worked hard to promote interest in Cypriot archaeology, and so in 1974 there were 20 teams operating on the island, including six recently arrived American teams. The American Schools of Oriental Research (ASOR – renamed the American Society of Overseas Research in 2021) sponsored one at Idalion (near modern Dhali). ASOR's traditional focus was on the lands of the Bible, but Cyprus could certainly lay claim to its place in

Stuart and Laina Swiny.

Christian history. The missions of St. Paul and St. Barnabas, followed by the conversion of Roman Proconsul Sergius Paulus to Christianity, meant that Cyprus was the first province to be governed by a Christian. ASOR President George Ernest Wright was considering the establishment of a school or center, but the 1974 division of the island caused those plans to be abandoned.[7]

However, the idea lingered and early in 1977 ASOR, now led by Philip J. King, voted to create a center for archaeological research with the strong support of both Karageorghis and Ambassador Crawford, who would soon depart and be replaced by Ambassador Galen Stone. A notice appeared in the April 1977 ASOR Newsletter that read: "In response to the invitation of the Department of Antiquities of the Republic of Cyprus, the American Schools of Oriental Research has decided to establish an institute in Nicosia to facilitate American archaeological work on Cyprus. This institute is envisioned as functioning like other ASOR institutes throughout the Near East and the Mediterranean area. It will serve both as a research center and a depot for excavations. All American expeditions and individual researchers will be eligible to use the services of the institute to a greater or lesser extent depending on the degree to which they choose to affiliate with ASOR. By sharing services of specialist personnel, dig equipment, archaeological reference collections...needless duplication will be avoided and American archaeological research in Cyprus will be enhanced."[8]

Originally, the new institute was to be called the "Cyprus Archaeological Research Institute," but the RoC requested that "American" be added to the title; thus the institute became CAARI.[9] "Karageoghis was familiar with the British schools in Rome and Athens and wanted CAARI identified with a nation," explained Stuart Swiny, CAARI's third director. "It made it more official and, if something went wrong he could always blame America."[10] However, as Swiny observed, because Cyprus was small and easy to navigate, and suitable accommodations were inexpensive and plentiful, a seasoned archaeologist would hardly have need of the services CAARI could offer. However, "for newcomers in the field, especially students, an archaeological center would provide a distinct advantage." Indeed, Swiny noted that student involvement grew from a handful of students in the late 1970s to a steady flow in the 1990s numbering in the hundreds.[11]

ASOR quickly named Dr. Anita Walker of the University of Connecticut as the first Executive Director of CAARI, but it realized that it could not bear the full cost of the new institute alone. Enter the Cyprus Fulbright Commission and the United States Information Agency. At its June 9, 1977 Board Meeting chaired by Public Affairs Officer Robert Jellison, the Board voted to support a grant of $15,000 (approximately $65,000 in 2020 dollars) to support the salary of the new director pending Washington approval, which was quickly granted.[12] There was just one catch. The Director had to be an American citizen. Dr. Walker was not.

"I was British and met an American post doc at the University of London and we married and that is how I came to America," explained Walker. "I had been in the U.S. for 19 years, had earned my Ph.D. and gotten tenure at the University of Connecticut, and had a Green Card. So, to get the grant I guess you could say I sold my soul; barriers were removed. We had the meeting in October 1977 and by December I was an American citizen."[13] Walker noted, with a laugh, that she was grateful that the speed of the process did not allow American authorities time to look too closely into her anti-war political activities in the 1960s.

She arrived in December 1977, leaving her husband and three teenage children behind in Connecticut but immediately hopped from Egypt to Israel to Jordan to visit the already established ASOR research centers. ASOR provided just $10,000 ($43,000 in 2020 dollars) to support a suitable building and run the new operation. "I spent more than that to run my household in Connecticut," noted Walker. Again, this is where the Commission and the Embassy stepped in.

"When Renos decided on something he would put his heart and soul into it, and he did that for the foundation of CAARI," recalled Walker. "I knew the important people in archaeology, principally Vassos Karageorghis, and the people at the Department of Antiquities and the museum, but Renos knew everybody and it was he who did a lot of the scouting for me to find a suitable premises for CAARI keeping in mind our tiny budget. He brought Lellos Demetriades on board – his law firm did our incorporation – but as Mayor he had access to so much and gave us an area for storage. Demetriades was very proud of Cyprus's archaeological history and thought the institute would be good for Cyprus."[14]

A suitable building (a former maternity clinic) was found at 41 King Paul Street in Nicosia, just a five-minute walk from the Department of Antiquities and Walker proceeded to set up shop. "I could not have done anything without the support of Renos and Stella and Vassos and new Public Affairs Officer and Board Chairman Mary Louise Tellich," said Walker. It was not just the support, but also the friendships. "Sometimes I would just buy some olive bread and sit at my desk and Renos and Stella would take pity on me and bring me home for lunch with them and Lou Tellich was a single woman and so we became very good friends and frequent lunch companions," remembered Walker.

CAARI held its first major event, an archaeological workshop, at the American Center in August 1978. Tellich and Kamenos pulled together the guest list for the reception. "Of course there were people from the Department of Antiquities and the museum, but there were also people interested in philanthropy, like A.G. Leventis and other movers and shakers that I would not have known. Renos and Lou did that," said Walker.[15]

Walker's term as Executive Director would end in the summer of 1979 and be handed off to Ian Todd of Brandeis University, another Brit who would hastily become an American citizen, but not before a crisis that threatened to end CAARI before it could get off the ground was averted. "A year in, ASOR suddenly decided that it could not afford to support us," said Walker. "Renos was furious and threw down his cigarette and said 'this is an insult…it is an insult to Cyprus and to the Department of Antiquities,' and he went to Ambassador Stone. It must have been the combined pressure from Renos, Ambassador Stone and Vassos that convinced ASOR to reconsider. We were a very small acorn in 1978-79 and an outlier when it came to ASOR's primary mission."[16]

There was no such wavering from the Fulbright Commission. It was committed to providing the salary of the Directors, but when Ian Todd left sooner than anticipated Swiny took over as Director on a temporary basis to bridge the gap. Swiny, like Walker and Todd, was another British citizen and the Fulbright Commission could not cover his salary. He was not an American citizen and it would have been a lengthy procedure for him to become one. What to do? "Renos managed to change the terms of the grant so that instead of going to me, it went to CAARI," explained Swiny. "Renos told me that it was all very difficult and that they were working on it and by his dead-pan tone I was sure he was going to tell me that it could not be done," remembers Swiny, "but then he said 'we have sorted it out' and so that was typical Renos. He had to pull your leg a little."[17]

It also helped to have some supporters in Washington. So when Ron Ungaro, Chief of the Academic Exchange Programs at USIA, visited Cyprus, Swiny made sure to give him a good tour. Driving him in an immense white station wagon affectionately known as the "White Hoax," which had been donated to CAARI by the U.S. Embassy, Swiny took Ungaro around to different sites and introduced him to some of the American archaeologists working on the island. He also took him to a lecture by Karageorghis at the spectacular amphitheater at Kourion and "made sure that Karageorghis mentioned CAARI in a favorable way several times during his talk."[18] Ungaro came away suitably impressed and found some end-of-the-fiscal-year money to provide a grant to CAARI of $10,000 ($30,000 in 2020 dollars) to begin building a research library. Later more funds were received from USIA to supplement those raised in memory of Laina Swiny's father, in order to purchase and transport the large personal library of the late French archaeologist Claude Schaeffer, who had excavated at the great Late Bronze Age city site of Egkomi in Cyprus.[19] As Swiny has written, that collection – which, in 1984, became "The C.F.A. Schaeffer Library Given in Memory of John Irton Wylde"

– helped CAARI become a true research center. It would eventually become the first library in Cyprus to computerize its catalogue.

"I had followed the work of CAARI in Washington because it was a particular interest of mine," explained Ungaro. "I also liked the Cyprus Commission because it was energetic and Stuart was extraordinarily able. He was young at the game at that point, but he had enthusiasm that was second to none and he loved Cyprus and we got on famously. He was quite an innovator and it all fit very well with our interests on the island."[20] The United Nations' Gustave Feissel, who was involved with Cyprus throughout the 1980s and 1990s, agreed. "If I had to pick one person who was most influential in making CAARI what it was, I would have to say it was Stuart Swiny."[21]

In addition to securing Schaeffer's valuable library, Swiny was busy shoring up CAARI's finances to the point that after a couple of years the Fulbright Commission no longer needed to provide a grant to support the salaries or administrative costs of the institute. Some of that support would come from the National Endowment for the Humanities (NEH) in the U.S. However, with the arrival of USAID funds at the Fulbright Commission in 1981, there would be another vital way that the Commission could help, and that was by providing grants to scholars.

Todd had sat on some of the selection panels for the Commission, which Swiny could not do as a British citizen. Soon after the arrival of the USAID funds, however, the Commission decided to designate specific grants to support archaeology. "While I did not sit on the Board, both Renos and Daniel Hadjittofi would confer with me, whether officially or unofficially, and I definitely would have a say in who would get grants to come do research in Cyprus," said Swiny. "There were no archaeologists on the Board, after all, and they never appointed someone that I was not sure about." Kamenos, Board Chairman Dan Howard, and Lellos Demetriades were CAARI's vocal supporters on the Board. The first grantee arrived in 1983, Dr. Julie Hansen, who had completed her Ph.D. at the University of Minnesota three years earlier. She came as a senior scholar to study early agriculture on the island.

Hansen bounced from Minnesota to universities in Indiana and Manitoba and had, since 1976, worked in Cyprus off and on identifying plant remains, particularly at Ian Todd's excavations. However, when she received a call about the possibility of a Fulbright grant in Cyprus, she was, out of economic necessity, working for an insurance company in her hometown of Madison, Wisconsin. She applied, got the grant and that led to a very different career path. "It was great. CAARI had not been up and running very long, but Stuart was getting things set up," remembered Hansen. "I spent half my time at CAARI writing and the other half wandering up and down the valley where Ian had his excavations identifying plants. I met people from the Ministry of Agriculture and other archaeologists and Stuart made sure I was involved in things the Commission was doing and events at the Embassy. Stuart is a very social person and he was tireless."

"I started working with other archaeologists and started to give lectures, which prepared me for what I eventually did, which was to teach. The Fulbright grant led to another fellowship in Jordan and then one in England. It was a good background for me and certainly better than the insurance company," said Hansen laughing.[22] Dr. Hansen is today Professor Emerita at Boston University.

"Supporting any institution that had 'American' in the name was good in my eyes," noted Howard. "The Swinys and my wife Mary and I frequently met at dinner parties and we became friends. Mary helped Stuart with research and editing of a book he was writing. Stuart first suggested designating Fulbright grants for CAARI, and Renos and I discussed it and both thought that it would boost the prestige of both the Commission and CAARI. Stuart was a very good salesman."[23] When Daniel Hadjittofi ascended to the position of Executive Director of the Commission, Howard also stressed to him that archaeology should be supported by the Commission.

In commenting on one of the first Commission program proposals under Hadjittofi, Washington wrote: "...we are aware that Cyprus remains a major world center for archaeological research, and we would like to see archaeology remain part of the program, even if it is to a lesser degree. While we agree with the Post (Embassy Public Affairs Section) that the Cyprus American Archaeological Research Institute is becoming largely self-sufficient, we think it plays an important role and feel that greater Agency (USIA) support than just the salary of the Director (though certainly less than has existed in the past) is justifiable. The successful CAARI presentation at the Cypriot Embassy (December 1987), which drew a large number of attendees, made it clear that there is a great deal of private U.S. interest, and we hope that CAARI will continue to look for ways to increase its private sector contributions."[24]

Bringing Fulbright scholars to CAARI made the Commission staff's life easy, as CAARI would house them and take care of their needs, particularly Executive Assistant Vathoulla Moustoukki, who was hired by Anita Walker in her final month in 1979 and who stayed at CAARI for more than 40 years. "CAARI always worked closely with the Commission," said Moustoukki. "Renos, Stella and Daniel were all wonderful people, and bringing the scholars was so important." Moustoukki would be there to poke them to write their final reports to the Commission and noted that one young woman Fulbrighter had only one complaint in her report: "She complained that I did not find her a husband," laughed Moustoukki.[25]

The next year, three more scholars – Karl Petrusso, Clark Walz, and Patricia Bikai – arrived and throughout the remainder of the 1980s and the 1990s, this steady stream of American scholars continued. Swiny, writing in 2000, opined that "the names of past Fulbright fellows constitute a Who's Who of American scholars publishing on Cyprus topics: Bernard Knapp, James Muhly, Barbara Kling, Gloria London, Priscilla Keswani, Joseph Greene, Glenn Markoe, Ellen Herscher, David Reese, Jane Barlow, Pamela Gaber, Joanna Smith, John Leonard and David Roessel, among others."[26]

"I had wanted to be an archaeologist since I was a girl and I wanted to study Mesopotamian archaeology and the only school where you could do that as an undergrad was Yale," explained Gaber, "and they would not accept women in the program."

Gaber ended up at the University of Wisconsin, which had a study abroad program and she went to Israel and worked on several excavations in 1971 where she met Drs. Lawrence Stager and Anita Walker who had just obtained a permit to excavate at Idalion and were looking for field directors. "So, I asked them 'what's in Cyprus?'" said Gaber laughing. "I never looked back. I started digging in 1971 and did not stop until 2017."[27] That fieldwork would lead to her Ph.D. at Harvard.

"Yes, I was evacuated in 1974. I came back under Fulbright in 1985 and had my two daughters – two and five – with me. "Renos was very pleasant and energetic and Stella was the brass-tacks person, who would say: 'Oh, you have children? They can go to the Falcon School and here is where you get the uniforms.' And I became very good friends with Daniel Hadjittofi and we have lunch whenever I am in Cyprus," said Gaber, which was illustrative of the close relationship between CAARI and the Fulbright Commission through the years.[28]

With a growing library and a rising number of visiting scholars, Swiny turned his attention to finding a permanent home for CAARI. This was possible because of seed money in the form of a generous donation from Eve, the wife of the late Australian archaeologist J.R. Stewart. With the help of Demos Christou in the Department of Antiquities, in 1986 a two-story mansion house (locally a αρχοντικό σπίτι) located at 11 Andreas Demetriou Street within walking distance of the museum was found. Now Swiny had to find the funds to not only purchase the property, but to cover renovations; the house had to accommodate a library and lecture space as well as office space, while also being able to accommodate the visiting scholars. So renovations included an eight-room hostel on the second floor.

Again, the Fulbright Commission and Washington were prepared to help. At its April 27, 1987 Board meeting, it was noted that "the United States Information Agency has increased its allocation by $38,000. This amount will be given to the Cyprus American Archaeological Research Institute (CAARI) in the form of a grant to support its efforts in buying its own premises. An initial installment of $20,417 was already given to CAARI." (The total grant of $68,417 was equivalent to $157,000 in 2020 dollars.)[29] The hostel, known as the J.R. Stewart Residences, also includes the larger "Fulbright Suite" for longer-term stays. The Residence welcomes more than 100 scholars a year from dozens of countries.

On June 10, 1991, then President of the Republic of Cyprus, Dr. George Vassiliou, officially inaugurated the house. This is where CAARI is located today. After 15 years as Director, Swiny departed and turned over the directorship to Dr. Nancy Serwint for three years, followed by the Australian scholar/diplomat Robert Merrilees. Then, in 2003, came Tom Davis who stayed for eight years and very quickly joined the Board of the Fulbright Commission.

"I met Fulbright Commission Executive Director Daniel Hadjittofi early on and I slid right onto the Board and immediately got involved in bicommunal efforts," remembered Davis. "Two months before I arrived the crossing between the North and the South had opened up and allowed much more bicommunal work."[30] Up to that point, the Turkish Cypriots on the Commission Board had not been supportive of the CAARI Fulbrighters because when it came to archaeology, the scholars were only allowed to work in the South given the restrictions put in place by the Department of Antiquities.

"The Commission had been doing a great deal of bicommunal work which was seen by many in Cyprus as political and no one had ever thought of building a wall between the Commission and CAARI to protect CAARI, but I thought the Commission should be embraced and that we could use it as a lever with the government to be more aggressive in protecting archaeological sites in the North," explained Davis. "Archaeology is totally political because it deals with the issue of identity.

What is a Cypriot? Archaeology speaks directly to that issue. Fulbright was founded as a bicommunal institution and as a Board member it gave me the chance to get to know people in the Turkish Cypriot community and, perhaps, put in place some good practices and stop some bad practices, wearing my Fulbright hat."[31]

Davis also made sure that the residences at CAARI were open to other visiting Fulbright scholars, who did not have to be archaeologists to stay there. "I always wanted to have a couple of non-archaeologists in residence at CAARI. Fulbright allowed me to do that," Davis noted. "They benefitted by having an instant community and we benefitted by having people working in different areas of scholarship so that our archaeologists were not just in their own fish bowls."[32]

USAID, which was also supporting many bicommunal efforts at that time, provided CAARI with a grant of $35,000, drawn from an Anatolian research fund, to purchase Turkish books. "I allowed Turkish Cypriots to use our library. If they called themselves a Cypriot, then I welcomed them." Davis was not averse to wearing a CAARI hat or a Fulbright hat depending on the need. "I used the fact that the Commission was created in 1962 as a hammer from time to time...saying that I was not doing this as the CAARI Director but as a Fulbright Board member. That eased some tensions and allowed me to do some things in the North."[33]

When Dr. Andrew McCarthy arrived to succeed Davis in 2011, he took Davis's place on the Board. "I knew that I was going to serve on the Board before I arrived in Cyprus and my main focus was to do what I could to keep programs going and scholars coming to Cyprus," said McCarthy. "So, it was upsetting to know that funding was disappearing and that the Commission was facing shutting down. CAARI relied on scholars coming through and the long association with the Fulbright Commission was part of that."[34]

McCarthy did things in much the same way as Davis. Turkish Cypriots were regular visitors to the library and non-archaeologists were welcome guests at the res-

Hannah and Pamela Gaber.

idence. "The nice thing about CAARI is that it is a crossroads where people can interact," observed McCarthy. "Cross-pollination can occur across a range of disciplines and that is not a detraction but an enhancement." His multiple hats allowed him to work more productively with officials even to the point of doing some so-called "rescue archaeology" in the North. "I helped facilitate repairs to the roof at the Kyrenia Castle that protected the Kyrenia Ship and its artifacts."[35]

However, when the Commission closed, the new, much-reduced program could no longer offer dedicated Fulbright grants to bring American archaeology scholars to Cyprus year after year.[36] After having awarded more than 50 Fulbright scholarships affiliated with CAARI, one of the very last was given to that two-year-old daughter that Dr. Pamela Gaber had brought with her to Cyprus in 1985.

Hannah Gaber came to Cyprus as a Fulbright scholar in 2017 with a varied background as a photographer, journalist, and cultural anthropologist. "I received a Fulbright to do a research project that tries to determine if there are spaces where Cypriots from the two communities gather for reasons that have nothing to do with politics," explained Gaber, about her film that is still a work in progress as this is written. "So many of my earliest memories are in Cyprus as I followed my mother to digs. I remember going to pre-school here."[37]

"I remember the night I received an email telling me that I received the Fulbright grant," said Gaber. "My Mom jumped up and down and we drank an entire bottle of wine together by the fire as she told me stories about being a young archaeologist in Cyprus. It is probably one of my fondest memories."[38]

CASP
Cyprus American Scholarship Program

Eugene Rossides was furious.

In the summer of 1974, in the days after the Turkish invasion, Rossides found himself in a room with four Democrats, Representatives Paul Sarbanes of Maryland, John Brademas of Indiana, both Greek-Americans, and Ed Derwinski of Illinois, and Senate staffer Andy Manatos, who worked for Senator Tom Eagleton of Missouri. Rossides was a Republican and a former Assistant Secretary of the Treasury in the Nixon Administration, but Democrats controlled the House. He was in the process of founding the American Hellenic Institute (AHI), a lobbying organization, and he wanted the Congress to punish Turkey. He needed their support.

Rossides, backed by the argument that Turkey had carried out the invasion with U.S.-supplied weapons, wanted to see an arms embargo, and the discussion ranged over the options for doing just that. However, as the Congressmen and Manatos were about to leave, Rossides yelled out to them "Hey! These people need money."[1]

How much, they asked?

"I had not thought about it and had not talked to anyone about it, so I just threw a number off the top of my head – $50 million," remembered Rossides. "We got $25 million [$132 million in 2020 dollars] that first year and then it eventually settled into $15 million a year."[2] Manatos, who left the Senate rather than support a repeal of the Turkish arms embargo during the Carter administration, wrote the amendment in the Senate.

That money, technically Economic Support Funds (ESF) from US-AID, would continue to flow for nearly 40 years.

Initially, the money was used, via the U.N. High Commission for Refugees (UNHCR), to cope with the crisis created by the displacement of an estimated 225,000 Cypriots. After dealing with immediate needs, the money financed a program to build houses, schools, hospitals, senior homes, and orphanages, and to boost businesses.

A November 1981 report by the U.S. General Accounting Office (GAO) detailed these efforts in the years following the summer of 1974.

It noted that the United States was the only country giving sustained aid after the first year of the crisis and, after giving $25 million in the 1974-75 period, had contributed an additional $106.5 million between 1976 and 1981 (approximately $570 million total in 2020 dollars).[3]

The money was apportioned strictly according to the population of the island, with 80.95 percent allotted to the Greek Cypriot South and 19.05 percent going to the Turkish Cypriot North. Because of a shortage of hard currency in the North, much of the money that went to the Turkish Cypriots was used to buy equipment from abroad.   In the South, more than 60 percent of the money was devoted to construction of housing, either government financed low-income housing, or grants to purchase building materials for those families building their own homes, or towards the renovation of vacated Turkish Cypriot homes. The report estimated that 36,100 housing units had either been completed or would be completed by 1983 that would accommodate more than 160,000 residents.[4]

At the time the report was issued, there were two main issues the Con-

Eugene Rossides (top right), seen with President Nixon, was instrumental in getting the U.S. Congress to allocate funds for displaced Cypriots in the wake of the 1974 war. A conversation between Senator Claiborne Pell (center) and Ambassador Galen Stone, shown taking his oath, led to the creation of the Cyprus American Scholarship Program.

gress asked the GAO to address. First, did Cyprus still need the money? Its economic recovery had been robust and the vast majority of refugees had been housed. The report noted that the few remaining tent encampments seemed to be strategically placed near the new airport at Larnaca so that visiting officials would be sure to see them, and that Cypriot government reports dwelled on the past and not on the current situation in arguing that they needed the money to keep flowing. The second issue was a matter of recognition. Because the money passed through the UN-HCR, many Cypriots did not realize that much of the money came from the United States.

The politics surrounding the aid money was fraught. Greek Cypriot officials, still blaming America for the situation, were loath to give the U.S. any credit. Public Affairs Officer Dan Howard remembered the brawl that erupted over the placing of a plaque at the Makarios III Hospital in Larnaca where the U.S. had invested $10 million ($35 million in 2020 dollars). "The bastards did not want to allow a plaque that said the hospital was a gift from the people of the United States to the people of Cyprus and I said then there would be no damn opening," recalled Howard. Eventually, the government grudgingly relented after a protracted negotiation over the size of the lettering.[5] "We were not getting anything for our contributions and I went to President Kyprianou and complained and he finally gave a speech giving some credit to the U.S.," said Ambassador Galen Stone. "From my point of view, it was just conscience money."[6]

In addition to the GAO team, there were frequent Congressional delegations passing through Cyprus. Public Affairs Officer David Grimland, who was in Cyprus in the immediate aftermath of the invasion, noted that some Congressmen were genuinely concerned while others just wanted a photo with some refugees that they could put in a newsletter to their constituents in order to raise some campaign money and then get out of Cyprus as quickly as they could.[7] One of the most important visits, which occurred at the end of the 1970s, was made by Representative Clarence "Doc" Long (D-MD), who chaired the House subcommittee that controlled the funding going to Cyprus.

"It was a brief visit that was part of a larger trip with a larger delegation," remembered Tim Kernan, who served as a senior aide to the Congressman and accompanied him on the trip. "We met Ambassador Stone and we saw some of the new housing. I remember the conversation when Congressman Long observed that the USAID houses were nicer than the ones where some of his constituents lived in Maryland."[8] In retrospect, Board Chairman Dan Howard believed Long probably wanted the money to stop, but Howard also thought that if the money was going to continue, then why not support a scholarship program because "most of the money would go straight back to the United States."

Long could indeed have reduced or stopped the money, agreeing with USAID and the State Department, which both believed early on that the needs of the Cypriots had largely been met. In 1977, the State Department had asked for just $10 million, then nothing in 1978, $5 million in 1979, and $2 million in 1980 and 1981. As the conclusion of the GAO report noted: "We believe that the need for continued U.S. humanitarian assistance to Cyprus has greatly diminished." However, the report went on to say: "We recognize that there may be other foreign policy reasons to continue some level of assistance to Cyprus."[9]

"The pro-Greeks were sensitive to the Doc Long kind of criticism, building houses for Cypriots," noted Michael Van Dusen, a Staff Director for the House Foreign Affairs Committee at the time. "I knew Paul Sarbanes and he was an intellectual and I knew Rep. Brademas better. Both of them were leading the charge. They were very good friends with Lee Hamilton, who was Chairman of the House Foreign Affairs Committee. In terms of the scholarships it meant reaching out to young Cypriots. Sarbanes and Brademas would have been more sympathetic to that than a lot of other members because they were concerned about education. I thought it was a better use of the money than a lot of other things, such as building some white elephant. We thought that the education of the younger generation could also help try to bring young Greek and Turkish Cypriots together in the Ledra Palace and in the United States when they were doing their studies. Having them get to know each other was important. They did not really have the means to do that in Cyprus."[10]

By the time of Congressman Long's visit, Paul Sarbanes had won election as a U.S. Senator from Maryland. "Chairman Long was extremely close to Senator Sarbanes. He collaborated with him on many things that had to do with Maryland and he listened to him very closely when it came to things involving Greece. Certainly, he had a lot of influence with the chairman at the time and his input was welcomed," explained Kernan.

Kernan noted several other dynamics at work. "This was a member-to-member discussion. Member-to-member discussions carry a lot more weight than any other conversation they were having with the State Department or USAID, or the testimony given before the subcommittee by lobbying groups. Until you see member-to-member conversations, you don't know it. Also, remember that Baltimore (in Long's district) had a strong Greek-American community. You can't leave politics out of this.

There was a substantial and very active Greek community. It is very true that all politics is local." Kernan noted one other factor: "$15 million was a drop in the bucket in a multi-billion-dollar foreign affairs bill."[11]

"The $15 million annual appropriation to Cyprus was a signal of a political commitment to find a solution to the Cyprus Problem," said Diana Ohlbaum, a long-time senior aide to Senator Sarbanes. "That was the entire rationale – to signal the U.S. commitment. Cutting it would be a signal of a reduced political commitment and that was untenable. Our job was to make sure that the funds were used in a constructive manner. As long as Senator Sarbanes was in the Senate, it was kept alive.

"The Greek community absolutely should get a lot of the credit for sustaining the Cyprus earmark. I think because there is a fairly active Greek-American community – there were many organizations that would come with their lobbyists and they brought along heavy-hitters who were well known in the community and really had a lot of clout and this is one of the things that they would push for every year. I don't think most of them really knew a lot of the details about how the $15 million was used, but getting $15 million was a big ask each year. There were enough members of Congress who had sizable Greek-American communities in their districts to ensure this got in the appropriations bill each year. And as with any diaspora or advocacy community, there were debates about the proper legislative strategy, but everyone agreed on the $15 million for Cyprus."[12]

Marx Sterne was the USAID official in Washington who oversaw the aid to Cyprus and he remembers being reprimanded by his superiors when he wrote a report arguing that the funding be stopped. "I was told that politically I should know better," said Sterne. "There was no economic or developmental justification. There was nothing more that justified USAID's presence there."[13] For Rossides, it was simple. "It was not so much that it was important to keep the money going; it was a matter of could we keep the money going?" said Rossides. "If we could, then let's keep it going."[14]

Reading the transcripts of the markup hearings, one saw a kind of ritual. Officials with Greek lobbying organizations would read their scripts, which would vary little from year to year. A State Department official would try to defend the lower request arguing that in their judgment the smaller amount was justified. That assertion would be invariably rebuffed. In the spring of 1979, as the Senate prepared the FY-1980 appropriation for Cyprus, Under Secretary of State Lucy Wilson Benson argued that the appropriation could be cut from $15 million to $2 million because "the economic recovery is very nearly completed and the needs of the refugees have greatly diminished. State proposed \$5 million last year and so this is consistent." To which Senator Claiborne Pell (D-RI) replied: "It is, but not in the judgment of the Congress. It may well be raised again." To which Benson responded: "I suppose that it may be."[15]

Challenges could also come from other members of Congress. In another markup hearing in the same year, Senator Jacob Javits, a New York Republican, said that he noted Senator Pell's support for the \$15 million figure and had great sympathy for the refugees in Cyprus. He did not want to engage in a debate whether some of the aid was "gold plated" but asked couldn't the amount be reduced to \$10 million to help keep the overall budget within reason and still show support for the Cypriots? Senator Sarbanes asked to be recognized and reminded Senator Javits that the week before he had supported Senator Javits's amendment for funds in support of Soviet Jews. Senator Javits responded: "I withdraw my amendment."[16]

There was another important conversation going on at this time, and that was between Ambassador Stone and Senator Pell. "I had spent several years in India and there had been a successful U.S. scholarship program and the grants went to the top students and they did well and came back with an affinity for the U.S.," explained Stone. "So, I spoke to Senator Pell about setting up a scholarship program. We got much more from that than we ever did from the other things we were doing with the money."[17]

Pell was a natural ally. In 1973, he authored the legislation that created the Basic Educational Opportunity Grants for university study, later renamed Pell Grants, and he was a former diplomat who understood the impact of such programs. "The Greek-American community believed this was an important program and that was a view shared by Senator Pell," noted Chris Van Hollen, the current Democratic Senator from Maryland who was a staffer on the Senate Foreign Relations Committee at this time and wrote a report for the committee on the Cyprus situation. "I knew Gene Rossides well and he was a force. And I can confirm that Representative Long would have paid very close attention to Senator Sarbanes."[18] In the future, members of Congress would refer to CASP as "Senator Pell's scholarship program." Still, even Pell had to be sensitive to the fact that the U.S. government was building homes for Cypriots when citizens in his home state of Rhode Island needed housing. "Senator Pell looked at me and said 'Mr. Ambassador, there are people in Rhode Island that need housing aid more than the people of Cyprus," remembered Cyprus's Ambassador Andrew Jacovides, who had studied at Harvard Law with Senator Sarbanes. "And I said, yes, but the people in Rhode Island were not made homeless by an invasion that used U.S.-supplied weapons. And he looked at me and said 'you have a point, so I will continue to support this.'"[19]

However, it was not that simple. Now the Embassy had to make a formal proposal and to furnish a justification for the creation of a scholarship program. That task fell to Public Affairs Officer F. Weston Fenhagen and his new cultural assistant Christina Hadjiparaskeva, who had walked through the refugee camps, where she heard a consistent plea.

"I had to write several justifications for the CASP program. What the refugees would tell me is that 'they can take our land and our homes and our trees, but if my son has an education, they cannot take that away,'" remembered Hadjiparaskeva. "Very few women used to go abroad for study. After 1974 people saw how it was. Prior to 1974, a girl would go to high school, get a dowry, some furniture, and get married and start a family. All that they had to contribute to a dowry was now lost so they knew they had to make an investment in their daughters, too...before then it was always their sons, their sons, their sons."[20]

"After the houses were built and the Embassy thought that they should stop sending the $15 million every year, we had to figure out what to do with the money," said Hadjiparaskeva. "I said, look, I am from Strovolos. I did not lose my house. If I want to send my son abroad to study I can go to the bank and borrow money and send him, but the people who are refugees have nothing and there is no university in Cyprus. Create a scholarship program. Cypriots will get educated and they will do it in the U.S. and become ambassadors for the U.S. The grants that [the communist party] AKEL was giving out were the main argument. Students were going to Greece and Turkey and then the Soviet Bloc and then the U.S. We were worried about that."[21]

In the midst of the Cold War, a competition with the Soviet Union for hearts and minds was a potent argument. In a memo prepared by the Fulbright Commission, it was noted that in 1979-80, 12,619 Greek Cypriots were doing university studies abroad, with just over half in Greek universities. There were 1,726 Turkish Cypriots studying abroad, almost three-quarters in Turkey. About 1200 of those Cypriots were studying in the East Bloc, mainly in Moscow. There were perhaps 400 or so studying in America, most at their own expense. The Congress highlighted those numbers. With the support of key Senators, such as Senator Pell, and the Embassy, the following language was introduced:

"Assistance for Cyprus in FY-1981 ($15 million) is authorized for use in educational exchange programs as well as refugee relief. The analysis provided below justifies the new program. Scholarships for Cypriot Students: Cypriot cultural identification with the West, in large part an inheritance from the British colonial period, is visibly weakening, and the first generation of Cypriots to grow up after independence will be entering labor, professions, business and government in the next few years. Increasingly, students are attending university in the Soviet Union and Eastern Europe, where full six-year scholarships outnumber western scholarship opportunities of all kinds by an estimated two or three to one (exact figures are not available as the majority of scholarships to East Bloc countries are awarded directly by the local communist party and are not reflected in official statistics). Even excluding the large number of 'unofficial' scholarships known to be made available through the communist party, full official scholarship opportunities for study in the Soviet Union and Eastern Europe exceeded those offered by Western European countries, Canada and the United States. Already, many professionals, including secondary education, medicine, architecture and engineering are strongly influenced or dominated by persons who have studied at Soviet or Eastern European universities, and as costs continue to rise in the West, the number of students taking advantage of educational opportunities in the East also rises. At the same time, the Soviet Union and some Eastern European countries have mounted substantial cultural offenses in Cyprus. There is no university in Cyprus. All students interested in university education must study abroad, either on scholarship or at personal expense. ... Non-scholarship students have traditionally favored study (in descending order) in Greek or Turkish universities, the United Kingdom and Western Europe with Canada and the United States far behind, mainly because of cost. With costs for overseas students at U.K. universities increasing this year by 100 percent or more (depending on the course of study), students in increasing numbers will be looking for alternate opportunities wherever they can find them, including the Eastern Bloc. (There is some possibility that Cypriots at U.K. universities may be eligible for the reduced fees granted to students from EEC countries, but that matter is not yet decided.) Scholarship opportunities in the United States are extremely limited. Of 391 Greek Cypriot students in the United States in 1977-78, only 84 had full scholarships and 11 had partial grants; all nine Turkish Cypriots were on either full or partial scholarship. Currently, there are 40 Cypriots (32 Greek and eight Turks) on full or partial Fulbright scholarships for undergraduate or graduate study. The only other official

U.S. scholarships offered here are AID-sponsored awards for study at the American University of Beirut, where 49 scholarship students (40 Greek, nine Turks) are currently studying."[22]

The justification was accompanied by a chart showing the scholarship opportunities for Cypriot students and noted that 54 percent of the scholarships came from the Soviet Union and East Bloc.

Additional stipulations divided the money, setting aside $5 million for the scholarship program and the remaining $10 million for refugee relief. In response to Congressional inquiries USAID noted that it could, under its rules, support a scholarship program using ESF but that there would need to be a U.S. contractor to help with the administration of the program. The more natural choice might have been IIE, but the bid was won by the American-Mideast Educational and Training Services (Amideast), somewhat to the surprise of Amideast officials. Its main focus was Arabic-speaking Middle Eastern and North African countries, but it was an academic exchange organization.[23] The Fulbright Commission in Cyprus would put out the call for applications, help with the necessary testing, make the selections, and help the grantees identify U.S. universities that would be a good fit. Amideast would make the actual applications and seek additional scholarship money, especially for graduate students. Once the students were in the U.S., Amideast would disburse the money and maintain contact with the students, checking on their wellbeing and academic progress.

The RoC was not particularly enthusiastic about the scholarship program. It wanted the money to be used for housing and large infrastructure programs that would create jobs, but Ambassador Stone pushed and they accepted the program after a delay of one year. On November 9, 1981 the RoC sent a diplomatic note to the American Embassy noting that the Council of Ministers had approved the program on October 15, 1981 "in preferred fields of national development." The fields would be agreed to with the Planning Bureau. "All scholars will be required to sign an undertaking binding themselves to return to Cyprus on completion of their studies." The government pledged it would be generous in granting leave to civil servants seeking a higher degree.[24]

The other entity that largely hated the program was USAID, which was a development agency and generally did not "do" Europe, at least until the Berlin Wall fell and it began to work in the former Warsaw Pact countries. There were exceptions, such as Northern Ireland, but USAID judged that the money going to Cyprus could be better spent elsewhere. For them, the Cyprus program was largely a bureaucratic annoyance and as the years went on, it was sometimes a struggle to get USAID to transfer the money on time.

"I remember Renos came home and said there would be money from USAID and that we had to figure out how many scholarships, how many programs and how many people we would need to run the program," remembered Zavallis.[25]   At the April 3, 1981 Commission Board meeting Chairman Fenhagen hinted at the possibility that some of the USAID money might be used for scholarships. The hints grew stronger and at the September 24, 1981 meeting Fenhagen reported on his consultations in Washington and explained that the Commission would have a major role in implementing a $5 million scholarship program ($13.5 million in 2020 dollars) that would be spread out over five to seven years with priority given to undergraduates, refugees, needy students, and young women – all of whom must present "high standard academic credentials." Two weeks later, USAID Project Manager Elmer Fales and Amideast Vice President James McCloud came to Cyprus and met with the Board to go over the details of the program. It was agreed that a press release would go out to both communities and that appeared on October 15, 1981, just after the arrival of Ambassador Ray Ewing, who was succeeding Ambassador Stone. There was a lot of work to be done.[26]

A week later, a four-page Letter of Understanding between the Cyprus Fulbright Commission and Amideast was signed. Chairman Fenhagen's wife Betsy, who had already been working at the Commission as a counselor, would take primary responsibility for organizing the Commission's efforts and she would get help in a few months when Katherine Redmond came with her husband Paul to the Embassy and was hired by the Commission, although it was Amideast that disbursed her salary. While Redmond did not have a background in counseling, she had been a teacher and had a master's degree in education. The Embassy made it clear to Kamenos that Embassy spouses should be given first priority for these positions. Spousal employment overseas was a major issue for every Embassy, particularly where local labor laws or language prevented the spouses of American diplomats from working in the host country.

These CASP Coordinators worked at the Commission, but were paid and supervised by Amideast. "Renos was curious about what I was doing. He could be a bit gruff and charming and he was highly respected. He was Mr. Fulbright in Cyprus," remembered Redmond. "He seemed to know everyone and I think the students were a little intimidated by him. The main thing we wanted to know was their financial status. We did not think tax returns gave us a true picture and I think Renos would drive around to see if the parents lived in a new fancy house and were pretending not to have money," said Redmond. "The students were just great. They were appreciative and very responsive. Amideast made the decision on placement and tried to have geographic diversity in the university choices. I don't remember students complaining about the choice of schools."[27]

The Letter noted that $1.5 million would be allocated the first year and the remaining $3.5 million in the subsequent years. The Embassy insisted on this. They wanted the grants to be spread over several years so that the "shower of gold" would not only benefit those who happened to be entering university studies in that particular year.[28] A substantial part of the $5 million – about $1 million – would go to USAID, USIA, Amideast, and the Commission for administrative costs. It was anticipated that after approximately 60 scholarships the first year, the number would drop to 25 in the second. Steve Brattain, who was the Economic Officer in the Embassy and charged with overseeing the USAID funds, said "we thought it was a one-off."[29] In other words, that there would not be another $5 million the following year. That turned out to be wrong.

The response to the press release and subsequent ads was immense. There were 800 inquiries and 560 qualified applications were submitted by the short deadline of less than a month. Of these, 141 undergraduate and 41 graduate candidates were called for interviews. Over a six-day period, they were interviewed at the Ledra Palace by a panel that included American, Greek Cypriot and Turkish Cypriot representatives. Ultimately 62 students – 50 undergraduates and 12 graduates; 51 Greek Cypriots and 11 Turkish Cypriots – were chosen. Dropouts reduced that number to 57 by the fall of 1982. After that first experience, Fenhagen and Kamenos met at the Planning Commission and it was decided that only candidates with an average mark of 17 out of 20 or 85 out of 100 could apply. In Washington, Amideast was busy setting up the team that would place the selected students. That team was led by Kate Archambault and included Vice President Dorothy LaGuardia, and Mary Jeffers.[30]

Betsy Fenhagen, who had worked so tirelessly to get the program off the ground, did not stay long enough to see the first students leave Cyprus, as the Fenhagens were off to their next assignment in Zaire. However, she received a letter from Archambault, catching her up on the news of the first class. Chrysanthos Panayiotou arrived first, at the University of Central Florida for graduate studies in electrical engineering. All went smoothly and he was thrilled. Orhan Oge and Petros Appios arrived together at Tulane. Archambault noted they seemed to be quite "chummy" and wrote "this seems to be the case whenever we have pair-ups" (a Greek

Cypriot and a Turkish Cypriot). "Being Cypriot is more important than being Greek or Turkish," she wrote hopefully. American students who learned that they would soon be rooming with Cypriots wrote to Amideast to ask if the arriving Cypriots "spoke English"? Amideast staff took some of the students who were attending Washington, D.C. area schools shopping for sheets and pillowcases and such. Archambault said she felt like a mother. Yiannakis Mouzouris and Christos Philippou were unhappy with their first impressions of Texas A&I, and Amideast immediately set to work on organizing transfers. Mouzouris eventually graduated from the University of Kansas and Philippou from the University of Colorado. Amideast's Jeffers was planning travel to a number of campuses to see how they were all doing.[31]

Though records are not complete, of those first 57 CASP grantees, at least 40 are in Cyprus today – approximately a dozen are teachers and professors, another dozen senior managers or managing directors at private companies, and a half dozen are senior government officials, including the former Auditor General of Cyprus. At least six found a way to remain in the United States, one is a banker in Athens, and another a senior manager in London. At least nine went on to earn a Ph.D.

One of those was Chrys Panayiotou. In March 1985, Archambault wrote to Mary Howard, the wife of Board Chairman Dan Howard, who was working as a counselor for CASP. Panayiotou had called Amideast to request a change in his visa status from J-1 to an F visa that, theoretically, could allow him to avoid the requirement that he return to Cyprus for at least two years. Panayiotou had completed his master's degree in electrical engineering and found a position with the defense contractor Lockheed Martin, which was offering to pay for his Ph.D. Amideast immediately suspected he was trying to stay in the U.S. and that was confirmed a few months later when he applied for permanent residence status. When asked why, he told Archambault "well, you know I have been married for a year." Archambault wrote: "I must have shouted my reply 'to an American?!?' because both Mary and Susan came running in from the other room to see what was going on."[32]

Archambault wrote that she had long anticipated that some of the CASP students would, indeed, try to stay in the U.S., but it was a still a shock when it happened. She noted there were ways to get out of the two-year requirement, one of which involved marriage to an American, but that the RoC also could apply monetary penalties if a student did not return. As Archambault noted, however, some students saw this all as a reasonable price to pay, like a student loan.[33]

"There was an exchange of letters between myself and the RoC," Panayiotou confirmed. "Ultimately, we returned to Cyprus for two years. I worked as a technician and not an engineer. My wife worked as an accountant, but we were just scraping by. After the two years we returned to the U.S. Our first child was born and I shifted to a Ph.D. in education at Florida Atlantic. For many years I taught at university, but since 2013 I have run my own technology center at Indian River State College, supported by grants from the National Science Foundation."[34]

"I will remember the day I received the letter saying that I received the CASP grant until the day I die," said Panayiotou, still married to the same "American," Joan. They have five grown children. "I am so grateful to the generosity of the American government. This is my home now, but I return to Cyprus once a year and it is a little disheartening that I have not found an opportunity to do something there. I would like to give back. I have written a couple of books and the royalties support a couple of scholarships here. It has been my small way of giving back."[35]

One member of the first CASP class who always intended to return was Olcay (neé Gultekin) Firinciogullari. "I grew up in a village – Balikesir – in a close family and my goal was to become a teacher and return," said Firinciogullari. Why America? "When I was a student I had a teacher who recommended that we subscribe to two magazines – *National Geographic* and *Reader's Digest*. I was particularly impressed with *National Geographic* and the pictures of America. I knew I did not want to go to Turkey like many of my classmates."[36]

She was unusual in many respects, including that she was a young woman – just 18 – when she applied for the CASP and she did so on her own. Often, parents would accompany their children to the Commission and ask more questions than their children, who remained largely silent. "I know that I did very well in the interview and when I got the scholarship I told my father and his first reaction was to say 'no, I will not allow you to go to America – it is too far away.' Of course I cried a lot, but then my brother and my headmaster at TMK spoke to my father and he was not stubborn about it and let me go."[37]

The other thing that was unusual was that she wanted to go to a small university. "I was a little scared and did not want to go to a large university and get lost among 30,000 students," said Firinciogullari. "I like close and warm relationships." She applied to just four schools and was accepted at all, but chose little Grinnell College in Grinnell, Iowa with just about 1,500 students. She went as a chemistry major but in her sophomore year she wanted to switch her major to math. She did not think it would be a problem, but there was some pushback from Amideast and the Commission. Eventually they relented and allowed her to change.

"I received such a well-rounded education there. I was part of the international students organization and the folk dance group. I studied Spanish and psychology and anthropology. I am the kind of person who is interested in just about everything," said Firinciogullari. She attended the university's weekly lecture series and remembers seeing, in addition to many American speakers, Mikhail Gorbachev and Bishop Desmond Tutu. "I owe Grinnell a lot. I made many life-long friends there and we still visit each other and write regularly."[38] Eventually, Firinciogullari returned to TMK, where she taught mathematics for 31 years.

As that first class was heading to America, the Congress was busy providing a second tranche of $5 million to the CASP program. However, the Commission and Amideast moved cautiously, upping the number of scholarships in the second year from the planned 25 to 41. Like the first class, the vast majority returned to Cyprus, and today occupy positions as teachers and professors, managers, and there are also several engineers working for the Cyprus Telecommunications and Electricity Authorities. At least six more went on to earn their doctorates.

As this was USAID money, CASP was seen as a development program, a view shared by the Planning Commission in Cyprus, whose views were largely shared by Turkish Cypriot officials. Howard noted that Kamenos was quite strict in adhering to these guidelines when the selections were made. As such, 42 of the first 98 students received grants to study engineering and another 26 studied business. Nine more studied computer science and five majored in architecture. The remaining 16 were scattered among hotel management, social work, education, and the biological sciences. The applicants – and particularly their parents – caught on fast and applied for grants in engineering and business, even though a student's heart might have been in the arts.

One student whose heart was firmly in engineering was Alexandros Josephides, who received a CASP in 1984 to earn a master's degree in mechanical engineering. "I had done my undergraduate work in Ireland and I remember that Kathy Redmond said she had never heard a Cypriot speak like a Galway Man," said Josephides laughing. "Maybe it helped."[39] He chose the University of Michigan and, other than a complaint about the long winters, he found the multicultural experience at the university just as important as the academics.

"I am a Maronite, so a minority here in Cyprus, but the university was such a multicultural student society – different origins, different socioeconomic backgrounds. When you study in a place like the U.S. you see how they all come together. We need that in our own country, of course," noted Josephides, who, as this is written, is the Marine Manager for the Cyprus Shipping Chamber. He worked briefly in the U.S. and then returned and found an engineering job with J&P, a large construction company, and worked in Libya for a time. "I had made friends from all over America and when I worked in Libya there were a lot of Americans and it was easy to understand how to work with them – you just have to have an open mind."[40]

That said, Laina Swiny, who served as a CASP counselor for four years, wished that there had been more flexibility in the subjects that could be pursued. "There were so many professions that Cyprus sorely needed (she singled out museum management) that were not allowed and the island suffered because of that. I fought, as did some of my colleagues, but to no avail. It was the usual rationale... 'Cypriots know what's best for their island.'"[41]

I personally sat on one selection panel in 1989 when a young lady tried to convince us all that she "loved engineering," when her transcript and outside activities strongly suggested she wished to do something else entirely. She was not convincing and, unfortunately, we did not award her a grant. This limitation was noted early on by Amideast as a problem. They wanted to give more grants to young women, but most of the women were more interested in the humanities than subjects such as engineering and so there were fewer applicants. "There were so many qualified students we could have given twice as many grants and it was agonizing to see those who were not selected because many would end up at Patrice Lumumba in Moscow," said Howard.[42] The Planning Bureau and the Commission relented in 1987 and allowed some grants in the humanities.

One of those in the 1983 class who did not pursue engineering or business was Leondios Kostrikis, now Dr. Kostrikis and a professor of virology at the University of Cyprus. He was 11 in 1974 and a refugee from Asha, his family escaping scant minutes before the Turkish tanks arrived. He received a CASP and was accepted at New York University to study biochemistry.

"I don't remember who told me about CASP...perhaps when I was in the army," said Kostrikis. "I applied and interviewed and then there was a letter saying I had been awarded a scholarship and it changed my life. I had been a refugee living under a tree and then the United States takes me in and pays my tuition and fees and back then I could not really understand this. Why were they doing this? Was the American government crazy? There were Americans in my dormitory taking out loans to go to NYU and perhaps they are still paying those loans. Now I am 53 and I understand it and I try to do the same as much as I can."[43]

Dr. Leondios Kostrikis.

"Of course there was culture shock. New York is a very diverse city and there were these punk rockers and all kinds of people and I was trying to understand that and, yes, I went to one of the sessions that brought together Greek and Turkish Cypriots and that was uncomfortable. Some in the group could not handle it," remembered Kostrikis. "I don't know why, but since I was a kid I had thought about studying in the U.S. and I wanted to understand America. After 1974, there was a small wave of Cypriot immigrants to the U.S. and I think it became fashionable to study in the U.S. so a wave of students followed. I often reference my experience there when talking to people."[44]

Dr. Kostrikis found further grants to pursue his M.A. and Ph.D. at NYU in virology, and graduated just as the AIDS epidemic struck with full force. He joined a new well-funded research center in New York to work on the development of a vaccine. However, there was still the matter of the J-1 visa requirement and so when he was offered a position at the still relatively new University of Cyprus, he decided it was time to come home.

"I realized that the reason that I came to the U.S. is that I was supposed to go back home. It was designed that way. And, I had a girlfriend who is now my wife. She is French and was studying international relations at Columbia and she was going to France to do her Ph.D. in law, so returning to Europe made sense and tenured positions don't come along every day. Now we have two children, Yannis and Sofia. I hope they will be able to study in the U.S."[45]

Dr. Kostrikis notes that his experience in the U.S. has impacted the way he thinks about his work as an academic. "I have argued here that some graduate courses should be offered in English so that we can attract foreign students and Turkish Cypriots, and some of my colleagues do not think that we should accept Turkish Cypriots.   Now, I have become the first professor here to have a Turkish Cypriot Ph.D. student and she is a good student and will write a brilliant dissertation and go back to teach at a Turkish Cypriot university and always know that she was helped by a Greek Cypriot. That is how you bring people together.   About a third of the professors here at the university are American-trained and that is reflected in the mentality here, the open-mindedness."[46]

In 2020, many Greek Cypriots got to know Dr. Kostrikis very well as he headed the Government of Cyprus's efforts to combat the corona virus pandemic.

CASP did not replace Fulbright, and that program – offering both graduate and undergraduate grants – continued in parallel to CASP. One of those who received a Fulbright to pursue graduate studies in computer engineering was Fehmi Tokay. When he returned to Cyprus from Auburn University in 1986, he began teaching at Türk Maarif Koleji (TMK). TMK's roots were the English School. When the island was divided in 1974, the Turkish Cypriot students at the English School could no longer access the campus, so a satellite school was set up, which eventually evolved into TMK, for many years the only true English-language medium school in the North. As such, the vast majority of Turkish Cypriot CASP and Fulbright grantees came from TMK.

"In 1988 I was asked to start helping students fill out applications for schools in the U.K. and the U.S., and so I was a counselor. I was also writing administrative programs, so I was an administrator," explained Tokay. "In 1990 I was informed that I was the Assistant Headmaster." A decade later he would rise to the position of Head Master.[47]

Tokay remembers well the buzz in the school when the names of the CASP grantees were announced.   "There was a big competition among both the students and the parents to get one of these grants. It was a great opportunity to get out of the country and get a free education. Parents whose children did not get a grant would pressure me to write letters to Mr. Hadjittofi to complain that the process was not fair. Some students who were better off financially received the grants and some who were not as well off did not, so that created turbulence. It was also a great motivator. You had to work very hard to get one of the grants. Parents came to my office and told me that they really wanted their child to get the scholarship and go to America and not come back. They wanted them to stay in America because of the Cyprus Problem and the economic limitations. They just wanted their children to get out."[48]

Board Chairman Walter Douglas (1999-2002) remembered that there was a class rank at TMK. "The feeling among the parents was that if there were 10 scholarships for TCs that those ranked one through 10 should get them," explained Douglas. "Well, this one year it did not happen that way. We chose number one and then number eight and then number 13 and the parents hit the roof and we had to explain that Fulbright was about mutual understanding and that it was not just about grades. We want them to go over there to interact with Americans and to have the personalities and the smarts to do that. We found that a lot of the good students lacked the social skills that were part of the Fulbright standards and that is why. I remember there were these meetings and Daniel had to go over to TMK and there were these screaming parents and I get it… it was for their kids. This was everything."[49]

In the mid-1980s, tuition costs in the United States had not yet exploded. The annual tuition, room and board at a public university in 1982-83 averaged $3,200, while the average cost at private universities was more than double that at just over $7,100.[50] Still, this fell under the ceiling that USAID had imposed, so the grants were essentially full four-year and two-year grants. The original plan approved by USAID said that cost should not be a barrier if Cypriots were accepted by elite universities. In some cases, Amideast was able to get universities to pay some of the costs. Despite the short notice in the first year, CASP students received offers of $57,594 in grants from 14 different universities, and $33,630 of those grants were accepted. Cypriots landed in 41 different universities in 20 states, a pattern that persisted year after year.

When $5 million continued to be appropriated each year, the first response was to create another program for Short-Term Training (STT) grants, a program that would be very much in line with USAID's philosophy that this was, first and foremost, a development program. The program was initiated on December 30, 1983 offering training opportunities in the U.S. lasting up to three months, all expenses paid.[51] The Commission began cautiously, with 14 grants the first year and 17 the second and they were immediately popular. However, the money was still piling up in the Amideast accounts and if the funds were not spent within seven years they would have to be returned to the U.S. Treasury.

"There was a huge surplus of funds building up and Renos said we have to spend the money and give more scholarships or the money would be lost," explained Zavallis. "Renos had a meeting at the Embassy and he told me that they wanted to expend all the funds before they expire and they told him to hire more employees because the existing personnel could not handle the increase in work. We sat together and estimated how many people we needed."[52] "Renos and I agreed that we should spend the money as soon as we could because there was pressure to divert the funds to the renewal of the sewers of Nicosia (a joint project driven by the two mayors) for which the U.S. would get zero credit, just as it did for all the housing we built," remembered Howard. "I spoke to Richard Haass, who was then the U.S. Special Cyprus Coordinator. He was a young man full of energy...he applauded CASP and said that we were doing more good for the U.S. than most of the AID projects around the world. He never took any credit for it but I have a feeling that he may have helped the increased flow of funds."[53]

Some of the hires were spouses from the American Embassy. Others were local secretaries to help with the paperwork. One was Kyproula Kyriakidou, who came to the Commission as a 20-year-old and trained to become an accountant. Eventually, she oversaw the Commission's substantial accounts until its close in 2014, 30 years later. In addition, Daniel Hadjittofi's American wife came on board as well, hired not by Hadjittofi, but by the Embassy.

"The selection panels went on for weeks," remembered Zavallis as the Commission sifted through hundreds of applications. Dan Howard remembered his wife Mary was putting in 10- to12-hour days for months. In the end, 252 Cypriots received full or partial CASP grants in 1985 and another $100,000 in grants from American universities was offered ($235,000 in 2020 dollars). The following year, the Board introduced a stricter TOEFL test requirement for English skills, and while there were still more than 1,000 applications, 143 received CASPs. Only after this bulge of nearly 400 scholarships would the CASP program settle into a pattern of roughly 70 grants a year, although the number of STTs grew steadily.

Amideast was able to build on the reputation of earlier Cypriot students, and in the 1985 class four were accepted at Harvard, six at Cornell, five each at Columbia and MIT, three each at Penn and Vanderbilt, and, on the West Coast, three at Berkeley and two more at Stanford. One of those in the 1985 class who found a place at a hidden gem of a university, Washington University in St. Louis, was Mehmet Ali Yukselen. His road to America got off to an inauspicious start.

"I had one of the first appointments for an interview for the CASP at the Ledra Palace. I had never been in the Green Zone and I went too far and ended up on the Greek side and a soldier guided me back," recalled Yukselen. "In those days you thought about study in America as a question of: 'Can we? Should we?'...it was a great opportunity."[54]

He earned an undergraduate degree in civil engineering and thought about finding a way to stay in the United States, but then visited friends in Turkey and decided to apply to Bosporus University. "I applied late, but when they saw I had a degree from an American university it made a difference. I finished my Ph.D. in 1995."[55] Yukselen moved back and forth between Turkey and Cyprus until 2007 when he became the Rector of Cyprus International University. In 2013, he was able to return to his hometown as Rector of the European University of Lefke.

"When I came here it was about 3,700 students and now we are approaching nearly 12,000 from 80 countries," noted Yukselen. "I am not sure how many of the faculty are (CASP and Fulbright) grantees, but the impact was great. I know the scholarship changed my life so I try to be generous here. The grantees have created a kind of community...I know engineers, bankers, business executives, so many of the top people. These are people who understand America and what it is all about. It is excellent to have such a community on the island that is made up of people in both communities. It was, as I said, a great opportunity."[56]

Ambassador Richard Boucher (1993-96) noted that he, like the other ambassadors, had the same discussion each year. "The funny thing is the money. Every year that I was ambassador we had a discussion with the desk...do we really need this money? No. Could we cut it? Yes. Is it really worth the political pain of going to the Hill to cut it? No. So what are we going to spend it on? Scholarships were always considered to be the most valuable. You know we had better places to spend $15 million in an era of tight budgets but then we thought as long as we had the money, let's spend it wisely. I always felt the money spent on scholarships was well spent."[57]

And so, the CASP program's impact continued to be felt. In 1974, there were a couple of hundred Cypriots studying in America, many on Fulbright grants. By the end of the decade, that number had risen to about 700. But by 1985, after the CASP program generated so much interest, the number increased to 2200, just as the Congressional committees had hoped.[58] Of course, that number represented not just students receiving grants, but students who wanted to follow their friends or who had family connections in the U.S. or who had applied but failed to get a grant. If they were good students, the Commission staff could still help them find a university and, often, a package of aid as well. It was a stunning success, but the man who did so much to build these programs, to promote American education, and burnish the name Fulbright in Cyprus suddenly and tragically passed from the scene. Renos Kamenos's untimely death in 1986 meant that the stewardship of the Commission would pass to a young Fulbright grantee recently returned from America and it would be his task to lead the Commission forward.

With the arrival of the CASP funds and the expansion of the Commission, the Commission rented this house on Egypt Avenue, which would become its principal office for nearly 30 years.

DANIEL

In the summer of 1974, Asha (Ἀσσια) was a bustling agricultural village in the center of the Mesaoria Plain. It has existed since at least the 13th century and was, in 1974, divided into two parishes, St. John's and St. George's. It was prosperous enough for its 2700 inhabitants to support five churches – St. George, St. John Prodromos, St. Theodore, St. Spyridon, and the Virgin Mary, an ancient church that has now been restored by the UN.

Today, however, the other churches stand desecrated and gutted and some are used to store farm implements. Prior to 1963, some Turkish Cypriots lived in the village, but were driven out. In 1974, the Greek Cypriots would meet the same fate. A section of the village has been razed and a Turkish military base has been built in its place. There is no marker to show where so many of the residents lost their lives.

On August 14, Turkish military forces rolled into Asha. The men were separated from the women and children, but there was a dispute between two soldiers on what to do with 15-year-old Daniel Hadjittofi – should he go with the men or with the women and children? He was small and fair, and looked younger than his years. Finally, an officer broke up the tug-of-war and told Daniel to "go back to your mother."

Then he watched as his father, Tofis, and his uncles Giorgos, Vassos, Shialos, and Costandis were led away with the other men. He never saw them again.[1]

Hadjittofi, along with his mother Chrysi and sisters Eleni and Myrophora, were clustered with other families in a house for several weeks until the UN came to register them. His older brother Demetrios was in the military, so he was not in Asha that day. First, the family went to Larnaca, but they stayed in more than a dozen places in the coming weeks. "We had a tent and people donated clothes to us and we were okay," remembered Hadjittofi. However, the Grammar School in Nicosia had offered Hadjittofi a scholarship and so the family followed him to Nicosia. Ultimately, his family would receive one of the USAID houses, and it is where Hadjittofi's mother lived until her passing in 2023. "But in those days you would not say that the house was built with American help," noted Hadjittofi.[2]

Hadjittofi did well at the Grammar School, had strong English, and one of his teachers suggested that he apply for a Fulbright. "I was not too keen, but my teacher put me in his car and drove me to the Commission and Renos and Stella were there," remembered Hadjittofi. "Ah, the boy with nothing...we have a lot like you," said Renos. Hadjittofi said he felt a little discouraged, but his teacher said: "You will fill out the application."

"Daniel was very needy and Renos was shocked by his personal story," remembered Zavallis. "I remember Renos said he had to fight with the selection panel to get Daniel a grant. They wanted someone else, but Daniel was very needy."[3]

The travel grant and the Fulbright imprimatur led to Hadjittofi's acceptance at Hamilton College, a small liberal arts college in upstate New York with the motto Γνώθι σαυτόν – Know Thyself. Founded in 1793 and named for the first Secretary of the Treasury Alexander Hamilton, it has high academic standards, small class sizes, and a tradition of generous financial aid. Hadjittofi's aid package covered everything except personal expenses and he was able to have a

Daniel Hadjittofi at Hamilton College (top) and as a young Executive Director of the Cyprus Fulbright Commission.

part-time campus job – first in the library ("too quiet for me") and then as the campus postman. "I delivered everyone's mail and got to know everyone. I loved it at Hamilton," said Hadjittofi.[4]

He studied political science and economics and he met a young woman, Catherine Ann Orlando, a year younger than he was. As graduation approached, he thought that he needed to further his education. An

MBA seemed to be a good way to go. The Associate Dean at Hamilton, Dr. Sidney Wertimer, urged Hadjittofi to apply to the University of Texas at Austin where a Hamilton graduate – Michael Granof – had done very well. By Hadjittofi's own admission, he put the least amount effort he could into the application, still not sure that Texas would be right for him. "I was comfortable at Hamilton and the thought of moving across the country made me feel like a refugee again," said Hadjittofi. However, Dr. Granof nudged him to rewrite parts of the application and he was accepted into the program.

"If Sid Wertimer made a request of me, you can be sure that I would do what it took to ensure that it was fulfilled," remembered Granof. "In the case of Dan, it took relatively little effort to get him admitted to our program. He was bright, articulate, and somewhat reserved, but always friendly and got along well with the other students. He breezed through the program."[5]

Graduation came in 1983 and it was time to return to fulfill his two-year visa requirement. "I had idealized Cyprus, but when the summer heat hit I was gasping," said Hadjittofi. He and Cathy married in Cyprus, but there were no plans to stay long-term. Hadjittofi had been offered a scholarship to study toward a Ph.D. at Princeton. In the near term, however, he needed a job.

"I had written to Renos and he told me to come around because he might have a job for me and there was an offer of a job at a bank. There were only a handful of MBAs in Cyprus at that time. I did not come see Renos the first day, which he expected, so when I did come he told me I was too late, but then he put together a little test and I was interviewed by him and [Board Chairman] Dan Howard and Dan asked most of the questions," explained Hadjittofi.[6] He was hired as the deputy director and Howard made it clear that Kamenos's retirement was not too far in the future. It would not be too long before the deluge of CASP scholarships saw Cathy come on board as well part-time as a counselor.

"Renos came up with Daniel as the prime candidate and I had no idea that he had an American wife at the time. He was Renos's choice and I agreed," remembered Howard. "For the remainder of my time there, Daniel kind of faded in Renos's large shadow. Renos had the strength to resist efforts by political leaders, and sometimes even the Ambassador, to sway the selection process. Renos did choose Daniel in anticipation that he would succeed him. But Renos's passing was sudden and unexpected and he certainly did not anticipate that Daniel would succeed him so soon."[7]

Laina Swiny, who worked as a CASP counselor, remembered the dynamic in the office. "I remember Stella could tell Renos off from time to time, but I also remember her taking him his coffees. She was very professional and very warm and caring and very caring toward Renos. That was always my impression. It could have been an awkward situation in the office because Daniel's wife Cathy came to work in the office, too, so you had two husband and wife teams in the office. Such things could be difficult…but it always worked. It was also clear that Renos was grooming Daniel to take over."[8]

After two years at the Commission, Daniel and Cathy had their first child, Christopher, but around the same time Kamenos, who had rarely missed a day in the office in more than 20 years, started to have a little fever. It was the spring of 1985. "He was given antibiotics but, eventually, he went to a specialist and the diagnosis was pancreatic cancer," said Zavallis. "He went to Sloan-Kettering Cancer Center in New York in the early spring of 1986 and we stayed six, seven weeks. We returned to Cyprus in May and Renos died in June."[9]

Hadjittofi had been named acting Executive Director during Kamenos's illness by the new Board Chairman Jack Sears, but there was some hesitancy to name him Executive Director after Kamenos's passing. He was just 26 and there were some who wanted someone with more experience and gravitas. However, he had done a good job in his time at the Commission and Sears largely overruled any objections from the Greek and Turkish Cypriots. With Ambassador Richard Boehm attending, Hadjittofi was unanimously confirmed as the Executive Director of the Commission at its September 19, 1986 Board meeting. He grew a mustache to look older.[10]

There was much to do.

The growing Commission staff needed a larger space and they soon identified a colonial era house on Egypt Avenue near the Venetian walls of the Old City and up against the back of the American Center library. Renovations were undertaken swiftly as Embassy staff liberally interpreted rules for the use of security funds and USIA contributed as well.

While Kamenos was in New York, two Greek Cypriot students at the American University in Beirut (AUB), who had received USAID grants administered by the Commission – Panayiotis Tirkas and Stavros Yiannaki – were kidnapped by the Abu Nidal terrorist group on April 28, 1986. They were released on June 21, 1986, after an appeal by PLO leader Yasir Arafat.[11] There was obvious relief that they were returned unharmed. However, that ended the successful program with AUB and the staff had to scramble to find Fulbright grants and placement for the affected students. Tirkas and Yiannaki completed their studies at the University of Kansas.

Also, there was a new program to launch. As noted, the Commission did not wish to fund Ph.D. studies because of the uncertain duration and cost, but both Greek and Turkish Cypriots – with an eye toward the founding of universities on the island – wanted to support some Ph.D. candidates in the field of education. With the CASP program supporting a substantial number of both undergraduate and graduate grants, the Commission felt it had the leeway to use the Fulbright program to support a small Ph.D. program, but limited the grants to three years, which put significant pressure on the grantees.

One of those was Sonuc Demililer, one of the few Turkish Cypriots who had not attended TMK. She had studied in the United States with the financial support of an uncle who was a physician in Pennsylvania. She started at Susquehanna University as a biology major because her uncle dictated that she should become a doctor. However, she realized her English was not strong enough and that her heart was in education. She found a way to break away from her uncle's controlling ways and finance her education by working as a resident assistant at Beaver College (today Arcadia University in the suburbs of Philadelphia), where she received a degree in the teaching of English.

She returned to Cyprus and taught at the technical school, which eventually became Eastern Mediterranean University and, in 1985, received a CASP to earn her master's at SUNY Stony Brook. When she returned, she settled back in at EMU, but when the Ph.D. program was advertised, she leapt at the chance and completed her Ph.D. at the University of Southern California.

"When I came back EMU wanted me to return but I wanted to change a lot of things and that was blocked," recalled Demililer. "They thought I was too demanding. I guess my style had become somewhat American – clear and direct. I forgot the words you were supposed to use with your superiors."[12] She stayed at EMU long enough to feel she had fulfilled her obligation to them and then went on to Cyprus International University where she worked as the director of the Foundation School, and then to Girne American University, where she was appointed Vice Rector. She also worked briefly as a part-time counselor for the Commission in the early 1990s.

"I think my American education is reflected in my teaching and I hear this from my students all the time," said Demililer. "An American education gives you autonomy and a chance to learn and find your own way. It does not focus on the problem, but on the solution. Education is not memorizing stuff, taking the exam, and getting a grade. Education is solving problems and this is what I learned in the United States. Our education system did not teach us to ask questions. We were supposed to listen. Over there you could ask questions and have opinions and you were encouraged to be creative and it all gave you self-confidence and motivation."[13]

Another Cypriot who took advantage of the short-lived Ph.D. program was Dr. Stelios Georgiou, who would become one of the founding members of the education faculty at the University of Cyprus. Georgiou had paid his own way, in 1976, to the small Jersey City University where he earned his BA and MA degrees, before returning to Cyprus to work at the Ministry of Education. When the Ph.D. program came along, he said he was a bit "romantic" about it, pursuing learning for the sake of learning, and not necessarily aiming for a particular position in the hierarchy. He took the requisite tests, sat through the interviews and was accepted at Boston University. All seemed to go smoothly until the Ministry tried to intervene, arguing that he was "too junior" to receive such a grant. Both he and Hadjittofi pushed back. "The Ministry promised me another grant later, but a Fulbright grant is a passport to many things," noted Georgiou.[14] He prevailed and finished his doctorate in the required three years.

In addition to launching this program, Hadjittofi needed to quickly establish administrative control. Kamenos had handled the accounting himself, but Hadjittofi knew that he had to go through the books and establish his own system. The CASP program was largely handled by Amideast, but there still needed to be administrative accounts for each annual grant. The Fulbright programs had their own accounts, as did the still new STT program. Eventually, there would be more than 20 separate bank accounts to oversee. Kyproula Kyriakidou, who had started as a 20-year-old secretary, was encouraged by one of the CASP coordinators – Nick Ferro, an Embassy spouse – to take on more responsibility and he encouraged her to take a series of accounting courses, which Washington would pay for, to earn her certification. She would finish in 1988. She then became the Commission's primary bookkeeper, which Hadjittofi had also encouraged.

He also hired a program officer who would serve as his deputy when he was away. He chose Ioli Kythreotou, who had studied social sciences at SUNY Stony Brook and was awarded a master's degree in organizational psychology from Columbia. She had spent a year working at the Bank of Cyprus, but she was bored and sought a different challenge. "Daniel was my mentor. He taught me how to do the counseling and there was always training," said Kythreotou. "A year after I was hired, I went to the U.S. for training in Washington and then visited campuses in Boston and California and every part of it included training. Every few years there were advising conferences where you worked with advisors from other commissions. We became a very good team."[15] In particular, Kythreotou did a good deal of outreach, giving presentations at schools throughout Cyprus, making the point that study in the U.S. could be more than just a dream.

Then there was the matter of the selection panels. Kamenos had run a tight ship, but, as in the case of Hadjittofi's selection, there were opportunities for jawboning. Moreover, there was always the possibility that a selection panel member could give high scores to one particular candidate, while intentionally giving a competitor low scores. Given that little separated many of the candidates, who all came in with top grades, a couple of points could make the difference. Hadjittofi, therefore, instituted a rule that candidates's scores could not be more than 1.5 points apart on the six-point scale. "If one of the six panel members gave a student 5.5 and another gave that student a 3.0, then each had to explain their reasoning and one or both of them had to change their score(s) so the difference would not be more than 1.5 points," explained Hadjittofi.[16] Then the scores of all six panelists were added together for the final score. Given how academically strong the applicants were, the interview was often decisive.

However, the Commission was always going to have to fight the appearance of favoritism. Achilleas Demetriades, the son of Board member Lellos Demetriades, received a CASP for graduate work in international trade law at Georgetown University in 1986. He does not remember any comments concerning his father's position on the Board. "Of course, my father was not on the selection panel," noted Demetriades. "I had studied in the U.K. and had been called to the bar there and had worked in Brussels, but I really wanted the U.S. experience. I tapped into the Georgetown circuit, the Embassy circuit, and the law school circuit. I made a friend who was a staffer in the Senate and got to see how that worked and I interned at a D.C. law firm. It was all very interesting."[17]

In reality, some children of individuals connected to the Commission and the Embassy did receive grants, and some did not. You could not penalize the children for where their parents worked or served if they had done the work and received the grades. Occasionally, the child of an important Embassy contact, including the children of ministers, would fail to earn a grant and there would be backlash and pressure. But, overall, the Commission managed to resist outside pressure. There was one crack in this wall. In the early 1990s, due to pressure from the Ambassador and an Economic Officer, the Commission agreed that the Ambassador, as honorary chairman of the Commission, could select from the pool of applicants up to five individuals for Short-Term Training grants, although they would still have to go through the regular process and sit for interviews. In actual fact, Ambassadors rarely exercised this privilege.[18]

Achilleas Demetriades (top) and Ozdil Nami (bottom).

Hadjittofi recalled another instance: "There was a case of the son of a man who was close to President Clerides. "Clerides would send me messages from time to time, but this time he called me and said 'I have this person and if you can help, I would appreciate it.' He was very polite and I said, 'Mr. President okay, I will see what we can do.' Then the interview was scheduled and Clerides called me again and told me the interview is tomorrow and I said that I was aware of that. Then, we had the interview and he did not get a grant. I did not say anything to anybody but I called Clerides and I said 'Mr. President, we did not manage to give him a grant,' and he said 'that is okay, don't worry about it.'"[19]

However, Hadjittofi was not above a little coaching. When Constantinos Pitris, from a refugee family, applied in 1988, Hadjittofi took him aside. "His clothes were clean but old and he was soft-spoken. I told him he needed to speak up for himself and be more aggressive in the interview," said Hadjittofi. "He came from a farm family. His father raised rabbits."

Dr. Constantinos Pitris.

"Yes, I worked on a farm and shoveled manure...I found it a character-building experience," laughed Pitris.[20] He had good teachers and watching his father fix electrical items on his workbench had given him an interest in electronics. Midway through his military service he spoke with Hadjittofi, and applied and received an undergraduate CASP that took him to the University of Texas to study electrical engineering.

"Studying in the U.S. was really not an option, but the scholarship made it possible. It was unbelievable," explained Pitris. "I went through a list of the top engineering schools. Some, like MIT, were too expensive, but the University of Texas was in the Top Ten and I applied there and at some other schools." In the course of his studies at Texas he became interested in lasers. "I went there to study telecommunications, but that is what I like about the U.S. system. You have an idea of what you want to do and can end up doing something completely different. The system is flexible enough to do that."[21]

Pitris's work on lasers led to collaboration with a group doing biomedical engineering, and from there to his master's degree at Texas and his first patent for an imaging system to identify a form of cancer. That ultimately took him to MIT for his Ph.D. studies, and, indirectly, to Harvard's Medical School as well. "I was not going to leave Texas, but the fact that I ended up at MIT was very fortunate because their program had something that the others did not and that was a collaboration between the biomedical engineering school at MIT and the Harvard Medical School," said Pitris. "You could take classes at the medical school, get clinical experience, and work at the hospital for a couple of months. In the end, I spent an extra two years there to get my medical degree from Harvard because I could. It was an amazing experience."[22]

At that moment, the University of Cyprus was just starting up its engineering department and Pitris headed home. He was the third professor in the department. "It was a great opportunity, but if I had known how much work it was going to be to start a department, I might have stayed in the U.S. a little longer," he laughed. Today he heads the Kios Center at the University, a major source of research funds. "I did not know that Daniel had fought for me to get a scholarship. He did a great job of encouraging people."[23]

Washington noticed, too. In sending its comments on one of the first program plans produced under Hadjittofi, the desk officer at USIA wrote: "After a year of transition following the death of the former Executive Director, the Commission seems to have achieved more stability and a stronger and more focused sense of purpose."[24]

In addition, it did not take long for Hadjittofi to get a taste of the politics of the Cyprus Problem intruding into the Commission's work. At his second Board meeting in November 1986, it was agreed that the Commission would raise money for a Renos Kamenos Memorial Fund and would use the money to buy books to donate to libraries on both sides of the island. However, Turkish Cypriot Board member Niyazi Alioglu cautioned the Board that while the Turkish Cypriots would gladly accept such books as a sign of respect for Kamenos, an inscription in the books with Kamenos's name – a Greek Cypriot name – would be too politically sensitive in the North and should be excluded.[25] And a year later, when a Greek-American Fulbright professor came as a consultant, it was decided he would only work in the South because he would not be accepted by the Turkish Cypriots.

In August 1989, the Commission dealt with another tragedy when CASP student Christos Americanos drowned off the coast of New Jersey. An honors student at the Stevens Institute of Technology, Americanos was swimming with friends when a strong undertow took him under. "It was such a tragedy," said Hadjittofi, who gave a eulogy at the funeral.

The late 1980s found the Commission taking on several new programs; these included the Hubert H. Humphrey grants for mid-career professionals, and another attempt at the Fulbright Teacher Exchange program. The Humphrey program, which offered primarily civil servants the chance to spend one year in the U.S. for a combination of studies and practical experience, started and ended rather quickly. Cypriot supervisors were not enthusiastic about allowing their employees to disappear for a year, especially since the program required that they continued to receive their normal salaries. Turkish Cypriots, in particular, did not like it because it did not lead to a degree or any kind of professional credential. In the end, only 30 Humphrey grants were awarded before the program was abandoned. Hadjittofi remains perplexed to this day why the program was not accepted.

The Teacher Exchange program matched Cypriot and American secondary school teachers, who swapped jobs, homes, and even cars, but not salaries. The program has long been particularly popular in the United Kingdom where there was the common language (sort of) between the U.S. and U.K. The Cyprus Commission quickly realized that it had to supplement the Cypriot salaries, particularly for Turkish Cypriot teachers. Greek Cypriots largely stopped applying for the program after the first two years. "It was a huge deal," noted Hadjittofi. "The Cypriot teachers who went to the States had to teach a much heavier load, sometimes three times the classroom hours. The American teachers seemed to like it, but some broke their contracts because they could not deal with the bureaucracy or understand the culture. After a couple years [Board Chairman] Lane Cubstead told me 'you tried, but if it does not work, it does not work'."[26]

One teacher who did have a positive experience was Turkish Cypriot Idil Akcal, who had grown up in the U.K. and was teaching at TMK when she was chosen in the first year of the program in 1988. She was placed at Venice High School in Los Angeles, a 2,000-student school where the movie *Grease* was filmed. "It was very different. I had taught at smaller schools and certainly not as multicultural as Venice H.S. I had students from Mexico, Vietnam, Africa, all over," remembered Akcal. In one case, her students warned her about wearing a certain color scarf, lest it be interpreted as support for a particular gang. "Having taught in the U.K., I was used to the workload, but the teaching was much more student-centered. They are expected to participate. In Cyprus, we talked and they listened and there was very little interaction, but it was very different in the U.S.," noted Akcal.

One of the things she particularly liked was the support system. "There were so many counselors and so if you had a problem with a student, you sent them to their counselor. You did not have to deal with discipline or with parents – you just taught." This came into play in the only truly negative experience she had during her academic year in California. She found a boy sleeping in her classroom and when she nudged him awake he became belligerent and so she sent him to his counselor. The next day there was an envelope on her desk. There was a single sheet of paper with the words "just to let you know, EOKA still exists."

Akcal was stunned. "Not even the teachers seemed to know where Cyprus was and someone knew about EOKA?" thought Akcal. "I took it to the administration and explained what it meant and they took it all very seriously. Apparently the boy had a relative who had fought in Cyprus in 1974. They asked me if I wanted to take action and I said no. They removed him from my class and I never saw him again."

"Teaching for a year in the U.S. was the best experience of my life. My husband and I made a number of friends. We connected with Cypriot CASP students in Southern California. I even went to my first prom," said Akcal. "Those experiences stick with you."[27]

Her American counterpart, Connie Barrett, completed her 10 months at TMK, but ran into a little "political" trouble at the end of her stay. She gave a radio interview to one of the main Turkish Cypriot radio stations "Bayrak" and in it praised her Turkish Cypriot hosts and "the beautiful cities of Morphu and Kyrenia in the Turkish Republic of Northern Cyprus." Hadjittofi was called by a Greek Cypriot journalist from the nationalist publication *Kyrikas* and the resulting article charged that an American Fulbright scholar had publicly communicated "scandalous propaganda for the TRNC." The Commission considered issuing a brief statement, but in the end decided to ignore the article, as well as give Barrett a little coaching.[28]

"I tried to put out fires before they got into the papers," said Hadjittofi. "One of the issues was discussed in parliament at one point, but I would call people up and ask 'what the hell are you doing? Are you trying to destroy us?' Then they would back off and turn their guns on the Embassy and leave us alone."[29]

As Hadjittofi settled in, two more significant issues surfaced. The first was the end of the seven-year period of the first CASP grant. Under the law, any of the $5 million not expended – known as residuals – had to be returned to the U.S. Treasury. The problem was, the Commission was unsure how much that might be, if anything, given Amideast's control of the accounts. The residuals could be created in a variety of ways—students who had been allocated a grant but had withdrawn at the last moment, or had received aid from their universities, or had finished early. "We were having trouble finding out how much was actually in the residuals from Amideast," said Kyriakidou.[30]

After a couple of years of running its end of the program in Cyprus, the Commission had wanted control, including financial control, transferred to USIA and the Commission, with Amideast playing a supporting role and, as such, reducing the amount it charged for administration. Howard had tried and failed to effect this change during his tenure as Board Chairman. However, things came to head in the winter of 1989 when the Commission learned that there was approximately $7.5 million in the residual account that soon would have to be returned to the Treasury. At the same time, Amideast proposed an amended Letter of Understanding between itself and the Commission whereby Amideast would assume almost total control of the CASP program on the ground in Cyprus. Both the Embassy and the Commission found this wholly unacceptable. In cables in January and April, Board Chairman Lane Cubstead argued that given the politically sensitive nature of the CASP program, day-to-day operational control was best left in the hands of the Commission.[31]

This set off negotiations that lasted into the summer. Under the new arrangement USAID would transfer the $5 million to USIA each year and USIA would in turn transfer it to the Commission, which would control the money with accounts in both Cyprus and the U.S. From USIA's point of view, once the money was transferred to the Commission it ceased to be U.S. Government funds and became Commission funds, controlled by the Commission and its Board. In addition, the Commission had the choice of retaining Amideast as its partner or, perhaps, striking a new arrangement with IIE. There had been some frustration with Amideast, not only over the lack of prompt information concerning the residuals, but also over the fact that IIE seemed to have more success in negotiating aid packages for students to supplement their grants. In the end, however, the Commission decided to stick with Amideast. The final agreement was signed on August 2, 1989. It also provided an extended deadline for expending the residuals.

Hadjittofi traveled to Washington at the end of that summer and, in a memo to the Board Chairman, noted that he "spoke with everyone at USIA who was remotely involved with the Commission." He also noted that USIA officials were congratulatory and "euphoric" concerning the new arrangement and that the USAID officials he met with were defensive at first, but "after a battery of questions" became more open and agreed the program was valuable and that it should continue. Even discussions with Amideast went well. On the issue of retaining the residuals, Hadjittofi did some networking with members of the Greek lobby – and they in turn lobbied members of Congress. The Embassy and USIA pushed as well, and eventually an agreement was reached to allow the Commission more time to expend the funds.[32] "Yes, the Greek lobby played a central role in getting the extension of the money," noted Hadjittofi. Several years later, the Commission only had to return $274,231 of the $7.5 million. Much of that $7.25 million was ultimately devoted to scores of programs on communication, conflict resolution, and bicommunal interaction, which is the subject of the next chapter.

His interaction with members of the Greek lobby was not serendipitous. When Hadjittofi took over as Executive Director, he had to find his own style. His instinct was to be more public in promoting the program, but Kamenos, who had come with his own network thanks to a large and prominent family, taught him to fly more under the radar to protect the program. Attracting too much attention could have political consequences. "Renos was always low key. I realized very early on that unless I stayed below the radar I could be a target," explained Hadjittofi. "We provided education, so people tiptoed around us, but I started to grow my network. I met with President Kyprianou and President Vassiliou. I was invited to join their parties, but said no because I wanted to stay neutral. I was able to express my views to them in a way that was not critical."

The creation of a network was actually in Hadjittofi's contract with the Board. Among other things, it said that the Executive Director must deal with "politically sensitive issues involving implementation of exchange programs and workshops" and "that he must develop and maintain a broad range of the highest level contacts to include ministers and vice-ministers in the ministries of Education and Culture, Foreign Affairs, Labor, Justice, Interior, the Ombudsman, and Social Welfare; with members of parliament; with deans and rectors of universities; with NGO directors; with mayors and representatives of local governments; with representatives of international organizations; directors of cultural institutions to support Fulbright goals and objectives."[33]

There was one other important item on Hadjittofi's agenda during his visit to Washington, and that concerned the idea of an endowment. Like Economic Officer Steve Brattain, many thought the allocation of $5 million for the CASP program would be a "one-off." A senior official with Amideast, familiar with the ways of Washington and a mercurial Congress, noted that for a scholarship program to last as long as five years would be a miracle. And yet, the CASP was now seven years old with no sign of stopping. That same summer, the House Subcommittee for Europe and the Middle East authorized $15 million again for Cyprus for fiscal years 1990 and 1991, noting that the funds were "an important expression of Congressional concern for the Cypriot people and a demonstration for the peaceful reunification of the island." The bill included the following language:

"The subcommittee also supports maintaining the Cyprus American Scholarship Program (CASP), which has been the principal instrument in shifting the preference of Cypriot students toward the United States for education in many important fields. This valuable program started in 1981 and some 80-100 Cypriot students are now funded annually for higher learning in the United States for various degree programs or short-term technical education. The subcommittee notes there has been a $7,500 cap on the amount of tuition, which this program will provide for one year of study. Such a cap may make sense for most of AID-supported scholarship programs, but the subcommittee feels the Cypriot program is unique and the Embassy in Nicosia should have full flexibility given to program directors to waive the cap based on need or proposed place of education.

"The subcommittee notes the important work of the Fulbright Commission in Cyprus, which has been in operation since 1962 and which has overcome some rough years during the years of high tension in Cyprus. It remains a vital bicommunal institution that is fully recognized in both communities. The Commission operates on an annual budget of $250,000 (which was the amount provided by USIA for the Fulbright program alone), which limits its work and makes it difficult to maintain its activities and achieve its goals. The subcommittee believes that since adequate funding has been available for educational activities, consideration be given to two new avenues to enhance the work of the Commission. First, the subcommittee thinks the Fulbright Commission can be utilized to manage some AID-funded bicommunal activities in Cyprus.

"Second, the subcommittee believes that consideration be given to setting aside $1 million of the funds made available for Cyprus to set up an endowment for the Fulbright Commission, whose annual interest payments could be used to supplement existing annual USIA fund allocations. This procedure has been used elsewhere to good effect and the subcommittee believes it can work on Cyprus at a time when it is clear annual USIA allocations are unlikely to increase. The subcommittee therefore, requests the Department of State, AID, and USIA to examine this possibility and report back to the subcommittee by January 1990."[34]

That did not happen, however, as the Senate stripped the language concerning $1 million for an endowment out of the House bill before final passage. Nor did the Embassy take a cue from the Congress and allocate more of the $15 million to the Commission for bicommunal work. Still, the Commission was determined, believing the CASP allocation would not last forever. Board Chairman Cubstead had sent Hadjittofi on a brief trip to Israel to see how its Commission had gone about establishing an endowment. At the September 15, 1989 Board meeting, Lellos Demetriades suggested perhaps setting aside a portion of the RoC's contribution to create an endowment given that it was legally impossible to use the residual CASP funds. The government's contribution had, over the preceding years, risen to 25,000 Cypriot Pounds ($105,000 in 2020 dollars) annually and at the October 19, 1990 Board meeting it was decided that CP20,000 of that would be set aside to create an endowment, and that this would continue in the years that followed. There were also a few small contributions from local companies, including Universal Life Insurance Company and the Paraskevides Foundation, but nothing substantial or sustained.[35]

By 1989, Hadjittofi's idea of returning to the United States had faded, as his hours at the Commission grew longer. At one point, Cathy complained that Christopher, then four, hardly saw his father and they needed to bond. "I thought that this bonding stuff was some sort of American idea, but I agreed to take an afternoon off and take Christopher to a small piece of land our family owned with some fruit trees very near the Green Line where you could see the Turkish emplacements," remembered Hadjittofi. "As we were driving there Christopher said 'you know Papa I am not afraid of the Turks.' And I asked him why he would be afraid of the Turks. They are people like you and me. 'Yes, I know, Papa, but I am strong and I will defend you'...and when we got there he picked up a rock to defend me and I realized he was scared and I was asking myself where is this coming from? Our household was an American family. I worked with Turkish Cypriots...I never spoke negatively about the other side, but TV, relatives... it all was making our kids scared. And I had a flashback about my own story and I realized I had to let go of any feelings I still harbored because it was going to impact my kids."[36]

As the Commission took its first steps into bicommunal work, there was always the hope that the experience of an American education in a multicultural society like America would help shape individuals who would return to Cyprus and help push the process of reconciliation forward. That was certainly the case for two Turkish Cypriots – Ozdil Nami and Dr. Ahmet Sözen– who took similar paths to America. Both went to TMK, both went to the English-language Bosporus University in Istanbul, and both received CASPs to do their master's degrees – Nami in 1989 at UC Berkeley and Sözen in 1992 at Syracuse. Nami earned an MBA and returned to Cyprus and Sözen stayed on to do his Ph.D. in political science at Missouri-Columbia, writing his dissertation on the Cyprus Problem. Both had long dreamed of studying in the U.S.

"Studying in the U.S. was an ambition from secondary school," said Nami. He remembered crossing into the Buffer Zone for the interview for the CASP. "It was quite an emotional experience to cross the checkpoint at that time...you needed special permission and I remember the sensation I felt when I stepped across the border, because you were normally not allowed. And then you are walking freely and nothing bad happens and you are meeting people and it is all so normal and you wonder why you have been kept from crossing."[37]

For Sözen, family led him to America. "I have two older brothers, both engineers, and they were my role models. One is now a U.S. citizen teaching at Grand Valley State University," he explained. "As an undergraduate, I started in physics but realized I had skills in the social sciences. I think the U.S. is just better for graduate work than Europe. In doing my Ph.D. there were many classes in theory and you had the chance to teach and that prepares you for your career. I have a friend who did her Ph.D. in Europe and I tease her that she does not have a Ph.D. in political science but in the narrow subject of her dissertation, because that is all you really do."[38]

Beyond his education, study in America taught Nami another lesson. He had hardly put his bags down when his host said that he needed to find housing and that they were returning to Berkeley so he could start his search. "She told me that I had two days to find a place and I said but I do not know anybody. In Cyprus or Turkey there was always someone you could call to help you with a problem but my host said, 'well, this is life and you have to figure it out'." Fortunately, Nami stumbled upon two other graduate students in the same MBA program – one from Switzerland and one from Japan – who were looking for a third person to share a flat. "So, my education started the day I arrived – the importance of self-reliance."[39]

When Nami returned to Cyprus he planned to be a businessman and help run his father's business, but a twisting path took him into politics. When he was fulfilling his military service he was appointed as an interpreter for a Turkish force commander and he came to the attention of Rauf Denktash. When he returned to the business of business he did some university teaching on the side and organized several conferences. This led to an offer to host a television program on money and financial matters and that, in turn, led to a role as an economic advisor to Denktash. Ultimately, Denktash integrated Nami into his negotiating team but there would come a breaking point. "I remember Ambassador Richard Holbrooke came to Cyprus and I was there and he said to Denktash ... 'Mr. President something big will happen and the UN will prepare a draft settlement document based on everything that has been discussed throughout the years and this will be an opportunity to settle the Cyprus issue with two constituent states as you require and this needs to be done because the EU has decided to enlarge the EU and we want to see Cyprus in as well as Turkey. So the Cyprus issue must be resolved.' And Denktash said 'we are not interested in settling the issue like that anymore. I want a two-state solution...two independent states.' At that point I realized that I could not work with him anymore. I saw that we had achieved what we wanted but he moved the goalposts farther away. So, after a few months I excused myself and left."[40]

Nami later agreed to have his name placed on the candidate list for the Republican Turkish Party led by Mehmet Ali Talat, and in 2003 he was elected to parliament. When Talat was elected president in 2005, Nami was added to the negotiating team and eventually became the lead negotiator. However, when Talat lost to Dervis Eroglu in 2010, Nami returned to business. "My education at Berkeley really opened my eyes on how people of different cultures and ethnicities and diverse backgrounds can overcome prejudices and learn to talk to one another."

Sözen's path was anything but direct, as he first involved himself in the conflict resolution work sponsored by the Fulbright Commission. Then, in 2008, when Talat and Dimitris Christofias began to talk, Sözen was pulled into the government and a power-sharing working group. "I had been writing academic and policy papers and I saw how proposed confidence-building measures were just flushed down the drain by both sides," remembered Sözen. "I thought if those could have been implemented in the 1990s we would be living in a different Cyprus today."[41]

As the Humphrey, Teacher Exchange, American University in Beirut, and Cleveland International Programs fell away one by one, the Commission was, one could say, concentrating on the basics – Fulbright grants, CASPs, American scholar/consultants, a handful of American Ph.D. students – mainly at CAARI – the growing number of conflict resolution programs, and STTs. STTs in particular were increasingly popular after one early glitch was worked out – civil servants who applied who did not always have permission for a leave of absence from their bosses. That permission would quickly become a prerequisite. In 1988 there were 20 STTs granted and by 1991 this number had doubled to 40 and by 1993 to 57 and it stayed in the 60-range for more than a decade. "This was a compromise with the Greek Lobby to support development in Cyprus," said Hadjittofi. "The Planning Commission gave us their priorities and it created the illusion that they have some control of the process, but they did not." For example, the Greek Cypriot Foreign Ministry expressed its opposition to bicommunal STTs, but the Commission organized some anyway. One sent a dozen Greek and Turkish Cypriots to the U.S. in connection with the development of the Nicosia Master Plan, a major project funded by USAID. That said, the politics generally made bicommunal STTs too difficult and the Commission would eventually give up on the concept even as the conflict resolution work gathered force. STTs would send people for training in a wide variety of disciplines, all expenses paid. "You learned a lot about a society by the kinds of programs people applied for," noted Hadjittofi.

Sevina Floridou cast her mind back to a particular rocking chair as she sat in her cluttered home office in a 100-year-old house on the old colonial road in the Marathefto-Geitonia area of Limassol. The chair sat in the office of Professor Michael Tomlin at Cornell. Her STT in 1995 allowed her to take classes in architecture and conflict resolution and her ongoing conversations with Dr. Tomlin allowed her better conceptualize the work she wanted to carry out in Limassol to preserve the city's history, but in a way to help both communities understand some of the things they shared. "I would sit there and gush this way and that and Dr. Tomlin would say 'right'...and he would crystalize my thoughts into one simple sentence and I would wonder 'how can he do that?'" Tomlin also stressed the importance of writing in order to make one's case as to why the preservation of a building or an area was important.

Floridou's father was Turkish Cypriot and had received one of the grants from AKEL to study in the East Bloc – in his case Bulgaria, where he met Floridou's mother. But while born in Bulgaria, Floridou grew up in Nicosia, went to the Junior School, and married a Greek Cypriot. She was working toward a Ph.D. in historic preservation in Bulgaria in the mid-1980s when the political situation grew problematic and she returned to Cyprus, deciding to reside in Limassol. "I thought it was a precious little corner of the Mediterranean, but its history was being destroyed bit by bit," remembered Floridou. She helped organize tours with the Union of Architects and they proved to be very popular, an idea she got from the Chicago Architectural Foundation. "At that time, there was no castle area...it was closed off...dark. There was no pier. The waterfront area was dangerous. There was no marina, there was no Rialto, there was no Hero's Square, there was nothing."

She remembers how her training at Cornell and learning how to communicate in the conflict resolution seminars prepared her for going before planning bodies in the fight to preserve historical structures. "There was a little Christian church and a little Dervish mausoleum in Limassol that were going to be destroyed by a new highway and I went before the

Planning Board in Nicosia and asked 'who will take political responsibility for destroying a mosque?'" said Floridou. "Both are still there, but I did not save them, the saints did."[42]

When Nicolas Philippou received the first of two STT grants in 1991, he represented the kind of grantee the Embassy's Economic Section enthusiastically supported. A businessman, a graduate of the University of Rhode Island, and someone who wanted to do business with the U.S. is someone whose ambitions dovetailed with Embassy goals. He received a second STT grant in 1998. Both were for business programs. (By rule, there had to be a minimum of five years between grants if someone was fortunate enough to receive two grants.) The first grant took him to Columbia and to the University of Michigan at Ann Arbor and the second to Stanford.

"Both were six-week programs and both were good, though I liked the Stanford way of approaching things," said Philippou. "They enhanced my education but I have given back by doing business with Americans and creating jobs there. Not a lot of Cypriots do business with America. To do that you have to get into the mind of American businessmen and you have to understand their concerns. We are a very small market and so you have to explain all the reasons they should do business here. I have done a lot of different deals – large and small – and am always looking."[43]

The relative stability in Cyprus in the 1980s and 1990s meant that the Commission could bring a steady stream of American Fulbright scholars, and that included the growing number affiliated with CAARI. However, the largest number were involved in education; over the 52-year history of the Commission, more than half of the 170 scholars were in the field of education. In the 1980s, these were still scholar/consultants because while there were a variety of tertiary institutions on the island, neither community had established a true university. The Greek Cypriot Ministry of Education had produced a report in 1976 concerning the establishment of a university and the Board of the Fulbright Commission had taken note. At its meeting June 29, 1976 the Commission agreed it should "involve itself extensively" in the planning for the new university, which it hoped would be a vehicle for bringing the two communities together.

There was another idea that had floated around since the Kennedy Administration that the U.S. would fund the establishment of a bicommunal English-language university that would be similar to the American University of Beirut or the American University of Cairo. In December 1989, Special Cyprus Coordinator Nelson Ledsky put forward a series of 10 confidence building measures, although he only expected one or two, if that, to get off the ground. One was a university, but he did not hold out much hope because neither the Greek Cypriots nor the Turkish Cypriots were in favor of such a plan.

At a hearing of the Subcommittee for European Affairs of the Senate Foreign Relations Committee in April 1991, Ledsky explained the situation to Subcommittee Chairman Joseph Biden and the other members: "We have talked to both the Republic of Cyprus and the Turkish Cypriot community about working together to establish, under American auspices, such a university," said Ledsky. Senator Biden then noted that he had recently spoken to Senator Charles Percy (R-IL) "who believed that he could raise a significant amount of money to put such a university in place and actually be prepared to put together a very distinguished board that would take a keen interest in such a university." Ledsky responded that he was not aware of that initiative, but that over the previous 18 months neither community in Cyprus had shown very much interest. "They have told our USAID people and others who have come to the island that this is a noble idea, one that could help build a sense of community on the island, but that each, for political reasons, must proceed with its own university at the present time," explained Ledsky. "They said come back at another time." Senator Biden expressed the view that it would never happen and Ledsky noted that it would remain on his priority list because it had repeatedly been mentioned by the UN and was on the Secretary General's priority list; further, that it was an idea associated with the U.S. Senate for more than a decade; and finally that it was an idea that, in principle, each of the communities had endorsed from time to time. Nothing, said Ledsky, was as important as breaking down language and educational barriers on the island. Biden thought this was an example of the futility of the current policy. "If an idea as benign as this, with the support of the UN, the Senate and the Administration cannot get out of the dugout, let alone first base...then perhaps much stronger medicine needs to be applied."[44]

Lellos Demetriades was a strong proponent for the university and Board member Dr. Charis Menelaou of the Ministry of Finance was a member of the planning committee for the new university, hoping it would be bicommunal. However, as the *New York Times* reported in March 1983 in an article entitled "Cyprus Needs A University, But Gets Talk," the issue of a new university was "highly charged politically, as it involves tensions stemming from the division of the island into increasingly estranged zones of Greek Cypriots and Turkish Cypriots."[45] The Commission would have to tread carefully. In that *Times* article, Dr. Nicos Vakis, a 1967 Fulbright grantee, who headed an organization called Friends of the University, expressed the hope that the university would get off the ground that year and that it would serve both Greek and Turkish Cypriots. Ultimately, however, it would take a little longer and it would not serve both communities. The University of Cyprus was finally established as a predominantly Greek-language university in 1989 with its first class entering in 1992. As a result, the Commission distanced itself from the university.

"Our hope was to have a university that would have English instruction and be bicommunal," said Hadjittofi. "When the nationalists gave some specious reasons for the university to be primarily in Greek, it meant that no Turkish Cypriots would be able to attend. Sofianos was furious and so was I. Since the university was not going to serve our primary objective of reconciliation, we lost interest. The fact that Fulbright scholars would be unable to be visiting professors was actually secondary."[46]

As these ideas were discussed, the Turkish Cypriots were busy expanding the Higher Technical Institute in Famagusta, which had been established in 1979. In 1986, the TRNC, working in concert with Turkey, upgraded the Institute to an English-language university and named it Eastern Mediterranean University. By 2021, there were nine colleges and universities in the Greek Cypriot South, while in the North there were some 25, many backed by Turkish investors that brought international students and hard currency to the North.

The Greek Cypriot Ministry of Education was concerned about the issue of accreditation and asked the Commission's help in bringing in an American Fulbrighter to work on the issue. That is how Dr. Fred Hicks came to Cyprus in 1990, one of a number of Fulbrighters that the Ministry found useful enough to bring back at its own expense. In Dr. Hicks's case, he would return to Cyprus frequently during a five-year period. For most of that time, Hicks worked with Stavros Philippides at the Ministry of Education. "Stavros was an outstanding individual," said Hicks. "When I first met him, he was in the middle of a number of issues. If you know anything about Cyprus, it is always politics, politics, politics. He had a strong moral compass and he was not going to succumb to any pressure."

Philippides wanted to establish benchmarks for accreditation for the many and varied tertiary institutions on the island – that ran the gamut from a business school affiliated with a British university to a training school for hotel and tourism workers. Most were for-profit institutions and owned by prominent Cypriots; that is where the politics entered in. Over a period of five years, Hicks and Philippides established the benchmarks, had the schools undertake self-evaluations, and brought an American accreditation team from South Carolina to Cyprus to move the process forward. Initially, there was an attempt to make the process bicommunal, but Hicks soon realized he was mainly working for the Greek Cypriots. In the end, however, the members of the final accreditation team, headed by Hicks, were chosen by the Ministry of Education. But Philippides's retirement meant he was not there to oversee things. "I think we established some good standards and we recommended accreditation for a couple of schools," said Hicks. "It started out with great promise, but I am not sure that they were ready at that point to have the accreditation standards fully implemented."[47]

When Dr. Marla Stone arrived in January 1991 to help with science education at the primary level, she was met at the airport by Kypros Kyprianou. "Kyp was a physics teacher, a linguist, a concert pianist, and a visual artist – an amazing person," noted Stone. Kyprianou described Stone as "friendly, lively, at times exuberant, and indefatigable." They made a dynamic team and became fast friends.

Stone began by observing how science was taught at multiple schools; Kyprianou was at her elbow translating *sotto voce* the interaction between teachers and students. Ultimately, Stone wrote a report in which she noted that teachers generally dreaded teaching science. The reasons varied; science phobia, lack of resources, lack of guidance, and faulty messaging from the Ministry. Kyprianou explained that at "the beginning of every academic year there was a frantic effort to avoid the teaching of science, with the inevitable result that it was allotted to the newly appointed or young inexperienced teachers." But Stone then met a group of teachers who were trying to write a science textbook and that is where she ultimately focused her efforts. However, it would take some work to convince the Ministry.[48]

"I wanted the textbooks written by classroom teachers, and not someone who had not been in a classroom in 20 years," remembered Stone. "Of course, Ministry officials thought this unbelievable because teachers were not high enough in the hierarchy." Kyprianou added that, "The prevailing attitude was that textbooks should be written by someone with a Ph.D. who had published articles and books. I took no role in convincing the Ministry, but only note Dr. Stone's unbending will on matters where she thought she was right."[49]

They began by bringing the inspectors on board and demonstrating hands-on experiments like dropping marbles from different heights and angles, taking measurements, charting scatter patterns – doing science. Stone wanted to make the point that fancy equipment was unnecessary to teach science. Rocks, leaves, or milk cartons could be used. Then teams of teachers were created in five cities in Cyprus and Stone traveled to each in turn during the week as the writing of the textbooks for the first six grades commenced. When Stone's nine-month tenure as a Fulbrighter ended and she had to depart Cyprus, the process fell behind schedule – not helped by a teacher's strike – and the Ministry was convinced to bring Stone back as a consultant to push the project forward. "Dr. Stone had gained the esteem, respect and trust of people working with her. The feeling was that finally things were changing for the better," wrote Kyprianou. After the better part of another year, the process yielded results. "She left in January 1993 and the first and second grade textbooks were completed by the end of that year. They eventually expanded the program to write textbooks for other subjects. In all, 18 different textbooks were created, with Kyprianou using his artistic skills to provide the illustrations. To say that Dr. Stone had a profound impact is an understatement," wrote Kyprianou. Stone was delighted when Kyp wrote to tell her that Greece had purchased the Cypriot books – instead of the other way around.[50]

The Planning Commission wanted experts with very specific specialties and although the Commission would request them year after year it was not always successful. Sometimes, however, it got lucky. Dr. Allan Felsot's specialty was pesticide chemistry. He came in January 1992 and remembers the head of the Agricultural Research Institute's beautiful rose garden. He helped train staff in the use of equipment and thinks he helped them with soil analysis and the potato crop. He returned to Cyprus in 2016 for a conference and could not believe the growth.[51] Dr. Jacqueline Robeck came in 1995 to teach computer-aided clothing design. She was limited by a lack of computers that could handle the software she had brought, but worked with both companies and secondary school teachers during her semester in Cyprus. The Fulbright grant on her resume led to a position at the University of Louisiana at Lafayette, where she still lives and works. She stays in touch with friends she made 25 years ago and frequents a restaurant in Lafayette run by a man from Larnaca. Small world.[52]

By the mid-1990s, the Commission started to bring on more permanent Cypriot staff. Anna Argyrou joined the Commission in 1994 to work on conflict resolution programs, while the counseling load grew steadily. By 1993, the Commission was fielding 10,000 inquiries annually about study in the U.S. Its 1995-96 Program Proposal – adopted in December 1993 – noted that approximately 20 percent of Cypriots studying abroad were in the United States, an estimated 3,000 students. These numbers grew despite toughening test requirements. By 1995, the number of CASP grantees – full and partial – would approach 900 since the program began in 1981.[53]

One of those CASP students was Giorgos Zacharias, who was from a refugee family and who would head to MIT in 1993. "When the other boys in my class would doodle the numbers of their favorite football players, I would doodle 'MIT'," recalled Zarcharias. With a gift for mathematics, Zacharias wanted to go to "the best mathematics school in the world and that was MIT."[54]

His double major in math and computer science eventually earned him a scholarship from MIT to pursue his master's degree. He founded a fintech company and attracted millions of dollars from investors, sold that company and then financed his own Ph.D. at MIT. "I was 26 years old and raised $26 million for a start-up even though I had a limited visa status," noted Zacharias. "They were willing to take a chance on me. You don't find that in Cyprus or Europe. I would like to bring that spirit to Cyprus."

He eventually became the Chief Technology Officer of the travel website Kayak, supervising more than 200 engineers in Boston and Berlin. Beyond that he has created a number of online communities, including one that has thousands of members learning Greek. He has lectured at universities in Cyprus on entrepreneurship and he returns to the island every year. "The pull of family is very strong," he says. Eventually, authorities in the U.S. and Cyprus agreed to waive his visa requirement and he has stayed permanently in the U.S. "I have created hundreds of jobs in the U.S. and all thanks to Fulbright."[55]

In May 1990, former Congressman John Brademas – then the President of New York University – came to Cyprus, 16 years after he and the other members of Congress had met with Eugene Rossides and set in motion the funding that would fundamentally change the Cyprus Fulbright Commission and the lives of so many Cypriots. He used the occasion of the visit to raise the possibility of establishing a business school affiliated with New York University, but could not generate any interest among the Cypriots because of politics. He came as the guest of that Commission, and spoke to a standing-room audience at the American Center Library that included the Archbishop and the Attorney General. "Of course, he seemed to know everyone by their first names," remembered Hadjittofi.

"I asked him not to give a political speech and he smiled and said 'we'll see' and then he gave a political speech."

Brademas had not been in Cyprus for 13 years and he praised the "resilience, ingenuity and determination" of the Greek Cypriot people. He noted one important "Hellenic value" that his father had instilled in him "I will never leave a lot of money to my children, but I will give them a first-class education."[56]

Turning to the Fulbright program, he noted the contributions that numerous American scholars had made in Cyprus, but then listed some of the Cypriots who had studied in America thanks to Fulbright grants: "They included Andreas Aloneftis, Minister of Defense; George Achillides, Secretary of the Council of Ministers; Andreas Georgiou, director of the Inland Revenue Department; Vassos Karageorghis, former Director of the Department of Antiquities; Lucas Louca, an executive of the Cyprus Development Bank; Alecos Michaelides, vice president of the Democratic Rally Party; Panos Papadopoulos, director of the General Construction Company; Nicos Papaxennophontos, a member of the Public Service Commission; Panayiotis Peristianis, Director of the Cyprus Pedagogical Institute; and Nayia Roussou, senior program officer at the Cyprus Broadcasting Corporation."[57]

At that point, with the Commission approaching its 30-year mark, many other names could have been added, including the Greek diplomat Yiannos Kranidiotis, son of the Cypriot writer, poet and diplomat, who attended Harvard's law school on a Fulbright from the Commission, but who would die tragically in an air accident in 1999.

From modest beginnings, the Commission had grown – thanks to the efforts of Dr. Brademas and others – into a multi-million-dollar program that was not only sending hundreds of Cypriots to the U.S. to many of its finest universities, but was helping hundreds more find a way to America, tapping into a growing network of international student coordinators in universities across the U.S. However, in May 1990, thanks to the continuing flow of funds and with Congressional encouragement, the Commission was on the cusp of its most ambitious endeavor – trying to educate Cypriots from the two communities on how they might find a path to reconciliation.

CONFLICT RESOLUTION/PEACE BUILDING

Jean Monet, a principal architect of the European Union, is reputed to have said that if he had it to do all over again – starting from scratch – he would have begun with culture.

And so it was in Cyprus that, when the American Embassy and the Fulbright Commission plunged into the politically fraught realm of bi-communal programming and conflict resolution, it began with culture.

In 1990, the Embassy's Public Affairs Section had run a couple of programs that briefly brought Greek Cypriots and Turkish Cypriots together, a process that was never easy.[1]   In addition, USAID funding, via the UN, was devoted to coaxing Greek Cypriots and Turkish Cypriots to cooperate, particularly in the business community where there were common interests.   Some participated in these programs hoping they would contribute to a solution, while others did so purely out of self-interest.

USAID also funded efforts to rewrite textbooks in both communities, as many contained skewed and toxic versions of history that worked against any kind of rapprochement. Though, as one of the bicommunal activists pointed out, "I remember going through one of my daughter's revised history texts and there was nothing that I found that was out of line, but it is what the teachers say in the classroom that is the problem."

Of course, since its inception the Fulbright Commission had been bringing Greek Cypriots and Turkish Cypriots together, during both the interviews and the orientation sessions for the grantees. However, the Congressional pressure to do more bicommunally was growing. In the mid-1990s Congress amended the conditions for the annual $15 million appropriation for Cyprus, mandating that $5 million be devoted to bicommunal and conflict resolution projects. Support for such projects was also the reason the Fulbright Commission was given more time to spend the CASP residuals. One is left with the impression, however, that the Greek lobby did not pay close attention to how the money was used. It just wanted to make sure that Cyprus continued to receive every last dime.

Marcelle Wahba arrived as Public Affairs Officer and Commission Board Chairman in the fall of 1991. Wahba, an Egyptian-American, entered the Foreign Service through USIA's mid-career Arabist program, which was designed to bring fluent Arabic speakers into the Service.[2] She was tough and shrewd. "I remember going to Marcelle when a particular Greek Cypriot newspaper ran a story about the Embassy's activities that was completely false and I wanted her to push back," remembered Ambassador Richard Boucher. "Marcelle looked at me and sighed and said, 'I could but will you ask me to do it again tomorrow?' And I asked, what do you mean? And she said, 'this kind of stuff is in the papers every day.'"[3] Boucher wisely learned to ignore most of it. Wahba certainly had no illusions about the political environment in which she had to operate.

Ambassador Marcelle Wahba.

"The question was, could we get young Greek Cypriot and Turkish Cypriot artists together to see each other's works?" remembered Wahba. "We found two gallery owners who did not know each other to work together. The Greek Cypriot – Gloria Kassianidou – was quite conservative but strongly supportive of the arts. When we first approached her she was a bit stunned but we convinced her. It was the same with the Turkish Cypriot owner – Rezzan Nevzat. We had to get buy-in from Nicosia Mayor Lellos Demetriades, which was huge. He gave us the exhibition space at Famagusta Gate and insisted that the Turkish Cypriot artists come to the Greek side first."[4] They called the exhibitions "Brushstrokes."

"We had to get the two gallery owners to meet and we had to broker that," explained Wahba. "Kassianidou did not want to cross to the Turkish side because of the requirement that you sign a piece of paper.[5] Nevzat did not want to cross to the Greek side because it would put her in a bad light in her community. This was a big initiative in those days. I came to understand how scared the Turkish Cypriot artists were. They were young and had never met a Greek Cypriot."[6]

Wahba depended on two cultural assistants: Christina Hadjiparaskeva, who had the best political antenna in the Embassy, and newly hired Ipek Uzunoglu in the Turkish-Cypriot community. Uzunoglu was the only applicant not recommended by Dogan Yavuz, who – given his many years with the Embassy – was the "Bey" of the office in the North. However, Wahba wanted someone who was independent and just as tough, shrewd, and smart as she was and she found such a person in Uzunoglu.

No one should be surprised that it took three strong-willed women to pull Brushstrokes together.

"We had brought an American theater group to Cyprus and we were able to get the National Theater to agree to host them. Given that most at the National Theater were [communist party] AKEL members, they had been opposed to anything from the U.S.," noted Hadjiparaskeva. "The group performed in both communities and that gave us the confidence to try Brushstrokes. It helped that both Presidents Clerides and Vassiliou were supportive of bi-com programs. You can imagine the amount of work for Brushstrokes...to get permissions for the artists to cross, to ready the hall, print brochures and invitations, organize a reception, and to curate the exhibition."[7]

The Denktash administration decided that only the Turkish Cypriot artists would be allowed to cross, arguing that it was not safe for other Turkish Cypriots to go to the South. All was set, and then an incident in the Buffer Zone – a Greek Cypriot soldier was shot – the night before the opening meant it all had to be postponed for many months. "Marcelle did her best to console me," said Hadjiparaskeva.

When it finally happened, it was a triumph. "When we got the Turkish Cypriot artists to Famagusta Gate they were met with such enthusiasm. The press was there and the coverage was positive," said Wahba.[8] "We had 500 people...the very best artists and the most important political figures," noted Hadjiparaskeva. Next, they had to do it all over again, bringing the Greek Cypriot artists and their works to the North. There was no gallery space like Famagusta Gate, but they found an old church they could re-purpose. Hadjiparaskeva diplomatically asked the Greek Cypriots for their passport numbers and Uzunoglu pre-cleared them with Turkish Cypriot officials so that there was no requirement to sign any papers. "When we took the Greek Cypriot artists across in a bus the Greek Cypriot TV news cameras were at the Ledra Palace checkpoint and they were yelling at us and calling us 'traitors' and asking why we were going to the North," remembered Hadjiparaskeva. "It was in all the papers and on the evening news. We were not intimidated and it was a very big success. No one else from the Greek side came, except Lellos [Demetriades]. Lellos always came."[9] The events were so successful that the Embassy sponsored two more rounds of exhibitions, the second under Wahba's successor, Dr. Judith Baroody. At the second one, President Clerides bought a painting by a Turkish Cypriot artist and hung it in the Presidential Palace.

However, putting Greek and Turkish Cypriots in the same room was one thing; actual conflict resolution work was a whole different animal. The academic field of conflict resolution had grown out of a fusion of psychology and political science. From the early days of the discipline, Cyprus was seen as a prime candidate for conflict resolution efforts and attracted several pioneers in the field, beginning with John Burton. Burton focused on basic human needs that were non-negotiable. He argued that "conflicts over basic needs must be distinguished from 'disputes' about tangible, negotiable interests, and therefore conflict resolution must be distinguished from dispute settlement."[10]   Burton was an Australian whose early career was as a diplomat, but who later helped form the Center for Analysis of Conflict at University College London. In October 1966, after a lengthy visit to Cyprus, he set up a five-day workshop in London that was attended by two leaders from each community. The other participants were academics from the Center and three Americans including psychologist Herbert Kelman from Harvard. After a bit of a rough start, the workshop participants were able to clear away some misperceptions and move on to more analytical discussions that produced – in the end – some concepts that were conveyed to the leaders in the two communities. The workshop was credited with helping the two sides return to talks under UN auspices.[11]

Burton was followed by Yale's Leonard Doob, who had attended an informal 1973 seminar in Rome put together by the Center for Mediterranean Studies. It included a couple of relatively senior-level members of the negotiating teams for the Greek and Turkish Cypriots, and the workshop received wide press coverage in Cyprus. There, Doob received encouragement to put together a two-week workshop along the lines of ones that he had conducted to try to find ways forward in the Horn of Africa and in Northern Ireland. Doob spent four months in Cyprus meeting Cypriots in both communities, helped by Glafcos Clerides and his daughter Katie and Dr. Kyriacos Markides on the Greek side and Rauf Denktash and Duygu Orhon (née Yusuf) on the Turkish side. All was prepared. Two dozen participants were set to fly to Italy to meet for two weeks at a mountainside hotel in Tyrol. The departure day was July 20, 1974, the day Turkish troops invaded, and Doob found himself being evacuated with other Westerners by the American Sixth Fleet. The workshop never happened.

However, Doob felt compelled to set down some of his observations about Cyprus. He noted the extreme Greek and Turkish nationalism, and while individuals in both communities seemed eager to speak to an American professor, he wondered if it was because they "wanted to diminish my ignorance or gain sympathy for their political standpoint."[12] On both sides, there was the belief that the problem was in no way psychological, but purely political. A conservative supporter of enosis stated that Doob was trying to plant a magnificent seed upon barren soil. There was suspicion as to what an American might be up to. He was not confronted directly with the charge that he was CIA, though one newspaper speculated that he was paving the way for Secretary of State Henry Kissinger. It became clear to Doob that the workshop could not be held on Cyprus if it was to have a chance of being successful, but that raised the issue of cost and funding for travel, accommodation, etc. Though he tried, representatives of AKEL would not participate, probably because Doob was American. Indeed, given the nature of the communities Doob realized that outsiders would never be completely trusted.[13]

In conducting the interviews to choose the participants for the workshop and to weed out "troublemakers" Doob recorded a series of statements that included:

"Hate and suspicion are inevitable. They are a product of our history."

"The leaders of the intercommunal talks are puppets manipulated by Greece and Turkey."

"The situation is hopeless. They hate us."

"Neither community has any sense of identity with Cyprus; there are no symbols to which people can cling."

"No other country in the world has a ruling group whose principal aim is to abolish their independence."

"How can Cyprus possibly be independent when it is strategically important to the great powers?"

Doob concluded that only an effort by conflict resolution practitioners over a sustained period might be able to create something positive and where would one find the funding for that?[14]

Through his interactions with both Burton and Doob, Harvard's Kelamn became interested in Cyprus and conducted several workshops before turning his attention to the Middle East and the Israeli-Palestinian conflict, particularly after the 1967 war. The Israeli conflict would consume his efforts for decades.[15] Kelman had helped found the world's first center for conflict resolution research at the University of Michigan in the 1950s as well as the Journal of Conflict Resolution in 1957. While Kelman believed that conflict resolution work must, somehow, be connected to the leadership of the countries or societies in conflict, he also found it useful to work with "pre-influentials," which included graduate students and young professionals.

There were other attempts – some that involved multiple workshops and some that were one-offs – including Ron Fisher and a group of Canadians, the Norwegians via PRIO (Peace Research Institute of Oslo), and Czech and German groups, and, of course, the UN. What would make the efforts of the Cyprus Fulbright Commission different were three-fold. First, there were resources – in this case millions of dollars – available to make a sustained effort over years. Second, Cypriots would be taught to carry on the work in the absence of outside trainers. Third, the effort would be broadly based and include individuals that ranged from the leadership class to secondary school students.

At the November 1992 Commission Board meeting, when the annual program plan was to be approved, RoC priorities were discussed. However, Lellos Demetriades told the Board that the government priorities were all well and good, but that the Commission needed to get involved in conflict resolution. Dr. Chrysostomos Sofianos agreed, but wondered if conflict resolution was an actual academic discipline, ever mindful of the Commission's role as a scholarly institution. He was quickly assured that it very much was just that. "Of course I was supportive and I defended it because it was good for Cyprus and I have the same opinion today," said Demetriades in 2016. "The idea was very good," said Sofianos. "Provided we had the right people doing this."

"This never would have happened if Lellos and Sofianos did not approve," said former Executive Director Daniel Hadjittofi.

By that time, there was already a small peace movement on the island, which had established a "peace center" founded by, among others, Dr. Maria Hadjipavlou and Bekir and Fatma Azgin. Passes to cross were almost nonexistent, particularly from the Denktash administration. Denktash wanted to maintain the narrative that Greek Cypriots and Turkish Cypriots could not coexist, but members of the peace center would meet in Hadjipavlou's house and use diplomats to pass messages back and forth, or in some cases, drive them across in their cars with diplomatic plates. That's how Costas Shammas first met the Azgins.

In 1985, Dr. Kyriacos Markides returned to Cyprus with Leonard Doob and took another stab at assembling a group of Greek Cypriots and Turkish Cypriots, with Markides pulling together the Greek Cypriots and Bekir Azgin the Turkish Cypriots. Markides did so warily. Two years earlier he had tried to do something similar and the effort did not go well. Rauf Denktash's eldest son Raif was one of the Turkish Cypriot participants and his angry outbursts were particularly poisonous.

So, when Raif Denktash was again part of the Turkish Cypriot group,

Markides's heart sank. What happened next was surely unanticipated:

"I could not believe my ears. Raif Denktash was a transformed human being," wrote Markides. "He was the most enthusiastic among the Turkish Cypriots promoting Greco-Turkish friendship and finding a peaceful resolution to the ethnic problem. For an instant, I thought he was playacting. Perhaps he was a spy for his father. I was wrong. During our first break, I told him, 'I am really curious, Raif. What happened in the last two years that turned you into such an enthusiast for a solution? Sporting a bushy, black beard, Raif smiled and explained his radical transformation. 'I spent two years at Oxford University studying for my master's degree in international relations. I met and befriended a group of Greek Cypriots there, and I was stunned to realize that we were so much alike. I then vowed to work for peace.' 'I am so pleased to hear that,' I said. 'But how is it that your father is following the exact opposite policy on the Cyprus Problem?' 'I am willing to take risks,' he replied. 'My father is not.'"[16]

Katie Clerides and Costas Shammas (top) were important players in the early peace movement in Cyprus, as was Fatma Azgin (second from top) and Katie Economidou (third from top). Serder Denktash (bottom), the son of the Turkish Cypriot leader, joined the Oxford Group to provide "balance" given the presence of Clerides, the daughter of the president.

The meetings continued for a couple of months and then Raif Denktash called and reported that permission to cross had been withdrawn and the Turkish Cypriots were no longer allowed to participate. It was a puzzle. Then, while trying to digest the meaning of that call, Dr. Markides received tragic news: Raif Denktash had been killed in an auto accident. Dr. Markides, dispirited, withdrew. Yet, ultimately, it would be his wife– Dr. Emily Markides – who would step forward with a profound impact on the peace movement in Cyprus and, indirectly, on the Fulbright Commission.

Emily Markides was, around that time, establishing a Peace and Reconciliation Studies program at the University of Maine; this allowed her to travel to see other such programs, and significantly the program at the University of Iowa. That is where she met Ambassador John MacDonald and Dr. Louise Diamond. "I read their work on multi-track diplomacy," recalled Markides. "We met several times at conferences. We became very close friends. I convinced Louise to come to Cyprus and help out and she got to know Costas Shammas very well...she met everyone."[17]

Diamond convinced the National Training Laboratory Institute (NTL) to get involved in conflict resolution work and it funded her first visit to Cyprus in 1991. It was during this time she wrote a book with Ambassador John W. McDonald entitled *Multi-Track Diplomacy* and together they founded the Institute for Multi-Track Diplomacy in 1992. They were an odd couple. McDonald, a lawyer by training, had had a 40-year career in the American diplomatic service, serving in four ambassadorial posts. He was most certainly "old school." Diamond, as her colleague Lennox Joseph explained, was originally a Buddhist but had moved beyond Buddhism. "She had special audiences with the Dali Lama, so she moved in those echelons," explained Joseph. "She was very spiritual. I think a lot of people regarded her as gifted...not only in peace building, but in bringing people together."[18] She was also a woman

Louise Diamond.

driven by a certain urgency. She had battled cancer since her 20s and her brushes with an early death made each day precious. When it came to the pursuit of peace, there was no time to waste.

Their conception of "multi-track diplomacy" was that peace was too important to be left to the political leadership alone. Every level of society had a role to play and, in their book, they referred to it as a "systems approach to peace." They laid out nine separate tracks from the government to the business community to the media to religious leaders to private citizens. All had a role to play.[19]

Commission Executive Director Daniel Hadjittofi had known Costas Shammas for a long time and in the 1980s he would meet Kyriacos and Emily Markides. So, it was not long before Diamond found her way to the Commission's door. When Marcelle Wahba arrived in Cyprus, the gears of the Washington bureaucracy were finally, slowly transferring the CASP residual funds into Commission accounts. Wahba wanted to pursue programs that brought the two communities together. Ambassador Boucher asked Hadjittofi to work with Economics Officer Michael Meigs to come up with a plan to use the funds. If the Embassy had done it directly, it would have been seen as political. If the Fulbright Commission did it, it would be accepted. With support from the Board and a push from Wahba, the Commission jumped in with both feet. Soon, the first RFPs (requests for proposal) were posted.

"Of course, Louise Diamond was one of the bidders, and she came with a reputation of someone who did not take no for an answer," remembered Hadjittofi. "She asked me why we were using her language in the RFPs and I told her you should be happy because it gave her a distinct advantage, but there was no other language around. She was the one who had coined phrases like Track I and Track II diplomacy and all the conflict resolution phrases used by the professionals. Of course she won the bid. In subsequent years we tried to spread the grants around to other organizations, but Diamond always seemed to win a good share of the contracts."[20]

When the Institute for Multi-Track Diplomacy formed at George Mason University, it was literally just Diamond and Ambassador McDonald. In the summer of 1992, they took on an intern, Jamie Notter, who was completing his master's degree in international relations. "Ambassador McDonald welcomed me aboard," remembered Notter "and he pointed to a box on the floor of their rented office space and said 'that's your desk.' I literally had to put my own desk together. The first time I went to Cyprus I raised my own grant money."[21] Diamond would make multiple trips to Cyprus in this period and in November 1992 she helped the activists create a bicommunal steering committee to support the work.

Diamond could see that they were going to need help, and someone at the State Department, in conversations with Amideast, noted that they liked the book *Getting to Yes*, a primer on negotiation strategies written by Harvard law professors Roger Fisher and William Ury. Ambassador

Boucher noted that during his time in Cyprus they liberally distributed copies of *Getting to Yes* to Cypriot officials on both sides of divide. "I asked them if they read it and they said, 'yes, we have read it and we're doing that,'" remembered Boucher, who thought to himself "well, you're not doing it very well."[22]

The Conflict Management Group (CMG) had been formed at Harvard and Diamond reached out to them and law professor Diana Chigas in her search for partners to take on the growing conflict resolution effort. Again, Diamond's spiritual bent and Chigas's lawyerly approach would seem to have been a mismatch. "I got a call from Louise Diamond," said Chigas. "I did not know her and we came from different schools of thought around conflict resolution. She herself was spiritual – the John Burton approach, the basic human needs John Burton approach – which Louise represented...but not incompatible. A lot of people in our field were surprised that it would work."[23]

Diana Chigas.

Chigas noted that they really did not know anything about Cyprus, but she had met Maria Hadjipavlou, who was doing post-doctoral research at Harvard. Hadjipavlou, who had received a Fulbright from the Commission to do a master's in journalism at Kansas in 1979, had returned to the U.S. for her Ph.D. at Boston University. She soon met Herbert Kelman at Harvard, and he became a mentor and one of the readers of her dissertation. Hadjipavlou helped them prepare for the very first conflict resolution program sponsored by the Commission, which brought together 49 CASP students – 38 Greek Cypriots and 11 Turkish Cypriots – who were already in the U.S. They all met at Harvard for a workshop in May 1993. As Chigas noted, it was less than satisfactory given the nearly four-to-one ratio of Greek Cypriots to Turkish Cypriots. "You can't do real conflict resolution work when Greek Cypriots are talking to Greek Cypriots," said Chigas. That said, having equal numbers of Greek and Turkish Cypriots was, in itself, a political statement.

Hadjipavlou was joined by Ahmet Sözen as a facilitator, so that there would be a Turkish Cypriot discussion leader as well. Sözen was pursuing his master's at Syracuse's Maxwell School of Diplomacy and had earned a certificate as a mediator. Sözen remembers the tense discussions that occurred during the five-day program. "There were emotional instances where you could have deep interactions with Greek Cypriots," said Sözen, "particularly during role playing exercises. But we also had the chance to have more informal interaction, going out for a meal or drinks."[24]

Dr. Eleni Kyza participated in the program, just as she finished her undergraduate degree in educational technology at Boston University on a CASP grant. "I remember that I thought the program was very well organized and we all had to read the book *Getting to Yes* before we arrived," said Kyza, now a professor at the Cyprus University of Technology. "It was the first time I had ever gotten into a discussion with a Turkish Cypriot and remember there were some people with very strong opinions and others who were less polarized. That stayed with me – that there could be an array of opinions. I think I became more open to other points of view – it made me think twice."[25]

Some in the Greek Cypriot media saw things differently. In an article months after the workshop, the small, nationalist daily *Eleftherotypia* featured a lead story reporting on "shocking revelations" that the workshop was designed by the Americans to "undermine the Greek Cypriot cause, create a neo-Cypriot conscience, and alienate Greek Cypriots from their national identity." There had been earlier articles charging that the Peace Center had held "secret meetings" but this article directly attacked the Fulbright Commission's efforts. It charged, among other things, that the participants (whose names the paper claimed to have) promoted an education system with bilingual teaching; intermarriage of Greek and Turkish Cypriots; avoidance of the term "invasion"; joint or mixed political parties; a new anthem, universities, and sports teams; mixed delegations at international events; joint nudist beaches; and that Cyprus should become America's 51st state. The U.S. Embassy believed that such "exposés" would not be taken seriously, would quickly disappear, and further efforts by the Fulbright Commission would broaden support for the work. But the Embassy also warned that those opposed to conflict resolution efforts would use the media to try to create an adverse public reaction.[26]

One of the tools developed by Diamond was called "the History Walk," and over the years it became a staple of conflict resolution workshops with Cypriots. Greek Cypriots and Turkish Cypriots were asked to write down on pieces of paper key moments in Cyprus's history; each event on a separate piece of paper. Then the two sets of papers were laid on the ground side-by-side in chronological order and the workshop participants were asked to walk along the two rows of papers and read each one.

Harvard's Douglas Stone, one of the trainers, described what happened when they did this exercise with political leaders from the two communities a year after the Harvard CASP workshop:

"The people in the room said that 'everyone here is Cypriot and they know the history so we don't need two hours for this ...we can skip it,'" recalled Stone. 'You Americans might not know the history, but we do.' So we would say, let's just do it...it is on the agenda...and they said, 'well, both sides are going to be the same...but okay.' So it was unbelievably illuminating. The Turkish Cypriots would begin in 15-something during the Ottoman Empire and the Greek Cypriots would start in 1960. And there were some radical differences, even during the same year. People would come and look at these two radically different timelines and they would say, 'oh, this is a practical joke...you told the other side to make this into a joke' and we said that we did not tell the other side anything. 'But their timeline is just made up...it is completely silly.' So we said, well let's just walk through. They could not believe that there were things that other side thought were important and they did not think were important or that they put down things that they were not even aware had happened. Both sides thought that the way they thought about things was right. Of course, Greek Cypriots were going to call what happened in 1974 'the invasion'...what else would you call it? And the Turkish Cypriots, of course, were going to refer to the same event as the 'peace operation.' That just set off fireworks and people just struggled with what to make of this when the story in their heads – which they believed was THE story – was challenged by people who seemed normal. It took a while – sometimes days – in the workshops to process what they were hearing. For some, it probably took years."[27]

Younger participants, through the years, would generally have a more curious reaction, saying "Tell me more about that." For example, Turkish Cypriots always mentioned 1963. Greek Cypriots generally did not. Younger students, in both communities, also had a sense that the history they were taught in school was heavily laden with propaganda and they would make fun of it, noted John Ungerleider of the School for International Training (SIT), where many of the youth camps for high school-aged students would take place.[28]

Margarita Constantinides (now Constantinides Bradley) remembered doing the History Walk as part of her conflict resolution training when she had a CASP to study engineering at U.C. Berkeley. "I remember leaving that training thinking that these people [the Turkish Cypriots] are exactly like me culturally," said Constantinides Bradley. "I went in somewhat negative and left with some good friends. I remember the History

Walk. It is interesting that that method is part of corporate training so that members of a team can better understand one another, but the first time that I did it was at the workshop. These are tools that are used in U.S. corporate culture but doing it there where it was much more emotional, it was pretty powerful."[29]

A few months after that first CASP workshop, Diamond – with grants from the NTL, IMTD, and the U.S. Institute for Peace – brought together 20 Cypriots – 10 Greek Cypriots and 10 Turkish Cypriots – for a 10-day workshop at Oxford University. They became known as the Oxford Group. When news of the workshop leaked out, the reaction in Cyprus was electric.

The participants were called traitors. Threats were made. Journalists wrote that it was an Anglo-American plot to solve the Cyprus Problem behind the backs of the leaders. Most political leaders – in both communities – condemned the effort. The nationalist press in both communities was particularly virulent. Katie Clerides noted that her family name did not shield her from harsh criticism. Fatma Azgin, who would become a member of the Turkish Cypriot parliament, said simply "of course we were afraid."

The reality of what they were doing, of course, was more benign. Almost all the participants were the peace advocates that had been working with Diamond over the past two years. One notable addition was the younger son of Rauf Denktash, Serdar, who was invited to join the group. "I was approached by Ergün Olgun. He told me that Katie Clerides, the daughter of the President, would be there and that I would add a kind of balance to the group. I said right away that I would. It was my first experience with Greek Cypriots away from the island in such a setting," said Denktash. Some thought Denktash agreed so that he could act as a "spy" for his father; Denktash laughs at this today. "We never had that kind of father-son relationship where he said 'do this or don't do that.' I was free in my own thoughts, beliefs and actions. I was just curious."[30] Costas Shammas noted "that there was a 'spy' there reporting back to Rauf Denktash, it just wasn't Serdar." Clerides remembered that Serdar was quite hardline in his comments, but "on a personal level he was very nice and he even called my father 'uncle' because that is the Turkish custom to call a friend of your father's uncle."[31]

"I think that Oxford was organized very well...it was getting people together and sharing stories and then there were the evening events... eating together, singing together, dancing together," remembered Shammas. "But it was conversations about peace in Cyprus and whether it was possible to do – yes, it can be done. I think it was very well organized, because it was designed to bring the group to emotional levels and for the members of the group to speak about their experiences. I remember a particular time when the entire group of 20 people was in tears and it was necessary to bring the emotions to a high level so that eventually you can reach a point where the intellect can be brought to bear. It was intentional to bring emotions out and it helped the group to address the political issues."[32]

However, in the minds of many Cypriots, if you listened to what members of the other community had to say it implied acceptance and that was simply treason. And yet, the criticism heaped on members of the group also provided an opportunity. Upon their return, members of the group were interviewed, they wrote columns, and went on television and radio to explain exactly what they were doing, and that blunted – a bit – some of the criticisms. For others, with more open minds, it provoked some curiosity. In a way, it provided an opening for the Fulbright Commission.

Daniel Hadjittofi had been talking for a couple of years to Dr. Diamond about how a series of workshops in Cyprus might be set up and most of the ideas came from Dr. Diamond. There would be workshops to teach communications and listening skills that could be applied to everyday life, and not specifically seeking a solution to the Cyprus Problem. The direct goals were "breaking down stereotypes and misconceptions of the 'other' community; increasing understanding of the perspectives of the 'others'; and building trust between members of the two communities. The indirect goals were enabling the development of friendships and professional relationships; encouraging a focus on the future; and developing joint projects to address shared concerns on the island." Diamond wrote in her cover letter to Daniel Hadjittofi: "Thank you for all your support and encouragement. I look forward to working together in peace and friendship on this beautiful island."[33] The Commission also gave Anna Argyrou, who was hired initially as temporary, part-time office staff, the responsibility of managing the logistics of the conflict resolution work. Argyrou was just 26 and had grown up in the U.K. "I think it helped that I did not grow up in Cyprus," said Argyrou. "I was not a refugee and did not know how that felt. I was able to be pretty neutral and I think that worked better."[34]

They decided to test the waters in Cyprus by holding a bicommunal gathering for alumni at the Ledra Palace. Hadjittofi would issue the invitations in his personal capacity. Would Rauf Denktash give permission for Turkish Cypriots to come? He did. It was hard for him, or Greek

Cypriot authorities, to say no. The Fulbright Commission had existed before Turkish Cypriots had boycotted the government in 1963. "The name Fulbright was always used," noted Argyrou. "We were an apolitical education office and we could do things the U.S. Embassy could not. If the Embassy got involved, the immediate reaction was 'they are up to something' but we kept a low profile and used the Fulbright name when we had to."[35] Attendees at the amicable gathering in the Ledra Palace ballroom remember more UN security personnel than alumni. At that point, Hadjittofi said, "if we can do this, we can do more."

In May 1994, the first of eight programs that were launched that summer was called Project Leaders I. Unlike the scholarship competition, there were no panels or interviews to select participants. The Commission began with the individuals already involved in the peace movement. "We were not about to place an ad in the newspapers. It was all very sensitive and so we kept a low profile and there was no reaction from the public because they largely did not know the workshops were happening," explained Argyrou.[36] After that it was word of mouth and recommendations from people already in the program. As the years went on, this would cause some grumbling and jealousy – especially if a trip to the United States was involved – because some felt it was a closed community and that they had not had a fair chance to be selected.

Katie Economidou was called by Hadittofi and invited to participate in the group. She had received a USAID grant to study political science and philosophy at the American University at Beirut and later a Fulbright to study conflict resolution in a business setting at Harvard. When he called, she said no. "I hated the Turks," said Economidou. "I went to the rallies and the meetings to protest against them. The land my husband's family owned was the exact point where the Turkish troops came ashore."[37] However, Hadjittofi was persistent and called again and said it is just one day...you might find it interesting how conflict resolution works in a political setting and Louise Diamond will be there.

Economidou went out of curiosity and in one exercise Diamond paired them off one-to-one with a member from the other community. "Diamond asked us to try to discuss the Cyprus issue without using 'trigger words' such as invasion. She challenged us to find other words," remembers Economidou. "The Turkish Cypriot in front of me would not accept any other words to describe what happened in 1974 but 'peace operation' and I said there were massacres and rapes, can't you call it a military operation or just an operation and he said 'no – peace operation.' So, I turned to him and said there is no way that I can communicate with you at this moment, but I have made a deliberate decision to love you. I was astonished that I expressed myself in this way. I cannot explain it. That marked the beginning of my involvement."[38] That involvement has remained intense to this day.

In June and July, the Commission ran the program Project Leaders II in Cyprus, and the first of two VIP workshops with community and political leaders, just outside of Washington, D.C. "We were able to get a willing group together for the first VIP workshop, but the second was harder to find people who would agree to participate. Daniel made a lot of phone calls to get these officials to make the trip. It was very difficult," remembered Argyrou. "These were influential people and it was tough asking them to do this." In the early days of the bicommunal movement, participants who met with members of the "other" community would face criticism and threats, the possible loss of a job, and social ostracism. In these cases, the Commission would sometimes employ letters of invitation from the American Ambassador, which was a double-edged sword. On one hand, it raised the prestige of the program. On the other, it raised questions about American government efforts to "manipulate" the Cypriot participants.[39] Argyrou remembered one uncomfortable meeting when Daniel sent her to one official's house to urge him to go. "He was very nice and offered me coffee, but it was a hard ask," said Argyrou. "We eventually got 20 from each side."[40] "We were offering them a trip to the United States. Without that, a lot of them would not have participated," noted Hadjittofi.[41]

At Projects Leaders II and at the U.S.-based program, Dr. Diamond – always willing to try something outside the box – brought in Richard Moon, an Aikido sensei. Aikido is a modern Japanese martial art that roughly translates as "the way of unifying (with) life energy" or as "the way of harmonious spirit." Moon and his colleague Chris Thorson spent time with Cypriots each day at the two workshops. "Louise Diamond approached me at a conference. She had been studying Aikido for about six months at that point," remembered Moon. "She told me she learned more in 10 minutes with me than in the previous six months and I was eventually asked to work with the Cypriots. I always knew that Aikido dealt in some way with conflict resolution, but I was unclear how. I saw our charge was to help the participants to drop into a deep presence to help them engage. In the corporate world we used Aikido as a physical metaphor for dialogue."[42] Hadjittofi admits he was skeptical. How would the Cypriots react? "I thought many of them would think it was silly, but I was wrong." Thorson felt that because dance was so much a part of the culture on both sides of the divide that the Cypriots welcomed the chance to engage in physical movement after often tense discussions in the workshops. "If you can come to a sense of peace in yourself, you have a completely different relationship with the world. To my mind, our work was appreciated," said Moon.[43]

The programs were not inexpensive, especially when flying large groups and escorts to the U.S. Each contract could run hundreds of thousands of dollars, but the trips to America could leverage increased participation. That said, the political/community leaders largely went to listen but go no further, often fearful of engaging in a process that they did not control.[44] Four of the eight programs that summer were with either CASP students in the U.S. – again in Boston – or CASP alumni in Cyprus. Even among these younger participants, it was not always easy to find open minds. "Particularly the boys," remembered Argyrou. "If they had been in the military, it was hard to overcome the kinds of ideas about the 'enemy' that had been drilled into them."[45]

The fall of 1994 saw two major advances in the conflict resolution program. At the November 30 Board meeting, Chairman Wahba reported that it had become increasingly difficult to arrange space for bicommunal meetings and training with the UN and that perhaps it might be possible for the Commission to establish its own space in the UN-controlled Buffer Zone at the Ledra Palace crossing. The Board was supportive, but Lellos Demetriades, the mayor of Nicosia, warned that Wahba should move quickly, given that her tenure would soon end, but also quietly. Over the next few months, the Commission received permission from Washington to spend up to $250,000 in CASP residual funds on a structure. Approvals were also obtained from the Church, which owned the land; the UN, which controlled the area; and the Ministry of Foreign Affairs to erect a "non-permanent structure" that would be taken down "when the Cyprus Problem was solved." Foreign Minister Alecos Michaelides, who was close to the Archbishop and was a Fulbrighter (1963 – Georgia Tech) helped smooth the way. The Commission moved expeditiously at that point to put up a 250-square meter (approximately 2,500 square foot) structure that would include offices, a meeting space, a kitchen and bathroom facilities. The Commission would eventually spend $158,000 (double that in current dollars) on the building and it would be ready in the summer of 1997. It was christened The Fulbright Center.[46]

The second was the decision to bring in an American scholar in conflict resolution who would spend an extended period of time in Cyprus. Dr. Ben Broome, of George Mason University, was brought in on a three-month grant but would ultimately spend two and a half years in Cyprus working with members of the two communities to develop bicommunal projects. Indeed, Broome's involvement with Cyprus has never really ended. Broome, tall and laid back, began his work with Cypriots even before arriving in Cyprus when he was invited by Dr. Diamond and Diana Chigas to work with their group during the summer of 1994. By that time, they had formally established the Cyprus Consortium, bringing together the Institute for Multi-Track Diplomacy, the Conflict Management Group, and the National Training Lab. That helped him ease into his work, but it did not allay several concerns that he had.

Broome worked with the process called "Interactive Management," which had three primary phases. A knowledgeable group, over an extended period of time, would (a) collectively develop a thorough understanding of the current state of affairs, which would (b) establish a clear basis for thinking about the future, and then (c) they would, together, produce a framework for effective action.[47] He had used the method before with other cultures, but was concerned how it would translate to the Cypriot culture. For example, it was very American to have an agenda and a schedule and to pack in as much as possible. For the Cypriots, whose concept of time was much more Mediterranean, such schedules could feel oppressive and create

Ben Broome.

tension. There was always extra time needed for socializing. The process also demanded that the group stay focused on the future, but Broome found that Cypriots, in both communities, had difficulty pulling their gaze away from the past. In addition, Broome had worked in Greece before and spoke a bit of Greek. He worried that Turkish Cypriots would view him as biased. He also knew that Cypriots were polite and less confrontational and less likely to tell you what they thought. If you asked them how they were doing, generally "you would not get a direct answer." Chigas had a similar experience as she was of Greek heritage and also spoke some Greek. "If Turkish Cypriots met me the first time as 'the Harvard professor' things were fine," said Chigas. "However, if they happened to encounter me speaking Greek, then it would take much longer to gain their trust and for some it would never happen."[48]

The initial training by the Consortium had taught the group of peace activists that gathered with Broome – 15 Greek Cypriots and 15 Turkish

Cypriots, nine men and six women in each group ranging in age from mid-20s to mid-50s from across the political spectrum – how to listen and how to speak to one another respectfully. This began the process of helping them break down stereotypes and helping them understand that there were other perspectives. What Broome hoped he could accomplish with this group was to develop an actual plan of action that would move the peace movement forward – a movement that this group had fostered at great personal risk.

Over the more than two years of working with the group in Cyprus, the external barriers were considerable. Initially, Turkish Cypriots could not obtain permission to cross into the Buffer Zone, and so the work began mono-communally. If Broome traveled to the Turkish side, there would be paperwork and fees and at one point he was completely banned by Turkish Cypriot officials from going north until the American Ambassador intervened. No Fulbright scholar had ever been denied that privilege. "There was a lot of resistance," noted Broome. At one point, Turkish Cypriot officials issued public statements "condemning the conflict resolution activities and accusing those involved as being organized and trained by American spies to subvert the official policies of the Turkish-Cypriot leaders."[49] The participants faced threats and sometimes there was physical damage to their property. Slanderous articles about them appeared in the press.[50] If Greek Cypriots went to a session at the Ledra Palace crossing, when weekly demonstrations were occurring, they faced a torrent of verbal abuse. When Turkish Cypriot journalist and peace activist Kutlu Adali was gunned down in July 1996, it sent a chilling message. And when, a month later, Greek Cypriot Tassos Isaac was beaten to death during the "motorcycle protests" at Deryneia, followed by the killing of Solomos Solomou by Turkish troops, the feverish atmosphere made peace work virtually impossible for many months. Even events external to the island – the dispute between Greece and Turkey over the islet of Imia/Kardak – provoked tensions that spilled over into the work of the group.[51] Broome estimates that more than half the scheduled meetings were either cancelled or rescheduled because the necessary permissions to cross could not be obtained despite the efforts of the Commission. Argyrou noted that at times she and others in the office spent more than half their time filling out the requisite forms seeking passes.[52]

As Broome explained, even phone calls were a challenge. "There were only a few phone lines between the two communities and there was a limit of just three minutes on each call and the lines were quite poor," recalled Broome. "If security personnel from both sides would surreptitiously join the calls to listen in – as they inevitably did – the quality of the line would decline so you could barely understand what people were saying and, in any case, under those circumstances they would be reluctant to speak at all."[53]

The internal barriers to the group were equally daunting. The sessions were presented to Greek Cypriot and Turkish Cypriot officials as "training" but, as Broome explained, "they were never training. These people wanted to get together to try to understand what stands in the way [of a solution] and what do they want for the future. So, all the time I was in Cyprus, there was a clear problem-solving focus."[54] First the group had to work through the "prejudices, misconceptions, and mistaken information that were part of the education of all Cypriots." Greek Cypriots were shocked that the two groups had such a different concept of the past. Turkish Cypriots were shocked that when the two groups outlined their visions for the future that they were so similar. How could that be when their ideas about the past and how Cypriots had gotten to that point were so different? And, of course, the sessions were conducted in English, a second language for the participants and that made nuanced discussions difficult.

"There was an 'Oh my God moment' when all the members of the group realized that the solution to the Cyprus Problem was not as simple as they thought," said Broome. "Some Greek Cypriots thought that if you removed the Turkish troops, the problem was solved, but it was not. Then there was a reluctance to continue because it all seemed so hopeless."[55] In outlining a vision for the future, Greek Cypriots would inevitably place disarmament at the beginning of the process and Turkish Cypriots would place it at the end – though both, at the end of the day, wanted to see the departure of the Turkish troops. However, one of the core issues was identity and Broome noted that the group spent many months on the issue. Turkish Cypriots, who had traveled abroad, all had the experience of people assuming they were Greek if they came from Cyprus. Greek Cypriots wanted their vision statement for the future to speak of "Cypriots." Turkish Cypriots did not want their identities subsumed in this larger whole because they felt they would slip back to the minority status that was so unacceptable to them. Greek Cypriots felt they had been more than accommodating in other language in the statement toward Turkish Cypriot identity. Could there not be one place in the statement that referred to the collective term "Cypriot?" In the final collective vision statement the solution had to come from an outside party to the training. The statement read: "To empower Cypriots from both communities to envision a Cyprus where people could live in peace and to believe that this is possible now."[56]

During this time, there was also an attempt at internal interference from the Turkish Cypriot officials. Two additional Turkish Cypriots, with close ties to the Denktash administration, showed up uninvited stating that they wanted to join the group. While they were accommodated for a time, the primary members of the group never accepted them and their presence had a chilling effect on the discussions. At one point, the two tried to bring the process to a halt arguing that it was dangerous. In the end, they withdrew, stating that their presence was endangering their own political careers.

It was clear that Rauf Denktash thought that any process that suggested that Greek Cypriots and Turkish Cypriots could coexist was dangerous. Conflict resolution scholar Marion Angelica remembers that Denktash was invited to meet with a group of Cypriot youths who were participating in a Fulbright Commission conflict resolution program. "When he came into the room and saw the group he was disturbed that he could not tell who were Greek Cypriots and who were Turkish Cypriots," remembered Angelica. "They all dressed alike and looked the same. Then he asked the Turkish Cypriots to raise their hands. He assumed that the two groups would be sitting separately from each other, but they were all mixed up and sitting together."[57] None of that comported with the narrative that was central to Denktash's negotiating position.

By the time Broome departed in 1997, he was gratified that much had been accomplished. The primary group, after considering more than 200 ideas, had come up with a dozen ideas to promote peace and understanding on the island and it was finding funding from a variety of sources. In the final year, Broome helped create eight dialogue groups that brought together businessmen, educators, and other occupational groups to engage in a discussion about the future of the island and seek cooperative actions. This expanded tenfold the initial group of 30 to some 300 individuals. Most of all, Broome felt that the primary group, which had nearly broken down several times, could now move forward without the aid of outsiders. The work would be picked up by a series of other American scholars – in particular, Philip Snyder, John Ungerleider, and Marc Turk.

In 1997, the Commission added a new component – youth camps. They would send 40 young people – 20 from each community – aged 15 or 16 to the U.S. for three weeks of conflict resolution work and "team building" outdoor activities. "We were not really getting anywhere with the adult leaders, so we decided to put more emphasis on youth," said

Hadjittofi. Records indicate that the Commission received hundreds of applications in the beginning, but in later years a lack of cooperation from Turkish Cypriot officials reduced the applications from the North. Beyond the contribution to conflict resolution work, the Commission had another motive. It hoped that these young people might consider applying for CASPs or studying in the U.S. under their own steam. Early surveys suggested about 20 percent of the camp attendees actually did pursue their studies in the U.S.[58]

Douglas Stone, one of the Harvard trainers, was at the first youth camp in Pennsylvania. He remembered: "The kids were terrified because they were going to camp with these crazy, evil people and the first days were very tense and they had trouble talking to each other." An Amideast report quoted one of the counselors as saying: "They moved from feelings of hesitancy and skepticism to strong feelings of group identity in six days." "By the end, they were best friends," remembered Stone, "and we were worried because what happens when you go home and you can't have contact with this person anymore who has become your new best friend? And how would they explain that they were friends with someone from the other side? We did a re-entry component, but it was hard to imagine what they were going to face."[59] One might think that young people that age would be immune from the criticisms dished out by the nationalist press on both sides, but that was not the case. Even those teenagers who attended the camps were the object of public attacks.

Valentina Toumaniou and Burcu Barin were two of those campers. Both were 16. Toumaniou had grown up in Limassol. Barin's father was a refugee from Paphos. Toumaniou had seen an ad in the paper. Barin, a student at Türk Maarif Koleji (TMK), had been more or less urged to fill out an application by school officials. Toumaniou's mother was a bit hesitant – "it is so far and you don't know anyone." Barin's father was suspicious about the motivation for the program, but her mother said let her go. Neither had met someone from the other community. Toumaniou remembers going to the orientation with her father and commenting that the Turkish Cypriots looked like "normal people" and she was surprised that some had blond hair and blue eyes unlike the prevalent stereotype. "Don't laugh," said Toumaniou, "but at that time in schools in the Greek Cypriot part of the island no one discussed that Turkish Cypriots even existed...that on the other side of the island that there were people living there. It's funny, but that is how it felt."[60]

Barin flew out of Ercan Airport and Toumaniou left from Larnaca, with the two groups of campers connecting in Europe before pushing

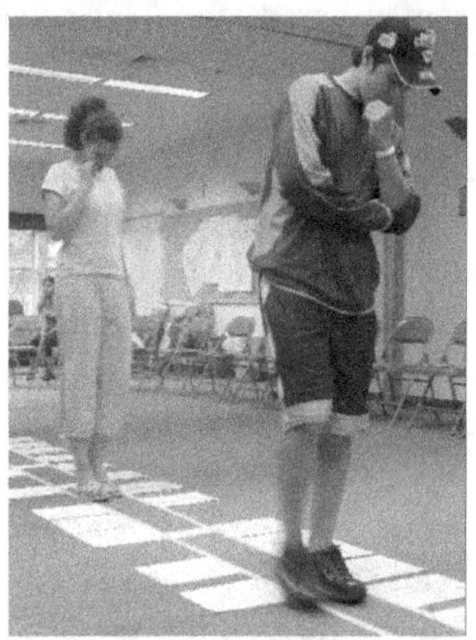

The "history walk" always came early in the youth camps and invariably provoked emotional discussions. They learned to agree to disagree. For older participants (below) the history walk could be a shock.

The BoldLeaders program in Colorado tested Cypriot Youth mentally and physically.

on to the U.S. together. It was just one more thing that the Fulbright Commission had to finesse. Greek Cypriot officials regard Ercan as an "illegal" port of entry and exit to the island. Through the years there were many such taboos where officials just agreed to look the other way. "They looked the other way in part because they could not question my patriotism – I was a refugee and had lost my father and my uncles. And I had a network of contacts," said Hadjittofi.[61] The group made their way to a camp near Waynesboro, Pennsylvania in the green, lush hills not far from the Gettysburg Civil War battlefield. Ten campers – five from each community – were housed in four cabins with escorts. Barin had expected large cities and shopping centers, not a small town. Many things were unexpected.

The camp was run by the Cyprus Consortium and Louise Diamond was one of the trainers. They began with the History Walk, which both Toumaniou and Barin remember vividly. "It was the first time that I heard that Cyprus was 'occupied'," said Barin, "and I had to ask what they meant. There were strong reactions from the other Turkish Cypriots and the Greek Cypriots reacted strongly when we talked about the establishment of the TRNC. Things got very tense and there was strong language and the facilitators had to stop the exercise and we returned to it the next day. Eventually we agreed to disagree."[62] "The camp was a very emotional experience and I did not expect it to be that way," said Toumaniou. "The History Walk is the exercise that I really remember. It stayed with me for a long time. It still helps me now. Whenever I hear statements in the press I know there is another perspective that we might be ignoring or that we never heard before. I did not agree with everything I heard on the History Walk, but I could not make the argument that it did not exist."[63] As one trainer put it: "We needed them to turn off the tape recorders in their heads."

Despite that tense beginning, the bonding of the campers did not take all that long. They were teenagers who shared many common interests and who were still exploring their identities and beliefs, and they were much more flexible than the adults. And, it was not all heavy political discussions. Much of the time was spent in outdoor activities, including team-building exercises where they learned to depend on each other. As the program came to a close, there was a "re-entry" role-playing exercise to prepare them for their return to the Cypriot environment. When they arrived back in Europe they split into two groups, once again returning to Ercan and Larnaca. Barin remembers it was emotional because it seemed that they would not be able to see their new friends again. Toumaniou said that trying to explain the experience to her friends in Cyprus was difficult and that they could not really understand it and she did receive some criticism upon her return. Although there was a follow-on meeting for the group at the Fulbright Center, not all the campers came; nevertheless, some friendships endured across the Green Line despite the obstacles. In the years that followed, both Toumaniou and Barin would apply for and receive Short-Term Training grants from the Commission, returning to the U.S.

The next year the Commission turned from the Consortium and sponsored two different youth camps with two new organizations – Seeds of Peace (SOP) and the School for International Training (SIT). Journalist John Wallach founded Seeds of Peace in 1993 when he brought together 45 young people – 15 each from Israel, Palestine, and Egypt – to a camp he had established in Maine. SIT is part of World Learning, a non-profit organization founded in 1932 and headquartered in Brattleboro, Vermont, which began by promoting international exchange. SIT faculty member John Ungerleider was one of the Fulbright scholars who spent time supporting the Commission's conflict resolution efforts in Cyprus in 1997-98, then returning to Vermont in the summer of 1998 to welcome 40 Cypriot campers.

Despite being the newer of the two organizations, Seeds of Peace gained political prominence in the U.S. and the Embassy pushed the Commission to use them. "We had problems with Seeds of Peace," explained Argyrou. "They would do programs with kids from several different countries and there would be a ceremony where they would raise all the countries' flags. We told them not to do it with the Cypriots because it was too sensitive, but they did it anyway, raising the flag for Cyprus but not for the Turkish Republic of Northern Cyprus and that caused a backlash."[64]

Dr. John Ungerleider led the program at the School for International Training.

Walter Douglas, who succeeded Dr. Baroody as Public Affairs Officer and Board Chairman in 1999, thought it was ironic that the Bicommunal Support Program was allegedly founded to deal with conflict resolution programs that were deemed too politically sensitive for the

Fulbright Commission, "but it turned out it was for programs that were too politically sensitive in Washington," noted Douglas. "Because once you have all this money, people would lobby to have their NGOs given grants. Seeds of Peace clearly had an inferior program to SIT, but there was political pressure from Washington to use them, so we used BSP to send kids to Seeds of Peace camps. They were just putting the Cypriot kids into programs with Israelis and Palestinians and that had nothing to do with Cyprus."[65]

As a result, SIT won the bids for more than half the Commission-sponsored camps between 1997 and 2011. However, the Commission did try other organizations and in 2006, 2007 and 2008 it gave grants to a program called BoldLeaders.

BoldLeaders grew out of a program for at-risk youth in Denver, Colorado, which was modified and used with young adults in Northern Ireland. "Our program was not really about conflict resolution," said founder Michael Donahue. "It was about leadership and it was about asking the kids 'how are you going to be human with each other?' They spent 24 hours a day learning to speak to each other, deal with each other, and getting out whatever emotions that they had. We saw a lot of anger at times...saw a lot of that and then they would pair up and spend a few days with an American family and we would get back together and we called it 'going on the road.' They would climb mountains, canoe rapids, and camp in the desert. The kids would be floundering and they were petrified and they were screaming at each other and we said 'hey, we trained you how to do this so work it out and they worked it out.' They became real pros and it was great to see."[66]

Birkan Uzun was one of those campers and his experience was a factor in returning to the Commission, applying for and earning a CASP grant, and ultimately studying computer science at MIT. "The camp was definitely a factor. I came to see the U.S. as a land of opportunity," said Uzun. "I had not really had much contact with Greek Cypriots, but I made a number of friends at the camp who I am still in touch with and Michael Donahue is still a mentor. It was a great program."[67] After the Commission had helped him through the application process to 13 American schools and he had received his acceptance at MIT, he turned down the CASP grant and accepted financial aid from MIT so that he would not have to fulfill the requirement to return to Cyprus for two years. Today, Uzun works for Amazon in Seattle, Washington as part of a team designing some of the company's most complex and advanced technologies. However, he still thinks about returning to Cyprus.

"Yes, I imagine returning to Cyprus at some point," said Uzun, who ticked off several ideas for education and healthcare that could improve government and life in general in the Turkish North. "But the biggest problem is how do you actually do it? It would require a good team and buy-in from the community. I hear the same story from a lot of people. They study in the U.S. and go back to Cyprus but they end up going back to the U.S. or perhaps to somewhere in Europe ...it is not a very open-minded place. Every time someone tries to change something it gets shut down. I had a conversation with the Chief Technical Officer at Kayak [CASP-grantee and MIT grad Dr. Giorgos Zacharia] about technology and Cyprus. You hope that if some like-minded people get together they can do something."[68]

Costas Georgiades agrees. He was at BoldLeaders as a 16-year-old in 2008 and ultimately studied in the Netherlands. "Cyprus is a closed society and the mentality is more or less the same on both sides," he observed. "There is no way that an individual can make an impact and so you need others to rise with you and I think that BoldLeaders gave us the skills to make that happen. But while many young people want to go back they feel that it is them against the world. My vision is to go back and be part of a network and then start building something."

Georgiades finds that he is in touch with more Turkish Cypriots than Greek Cypriots, and his conservative family had trouble understanding this. "The push-back started before I went. I come from a family – like my grandparents – who had been part of the generation that fought against the British and were a bit conservative." In contrast, he found the participants in the program came with a particular mindset that is still evident today. "They are all trying to bring change, whether they are in the corporate world or they are working directly in conflict resolution in Cyprus. The toughest part of coming back was a battle...not with myself, but with my environment, with my peers, and others. They had never visited the North and could not imagine what it would be like to spend three weeks with a Turkish Cypriot. It was hard to find my place and my space and that motivated me to stay in contact with the group."[69]

The final camp was held in 2011, returning to SIT. John Ungerleider notes that through the years they learned as much from the campers as the Cypriot teenagers learned from them. "A lot of the methods we used for youth camps evolved from the work we did with Cypriots," said Ungerleider. At times the road could get bumpy. "Sometimes we would deal with stereotypes that Greek Cypriots and Turkish Cypriots have of each other – murderers, dirty – really bad stuff. Then we ask, what about the people that you have just met? It could be really divisive."[70] When a Turkish Cypriot girl wore a TRNC t-shirt, a Greek Cypriot camper relayed that to his father, whose brother worked at the Foreign Ministry, who informed the Minister, who called the American Ambassador, who called down to the Public Affairs Officer, who called Hadjittofi, who called SIT and Ungerleider to see if they could set some boundaries on certain symbols. The girl had no idea she was doing something provocative and had even asked some Greek Cypriots to sign her shirt as a gesture of peace. Just another day at the office at the Commission.

Ungerleider always took the campers to Brattleboro Village Pizza, which was run and co-owned by a Greek and a Turk. "The kids could not believe it," said Ungerleider. "And yes, music, dancing and even cooking were part of the camp experience as well. When the campers prepared traditional Greek Cypriot and Turkish Cypriot dishes, they were the same dishes, but they just knew them by different names. They would argue – 'that's not how my grandmother does it!' – but I have to say that over the years we saw a real decline in cooking skills and I worry about traditional culture in Cyprus."[71]

In addition to the youth camps, the Commission was still funding programs with CASP students in the U.S., especially after adding a requirement that grantees take at least one course that could be regarded as American Studies. Not all the students would take the courses, and so the Commission set up summer programs that would bring groups of students from both communities together. "Everything we did had a conflict resolution component," noted Argyrou. However, as the years wore on – especially after the checkpoints opened in 2003 – the conflict resolution portion could get lost. "I would receive calls from students about the youth camps asking if the Commission was the place where you applied for a 'vacation' in the U.S.," said Argyrou. Still, over 14 years more than 750 Cypriot teenagers experienced the program and a substantial number, like Birkan Uzun, would go on to study in the U.S.

The year the youth camps were started, 1997, turned out to be a tumultuous year for the Commission's conflict resolution efforts. In addition to Ben Broome's dialogue groups, the Commission funded a series of workshops for managers, including two in the U.S. for senior managers. In all there were more than a dozen programs, all of which had substantial numbers of participants, from labor leaders to local government officials. A group of 19 Cypriot journalists that went to Washington in the spring of 1997 was given special attention – acknowledgment by State Department Spokesman Nick Burns at the daily briefing, a brief encounter with Secretary of State Albright, and attendance at an event with President Clinton. A small Turkish monthly publication, *Kibrisli*, charged that the journalists had "submitted their bodies and spirits to America with no hesitation" for a trip to the U.S. and $600 in meal money. It concluded that the "brain-washing activities" were continuing with the force of money.[72]

The Commission sponsored other programs that offered special opportunities for one Greek Cypriot and one Turkish Cypriot. For example, a tax program at Harvard in 1994. Lazaros Lazarou was the Greek Cypriot participant and it led to a master's in public administration from Harvard, after which he returned to run a district tax office in Limassol. He was appointed, at age 32, Accountant General by President Clerides. Today he is one of 28 Auditors-General for the European Union. "Of course, the American training was valued," said Lazarou. "The name Harvard University opens doors. If it was not valued, I would not be where I am today."[74]

At the same time, the American Embassy increased its bicommunal effort. Ambassador Ken Brill arrived in Nicosia in July 1996. Two phrases that described Brill were "hands on" and "aggressive." His appointment of a Special Assistant for Bicommunal Affairs in December 1996 was somewhat serendipitous but illustrative. Public Affairs Officer Dr. Judith Baroody's husband Richard Krueger was a retired Army officer and had acquired a position teaching a political science course at Intercollege, which would become the University of Nicosia. All instructors were required to give periodic public lectures. Krueger had put together a lecture on the relative military strengths of Greece and Turkey and at the weekly Country Team meeting Baroody noted that the lecture was that night and invited Embassy officers to attend. "Ambassador Brill was shocked," said Baroody, "and he said that Richard could not give that lecture because he had not cleared it with the Embassy. And I said, Sir, he does not work for the Embassy and within two weeks the Ambassador found a way to use CASP funds to create the Special Assistant's position."[74]

It was an interesting arrangement. Krueger would sit in the Public Affairs Section, but could not work for his wife. So he reported directly to the Deputy Chief of Mission, Deborah Graze, thus avoiding Department rules concerning spouses supervising spouses. The Commission would fund the position via a one-year grant of CASP residuals, but while Board member Dr. Chrysostomos Sofianos expressed the thought that a coordinator was not a bad idea, he was concerned that Executive Director Daniel Hadjittofi had been bypassed in this arrangement. There were other questions, but the Ambassador was asking and the grant was approved.[75]

There were two other interesting items of note at that meeting. First, Ambassador Brill had appointed his wife as an alternate Board member. That had never happened, although Mary Brill was certainly qualified. Second, DCM Deborah Graze attended, which was also irregular as the bylaws of the Commission provided no particular status for the DCM unless appointed to a Board position by the Ambassador. Graze nevertheless continued to attend most meetings.

Seven months later, Ambassador Brill attended the first Board meeting at the new Fulbright Center and had a new request – $500,000 in CASP residual funds to be given fast-track authority and used for bicommunal programs at his discretion. His rationale was that the Commission had to speed up the expenditure of the residuals before the extended deadline was reached. Several Cypriot Board members were uneasy. Lellos Demetriades questioned whether funds already delegated to the Commission could be delegated further, and suggested a subcommittee be created to approve the programs that would be funded by the half million dollars. Dr. Sofianos agreed, but expressed the thought that consultation with such a subcommittee was essential since it included the wisdom of others and protected the Ambassador if something went wrong, meaning if a program provoked a political backlash. However, his main concern was appearances. It was important not to jeopardize the status of the Commission as an independent institution. It could not be seen as an instrument of the Embassy. After Ambassador Brill's departure from the meeting, the Board approved the following language in the transcript of the Board proceedings: "The Board resolved to make available to the Honorary Chairman of the Commission an amount of up to $500,000 under fast track authority for implementing projects under the following terms and conditions. (1) That projects be related to topics, the nature of which the Board has been authorizing up to now. Such projects may take place in either Cyprus or abroad. (2) A sub-committee made up of one Greek Cypriot, one Turkish Cypriot and one American, each having an alternate and chaired by the Honorary Chairman of the Commission, be set up to evaluate proposed projects and grant approvals." The members of the sub-committee were then listed. Finally, (3) "if there is dissent from any of the members, the project will be submitted to the full Board for decision."[76]

With both the Commission and the Embassy engaged, the number of Cypriots involved in both conflict resolution and bicommunal programs swelled. "There were about 2,000 individuals engaged in these programs and we had some real momentum and then Denktash shut it down," remembered John Ungerleider. Denktash ordered that the checkpoints be closed and an end to passes in late December 1997, and many of the programs came to a screeching halt.

There were a few alternatives. One was to organize meetings at the sole bicommunal village in Cyprus, Pyla. Argyrou remembers driving down there with some peace activists followed by not-so-very-undercover police who would camp at an adjacent table to listen in on the conversation. Argyrou would puckishly ask them if they wanted a coffee. The other alternative was to not take no for an answer. The Fulbright Commission would push authorities – couldn't we have just this one pass? One would turn into two and special events might pry open the gates further. Even when the checkpoints were open, the process was often arbitrary and capricious. Louise Diamond was stopped at a checkpoint and fired back "you have a letter from the Fulbright Commission." "What letter?" asked the none-too-cooperative official. Spying the Commission's letterhead, Diamond retorted "that letter right there on your desk." After some grumbling, she was allowed to pass. Sometimes, the decisions were just malicious and cruel. Katie Clerides and Costas Shammas had first danced together in Fatma Azgin's garden, and on the day of their wedding Azgin believed she would be allowed to cross to attend the ceremony, but she was stopped. She gave the present she was carrying to the policeman blocking her way, and cried all the way home. She lamented that she just should have climbed over her garden wall, which abutted the Buffer Zone.[77]

The other alternative was to take the conflict resolution work off the island. Of course, it was more expensive but the Commission had the money and was rushing to spend it. Plus, the carrot of U.S. travel attracted new participants, still chosen by occupational group or via introductions provided by persons already engaged in the Commission's programs. That is what Fulbright scholar Marc Turk did.

Turk – and yes, his name was a bit of a show-stopper for Greek Cypriots – had been an entertainment lawyer in Los Angeles who closed his practice and began teaching mediation and conflict resolution courses in the law school

Marco Turk.

at California State University at Irvine. He sought an opportunity to do this abroad and noted that Cyprus was the only country in the Fulbright catalogue looking for someone in conflict resolution. The Commission brought him to Cyprus to teach mediation skills in the context of domestic violence. "Marc was very energetic and charismatic," noted Fulbright Scholar Marion Angelica. "He had a way of drawing people to him," said Argyrou. Turk arrived and ran an astonishing number of workshops, first in family mediation, but then expanded into many other fields. When the checkpoints were closed, he tried personally to get Denktash to reconsider. "Denktash told me what I was doing was fine, but that it would have to be done separately. He said you cannot tease the Turkish Cypriots with the idea that they can live together with Greek Cypriots and create false hopes," said Turk. "So, I asked some of the group members if they would like to do this off the island, in this case Oslo, and we put together a group of 26 Greek Cypriots and 26 Turkish Cypriots. There was one Greek Cypriot news reporter in the group who was a bit of a 'spy' and there probably was on the Turkish side, too, but I did not know who it was."[78] By this time some Greek Cypriot newspapers were running articles that Turk was CIA and that he was causing trouble, but he pushed ahead.

Oslo was chosen because PRIO was a co-sponsor of the effort, as was the Norwegian Fulbright Commission. In 1998, there were two sessions with the group in Oslo, with the goal of producing a Vision Statement for the future of Cyprus that dealt with real issues and would have an impact on the leadership of the two communities. That said, Turk stressed that he did not write the Vision Statement. The Cypriots did. They used role-playing to work through the issues and Turk noted that the Greek Cypriots who played Denktash and the Turkish Cypriots who played Clerides were better than the actual Denktash and Clerides. In between the two Oslo meetings, the group met in Pyla. There were impediments. Denktash tried to literally pull people off the plane going to Oslo, and one of the meetings clashed with a separate meeting of Cypriot business leaders that was being run by Special Cyprus Coordinator Richard Holbrooke. "Holbrooke had trouble getting enough Turkish Cypriots so he tried to raid my group and he tried to insinuate our group into his group for press availabilities but the people in my group wanted it to be low key and stay out of the press. We were able to resist all of that," noted Turk.[79]

While 52 Cypriots went to the first Oslo meeting, only 31 could attend the second, on December 7-11, 1998. Between the two meetings, six subgroups worked on the text of the 46-page statement.[80] Turk noted in a law journal article that after Oslo the group tried to get a hearing for the ideas that they had assembled, but were largely ignored. Argyrou remembers how hard Turk tried to get the media interested in the final product with virtually no response. "He was frustrated and very disappointed." Three years later, however, the *Cyprus Mail* in its Sunday edition published a front-page story on the efforts of the Oslo group, which called the product of their labors "shocking." The participants in the group were described as "hand-picked by the Americans" and "betraying the pain" caused by Turkey's invasion of the island. The article called Oslo a "pointless psychological effort."[81]

Turk would return and run more workshops, particularly in the run-up to the Annan Plan vote. "If you look at what was in the Annan Plan, many of the things we were talking about at Oslo made it into the Annan Plan," noted Turk.[82] Turk said that he could not have accomplished any of this without the support of the Fulbright Commission. "Daniel, Anna, and the staff made things work. Daniel kept extending me until I had to return to America for family reasons. It was a super organization that cared about people. They did everything to get the necessary permissions." Turk would write often about Cyprus and continue to return to the island. He never gave up hope. In a 2006 law journal article, he closed by quoting anthropologist Margaret Mead: "Never doubt that a small group of thoughtful, committed citizens can change the world. Indeed, it is the only thing that ever has."[83]

In the summer of 1999, Board Chairman Baroody was set to depart Cyprus as was her husband, Richard Krueger, the Bicommunal Coordinator. From the Commission's point of view, there had been too much interference and not enough coordination. During the 14 months that Marion Angelica was in Cyprus evaluating the conflict resolution programs on behalf of the Commission, she noted that Krueger was "asking me to do things that were not what Fulbright wanted to do. It was very awkward and I could feel the tension between the Embassy and the Commission."[84] Krueger was supposed to be talking with Hadjittofi, but he did not and the relationship between Argyrou and Krueger had broken down almost immediately. The solution was to interpose an intermediary – Karen Stefanou – Amideast's representative in Cyprus. She worked to support the Embassy's bicommunal programs. However, as Krueger was about to depart, the Commission argued strenuously for the position of the Coordinator to be eliminated. The situation was serious enough that, in the summer of 1999, Dr. William Bader, Associate Director for Educational and Cultural Affairs at USIA, came to Cyprus to meet with a large swath of interested individuals, but particularly Ambassador Brill. Upon his return to Washington, Bader wrote a cable to the Ambassador that read in part:

"The Commission's reputation is the result of many years of hard work that established its credentials as an organization with a proven track record for independence and very high quality programming. I am certain that we can resolve the complications, which the CASP program has occasioned of late, both for the Commission and its Board. My operating premise is that we can continue to have the Fulbright Commission administer the CASP programs as long as we respect the fundamental principles that govern each program undertaken by the Fulbright Commission, regardless of the funding source....The issue of the Bicommunal Coordinator, in my view, goes to the heart of the question of whether the Fulbright Commission will remain associated with CASP in the future. It was the Commission that conceived and introduced the coordination of bicommunal programs under CASP auspices. I think we now see that the creation of a special coordinator, separated from the Commission Executive Director and answering to the Embassy, created what is now perceived to be a very different dynamic. I now believe that we ought now to eliminate this position in view of what I have learned about the situation from many sources. It seems to me that the presence of Embassy Officers on the Board of the Fulbright Commission, including the Public Affairs Officer as chair...is sufficient to ensure that U.S. policy interests and the instructions of the Ambassador are taken into account in anything having to do with CASP, as well as the Fulbright program itself. Otherwise we should consider ways to separate bicommunal activities from the Commission altogether."[85]

Ambassador Brill rejected Bader's plea and hired a new Coordinator to succeed Krueger, perhaps with an eye to the fact that the United States Information Agency would, at the end of September 1999, cease to exist as an independent agency and its public diplomacy functions would be folded into the Department of State.[86] At the end of the day, the Bicommunal Coordinator continued to exist and the Commission kept using CASP funds to support conflict resolution programming. "You don't want to set up competing initiatives. You want them to build on each other," observed Harvard's Chigas. "After Brill things started to fracture and there was not as much communication. It wasn't that there was not good work, it was just that everyone was doing their little thing."[87]

Indeed, as the millennium dawned, the Commission's bicommual/ conflict resolution/peace building efforts were many and varied. This, despite the fact that the deadline to spend the $7.25 million in CASP residuals had finally come and the Commission was compelled to return the last $274,231 to the U.S. Treasury.[88] Conflict resolution had become an integral part of the Commission's mission. In 2000, Commission documents show 20 discrete programs, including three youth camps, several programs with CASP students, and a host of very specialized efforts – domestic violence, special education, sustainable planning, emergency management, historic preservation, educational administration, nursing care standards, handling asbestos, anesthesiology, and several music programs conducted by American classical violinist Peter Sulski. "In this period we tried to do bicommunal short-term training grants, sending Greek and Turkish Cypriots together on training programs in the U.S. We looked at the needs of the society and tried to create various programs. I have to say the STTs, although extremely successful in the dissemination of specialized knowledge to the Cypriots, did not work very well on the reconciliation front," said Hadjittofi. "They did not create the kinds of ongoing relationships we were hoping for."[89]

Sulski's participation in bicommunal programs was serendipitous. He was a violinist in the London Symphony at age 22. He had become involved with the Apple Hill Chamber Music Center, which brought several hundred young musicians from around the world to rural New Hampshire each summer to train and play together. The Commission and also the Embassy's Bicommunal Support Program sent pairs of Cypriots – one Greek Cypriot and one Turkish Cypriot – to the program on several occasions. Sulski played with Apple Hill during a tour of the Middle East in 1996, when he came into contact with the Cyprus Chamber Orchestra and, in 2000, he was hired as the principal violinist for that orchestra. Apple Hill set up his connection with the Fulbright Commission and Sulski was given an unofficial title – Bicommunal Coordinator for Chamber Music for Turkish Cypriots and Greek Cypriots. Sulski remembers the arrangement as controversial because the Cyprus Chamber Orchestra was a state orchestra and so he was, essentially, a government employee. "I did receive some criticism and so I had to be very discreet," remembered Sulski. He trained the young musicians separately, and was only able to arrange for the Greek and Turkish Cypriots to play together a few times. "When it happened, it was great," said Sulski. "I did it for almost three years, but one of the reasons I left was the politics. When you are a musician, you are a musician and that is what is important. When we played chamber music together it was stunning. That is what I remember."[90]

Another example of a needs-of-society program was in substance abuse awareness. Roxanne Kibben was invited to work with a community of Cypriots in Louisville, Kentucky, and through them she met a doctor from Larnaca. The Fulbright Commission found money to bring her to Cyprus, where she ran a whirlwind of programs leading Hadjittofi to ask her to come back. She received a grant as a Fulbright scholar and arrived in February 2001 and stayed for seven months. Over the next two summers, the Commission would finance a bicommunal group of Cypriots – 24 the first year – to travel to Minneapolis, where Kibben was based, to receive further training in substance abuse prevention. Kibben remembers the training began with the first group on September 11, 2001. "When I first arrived in Cyprus it was difficult to get the groups together. It was especially hard for the Turkish Cypriots. We ran all-day workshops on the weekends. I returned in the spring of 2003 when the checkpoints opened and that was one of the peak experiences of my professional life," said Kibben. "I'll admit I did not know enough about the politics, but I think that we made a difference and I hope that the participants remained in contact."[91]

When the checkpoints opened in 2003, Argyrou went into Hadjittofi's office and asked whether or not she still had a job. "I was not sure what to do," said Argyrou. "When the checkpoints opened, initially we felt we had won," said Hadjittofi. "We felt that people could get together at will but then we realized that, while the checkpoints were physically opened, psychologically we still had a lot of work to do. However, we also found that the interest in many of these programs had waned." Argyrou noted that "people would cross to see their former properties, but people were not really talking."[92]

After 2004, as CASP funds were reduced, there were usually no more than three or four programs a year – a youth camp, a conflict resolution workshop with CASP students – the "pre-influentials" – and an American Studies program. Argyrou organized a couple of other successful programs that involved taking groups to the U.S.; one for nurses, and several for high school counselors aiming to introduce them to the American educational system including visits to American university campuses. "That was my idea," said Argyrou, "and I am still in touch with some of those counselors and they say it was the best experience of their lives."[93] In 2011, the year of the last class of CASP scholars, the Commission did its final two conflict resolution programs – a youth camp and a program for the counselors. Ultimately, they would train 60 counselors who had access to some 20,000 students. In all there were 202 separate programs over 17 years. Well over $10 million was expended. Did it make a difference?

The Commission's efforts did not occur in a vacuum. Other countries and the UN supported various bicommunal efforts. The UN efforts were heavily supported by the $10 million annual appropriation from the Congress that was the other two-thirds of the $15 million pushed through year after year by the Greek lobby and friendly and determined lawmakers. Whether it was the Nicosia Master Plan, which saw the cooperation of Lellos Demetriades and Mustafa Akinci, or the promotion of ties between the two business communities, or the construction of the Home for Cooperation in the Buffer Zone, or the restoration of churches, such as St. Mamas in Morphu, or the founding of the Cyprus Institute of Neurology and Genetics to aid in the identification of the missing from the 1974 war, much of the money was spent trying to coax cooperation between Greek Cypriots and Turkish Cypriots or to ameliorate impediments to reconciliation.[94]

Dr. Diamond warned in her very first proposal that "human behavioral science is imprecise and does not lend itself to predictable outcomes." She also stressed that the emphasis of her project was on skills training and not on the specifics of the Cyprus Problem. Still, she wrote, "we may reasonably expect new attitudes, assumptions and behaviors to spread to inter-group relations between the two communities."[95] Measuring the success of the Commission's work depends on the specific goal. The Cyprus Consortium's goals were rather modest – to create a group of Cypriots who could communicate across the dividing line and train others to do the same. That was largely accomplished and thousands participated. "We basically worked ourselves out of a job," noted Chigas. Ben Broome's goals were more ambitious. He hoped to pull together a group of Cypriots who would develop multiple programs that would advance the peace process and grow the number of participants. He was partially successful. Marc Turk was, perhaps, the most ambitious of all, trying to create a vision statement that would serve as a roadmap to a possible solution to the Cyprus Problem. And although, yes, they created such a vision and, yes, some of the language from the statement is similar to language found in the Annan Plan, it seems that today Cypriots are no closer to a solution than when the Commission began its efforts. As Chigas observed, "the Cypriots chewed up and spit out everyone who tried including [the legendary Richard] Holbrooke."[96]

Certainly, there was skepticism about the Commission's efforts from the beginning. "The Commission's conflict resolution programs came along after USAID's bicommunal programs had been going on for some time," noted Ambassador John Koenig, who was a political officer at the

Embassy between 1994 and 1997. "They had boards and project grants and initially there was some skepticism that this would complement all that effectively, but I think it did."[97] Gustave Feisel at the UN, who was resident on Cyprus in the same period (1993-98), felt that in order for significant change to happen the "political leaders would have to decide to do something and at that time they largely decided to not do something."[98] Ambassador Richard Boucher had a similar take. "I thought it was a good use of the money," said Boucher, "but I never held out the hopes that the Track II folks held out. They did not have agency. This is something that has to be solved by government representatives –people who have a mandate. Establishing a common frame of reference is all well and good, but it does not get to the heart of things when you are dealing with land and houses and compensation."[99]

"In Cyprus, political life is based on the party," observed Katie Economidou. "You have to go through the party. The party has control. We [the bicommunal activists] did not try to bond with the parties. They became skeptical and attacked. They did not trust us. They would ask... Who are you? Are you trying to play the role of a leader? You are not elected by the people. You do not have the legitimacy to do what you do. You don't represent us."[100] There was a feeling that in some ways the Turkish Cypriot participants did more to connect with their political structures, even if Denktash represented the ultimate roadblock. Mustafa Akinci was deeply involved in the Commission-sponsored programs. Fatma Azgin was a member of the parliament. Hussein Gursan was head of state media in the Talat government. "Fulbright was the key to open the doors that were never opened," said Gursan. "It was not always seen as a peace activity, but an educational activity. The British also invited a group to the UK. But that was only one time. Fulbright was for more than 10 years. And they also gave money for bicom projects at that time. It was important for TCs, but we were acting against our government."[101]

Marion Angelica, who studied the Commission's conflict resolution efforts in 1998-99, reached the conclusion that the bicommunal movement created a third "tribe" in Cyprus. "I remember that when we were leaving Cyprus after 14 months, I was sad because instead of bringing two communities together, now there were three communities," said Angelica. "My take from all the interviews I did was that the Greek Cypriots still looked down on the Turkish Cypriots and believed that they had a superior culture, even though the Turkish Cypriots in the programs were well-educated, and the Turkish Cypriots sensed this. There was also a feeling in the larger community that people who wanted to make peace were betraying their communities. However, it was also my feeling that some of the participants in the program looked to the Fulbright Commission to solve the Cyprus Problem."[102]

Ben Broome thought that Angelica's observation about a "third tribe" was "right on target" but felt that Ambassador Boucher's definition of agency was too narrow. "Agency has to be thought about in a long-term time frame and how does change happen in this society?" noted Broome. "Is it a top-down process or a bottom-up process and then what kind of change are we talking about? Is it a negotiation that leads to a document that is signed and then goes to a referendum, or is it change in personal attitudes? How someone writes in the media, for example. So, in that sense, they had a good deal of agency, but perhaps not in the way that an Ambassador is used to thinking about."[103]

On the other hand, Dr. Ron Fisher, who was a research fellow and one of the "bodies" brought in to do the large volume of work with Louise Diamond and Diana Chigas, thought that Angelica's view was too pessimistic. "The work gave peace-oriented Greek and Turkish Cypriots the opportunity to build a social movement that would influence the peace process. And that is exactly what happened. Many of the people who are involved in the working groups were trained in the conflict resolution movement. They became a separate social movement and they had influence, especially in the North. They made a difference. That is my read." Fisher praised the support provided by Ambassador Richard Boucher, and also that of Daniel Hadjittofi. "His contribution was so outstanding. He was so level-headed and so committed."[104]

Activist Harry Anastastiou, who continued to run workshops at Portland State University with Birol Yesilada, even as the Fulbright Commission's work waned, concurred that the grassroots work was essential: "We knew that the two communities had to interact to try to repair broken relationships. It was imperative if there was to be a settlement. It was dangerous to have a successful negotiation because there had been zero preparation. You have to navigate it all and if you move too fast you will be crushed."[105]

Diana Chigas felt that one had to think of a much longer time frame, which was hard to sustain. "Daniel Hadjittofi really suffered through this," noted Chigas. "There was a point when I think Washington began to question the value of this work and there were certainly officials in Cyprus who wanted to spend the money on something else. However, I worked with these people for a decade or more and I did see evolution. It would go up and down, but the general direction was up. I think if you look at the situation now and the possibilities that exist that they would not have existed without the Fulbright Commission."[106] That said, Ambassador Koenig noted that there came a point when it seemed that the same people were being trained over and over again and the size of the "tribe" had reached its limit. The more cynical individuals in the American Embassy referred to some of these activists as the "usual suspects."

Katie Clerides felt that the conflict resolution workshops were a "revelation" in the sense that too often when we communicate we don't actually listen to what the other person is saying because we are focusing mentally on our counter-arguments. "These are very basic things that have become more part of myself," said Clerides, "but they weren't at that time. So I learned a tremendous amount and they changed my life, my whole attitude toward life." Of course, her life changed in another way when she met the man who would become her husband, Costas Shammas. "She was my prize from the peace work," said Shammas smiling and taking her hand. "However," noted Clerides, "I do think we had a wider impact. We did influence people. It took a long time and it was very difficult."[107]

"I think the workshops did give us a language and it gave us concert," said Hadjipavlou. "It gave us a new vocabulary that did not previously exist and it has become mainstream. I analyzed the language of [President Nicos] Anastasiades in the first three/four months of his administration ...what they were saying...and it is all conflict resolution words and phrases. I think the Fulbright Commission did create a third community in Cyprus in the sense that both the scholarships and providing people the opportunity to be with the "other" in that historical moment of our conflict made a difference. It was a cultural and educational center and not an American political – 'CIA' – kind of place because as you know there are all these conspiracy theories in Cyprus that create all this fake information. So I think, for us, it was like an oasis. The people at the Commission were so committed, so enthusiastic and so open to hear about our local needs and as well because we had a small steering committee that was important. We felt like a family, like a community."[108]

Certainly Rauf Denktash believed that the Fulbright Commission was having an impact. In an October 1994 interview with the newspaper *Kibris*, Denktash said "...the work started under the name 'Conflict Resolution Group' has taken the shape of unacceptable intervention in the internal affairs of the TRNC. The foreign embassies have no right to tell our people what their case is about and to guide them in the direction of interests of their countries. This work has gone out of control as time has gone by. Those of our people who have been participating in this work feel uneasy. So do we. These CIA methods should come to an end.

Bringing Greek Cypriots and Turkish Cypriots together at various levels is one thing – brainwashing is something else."[109]

"Yes, my father thought Fulbright was brainwashing his people," said his son Serdar. "He thought the programs might convince the Turkish Cypriots that they would be able to share power on the island. I think we learned in the workshops to take certain words not so seriously and to work past those words. It helped to ease the anger that both sides felt."[110]

Twenty-five years after the programs began, some of the participants remain in positions of influence. Ipek Uzunoglu also noted that some of the more than 2,000 alumni of the programs were sprinkled throughout the UN-sponsored technical committees that carry on the work of the peace process. Others still believe in the peace process but realize that a new generation must find a way to pick up the torch. Katie Economidou still meets regularly with a group of Greek and Turkish Cypriot women activists from the earliest days of the movement, "but now we talk mainly about our lives and our children."[111]

"The Commission took on a battle that wasn't its to fight, a battle for which it was ridiculed and resisted by self-serving individuals, a battle that almost everyone believed could not be won," said Hadjittofi, "but I think it demonstrated that Senator Fulbright was right when he said that education is a slow moving but powerful force." On a personal level, Hadjittofi's role helped him fight his own demons – the demons of 1974 – that could have easily consumed him. "I could not feed the dragon because my children would suffer."[112] As Dr. Lennox Joseph observed, echoing Louise Diamond who would succumb to cancer in 2015, "forgiveness is a gift that we give to ourselves."[113]

THE LONG GOODBYE

By 1997, the Cyprus Fulbright Commission had grown into a $6 million annual program ($9.7 million in 2020 dollars) made possible by the continuing flow of CASP funds. It maintained three offices and a staff of 17 full- and part-time employees when one counted the newly created position of Bicommunal Coordinator, the outside accountant, the caretaker for the Fulbright Center in the Buffer Zone, and the two counselor positions reserved for the spouses of American officers at the U.S. Embassy. Its detailed annual program plans would run well over 100 pages, and its annual University Fairs were attracting 1,000 attendees.[1]

The International Institute of Education figures showed nearly 2,200 Cypriot students in the United States, the highest number of Cypriot students for any country outside of Greece and Turkey.[2] The Commission's program plans showed a number closer to 3,000, based on numbers from the RoC statistics office, but it was clear that the combined Fulbright and CASP programs and the work of the Commission counseling staff were the catalyst. If the Congress's intent was to get more Cypriot students to the United States and fewer to the Soviet Union and East Bloc, it had succeeded beyond expectations.

The Board in the late 1990s became embroiled in a conflict with the Embassy. From left to right, Lellos Demetriades, Executive Director Daniel Hadjittofi, Board Chairman Dr. Judith Baroody, Dr. Mehmet Tahiroglu and Ali Cagansoy.

"I liked the Cyprus Commission because it was energetic and it existed on an island that had political strife," said Ron Ungaro, who was head of the Fulbright Program at USIA during this period. "They were enthusiastic about what they were doing and it was worth the government's resources and worthy of Washington's attention. It was an elaborate program, but geared to the needs and in conjunction with our overall goals in Washington. It was a good staff."[3]

With the exception of the conflict resolution programs, which were unique to Cyprus, the Commission had largely stripped down to the basics – Fulbright and CASP grants, Short-Term Training (STT) grants, visiting scholar/consultants, and counseling. Gone were the teacher exchange program, Humphrey grants, and the USAID-funded grants for the American University in Beirut. The Commission was handling more than 10,000 counseling requests a year, which included helping grantees identify and apply to schools, assisting non-grantees in finding financial aid, and walking students through the various tests required for admission to U.S. universities. Commission counselors were finding upwards of $1 million in scholarship offers from American universities each year in this period, and Amideast was finding another $100,000 to $150,000 in grants just for the CASP scholars.[4] It was also about this time that the Commission decided to set up its own testing center in conjunction with the Educational Testing Service (think TOEFL, SAT, and GRE) and Sylvan Learning Systems, hoping fees might provide a bit of extra revenue.

However, it was during this period that relations between the Commission and the Embassy became strained, and members of the Board and Commission staff feared that the Commission and its mission would be irreparably damaged.

It started with Ambassador Brill's intervention to set up the Bicommunal Coordinator position and to gain control over some of the CASP funds for Embassy-run conflict resolution programs. A wary Board had approved this but, as noted in the previous chapter, the Commission staff felt there was not a lot of coordination and too much interference. When Ambassador Brill requested that $500,000 in residual funds be reallocated for Embassy-led programs and the Commission Board agreed with the caveat that a three-person subcommittee be established to approve the various programs, Dr. Chrysostomos Sofianos got in a not-so-subtle dig noting that "although a dictatorship is the most efficient form of government and democracy the most frustrating, there are other criteria that make the latter preferable."[5]

A year later, on September 18, 1998, Ambassador Brill again attended the Board meeting. He explained that the previous year the Commission had received $6 million in CASP funds, so this year it would be reduced to $4 million to average $5 million a year. Brill said it was not enough now that residuals had been spent and in light of the aggressive bicommunal track that he wanted to pursue, he explained he had worked with the UN to divert $1 million from the funds that normally went to the UN-OPS from USAID ($10 million annually) for one year and he proposed that the money be divvied up: $3 million for scholarships, $500,000 for bicommunal programs, $500,000 for STTs, and the remaining $1 million for administrative costs (USIA, Amideast, and the Commission itself). Several Board members pushed back, particularly Lellos Demetriades. They questioned the amount proposed for conflict resolution at the expense of scholarships – the proposed budget would mean 10 fewer CASP scholarships – and argued that the bicommunal programs would not be openly voted on by the Board but instead largely driven by the Embassy. Demetriades referred to the prestige that the Commission enjoyed and noted that the Commission and its Board were constituted as an independent entity. No Ambassador had ever come to a meeting and proposed how the Commission should allocate its funds.[6]

Before departing, the Ambassador made his argument for the bicommunal funds, even if it meant a reduction in scholarships: "This is the premier group of its kind on the island; who better to be involved with bicommunal activities than the premier bicommunal organization on the island? And it is the right thing to do, to try to bring people together to help them think of each other as neighbors, to help them find ways forward, who better to be associated with it than Fulbright?" He said he had worked hard to get the extra $1 million for the coming fiscal year expressly for bicommunal programs and the Board should appreciate that.[7]

A week later, Demetriades requested that a special meeting of the Board be called. He took the floor and said: "I have heard rumors – you know Cyprus is a small place – that Mr. Demetriades is angry with the Ambassador for something or other; Mr. Demetriades wants to be difficult....I think you know where these rumors are coming from...I resent this kind of thing. I have 30 years on this Commission and I have been on excellent terms with every Ambassador who has come to Cyprus. I have nothing whatsoever against this Ambassador or the Embassy.... But I don't want this committee to be a rubber stamp. I am 66 years old and I have been in public life 40 years and I have not been called a rubber stamp by anybody."[8]

Demetriades's main objection was that the list of proposed conflict resolution programs given to the Commission from the Embassy had little information beyond the titles. On the Turkish Cypriot side, the concerns were a little different. Dr. Mehmet Tahiroglu noted there were rumors in the Turkish Cypriot community that could tarnish the reputation of the Commission, and stressed that – from the Turkish Cypriot point of view – they were most concerned about a reduction in the number of scholarships.[9]

From Executive Director Daniel Hadjittofi's perch there was really no choice but to accept the Ambassador's proposal. "My intention was not to have poor relations with the Embassy. If you look at the record, I have never ever refused something that the Ambassador asked me to do," said Hadjittofi. "I was charged with running a Commission. If an Ambassador bypassed the authority of the Board, in this part of the world one understands that the Board members would feel humiliated."[10]

At that moment, however, there was – unbeknownst to the Board – another issue brewing that in two months' time would bring threats of legal action by the Board against the Embassy and would roil relations between the Board and the Embassy for the next year.

One of the American spouses working at the Commission came into Board Chairman Dr. Judith Baroody's office at the Embassy. Baroody explains what happened: "She had been hired at Fulbright. She became unhappy in Cyprus...including her marriage. Her life was falling apart. She became more and more hysterical. She came to my office and for two hours she complained about the way that Fulbright was being run. She was crying. She was implying that Daniel was using the staff to do personal work for him and she implied that he was misusing funds. It got to be very ugly. The Ambassador was concerned about this as was the Management Officer. She would go into a lot of people's offices and complain and cry. She could be very compelling."[11]

Members of the Embassy staff, including the Ambassador and Deputy Chief of Mission, began to pull aside members of the Commission staff and ask questions and a few days before the November 20 Board meeting, DCM Deborah Graze walked into a Commission staff meeting with Board Chairman Baroody and Hadjittofi present and implied that Hadjittofi was under investigation.

At that Board meeting, after regular business was completed, Dr. Sofianos took the floor and noted that he was the alternate to Lellos Demetriades, but that Demetriades, H.E. Alecos Shambos, the Permanent Secretary of the Ministry of Foreign Affairs, and Dr. Andreas Phylactou, the Permanent Secretary of the Ministry of Education, who were not present at the meeting – and appeared to be protesting by their absence – had approved his statement. Dr. Sofianos's central point was simple. Daniel Hadjittofi worked for the Board, not for the Embassy. If there were allegations, the Board needed to be informed and the Board would decide what was to be done. Dr. Sofianos referred to Article Nine of Hadjittofi's contract that stated the Board was the sole judge of his performance.

Dr. Sofianos demanded a written explanation of the allegations because Graze's explanation at the staff meeting was vague and inadequate. Later in the meeting, Hadjittofi revealed that he still did not know what the allegations were. Dr. Sofianos said the Board was perfectly capable of investigating any claims and that "nobody would cover for anybody." He added that he was unsure what Hadjittofi would do legally, but "we plan to take court action as members of the Board, or an interim injunction to stop this proceeding as being illegal."[12] Later Dr. Sofianos stated that they would take such action with the greatest reluctance because once there was a court filing the dispute would be out in the public and the Commission's reputation would be damaged, not to mention Hadjittofi's.

Thomas Young, the Administrative Officer at the Embassy and the Treasurer of the Commission, tried to offer a justification saying that if allegations came to their attention they had a responsibility to investigate as it involved taxpayer funds.[13] The second argument was that their examination of the allegations was in such an early stage that they had not yet been ready to bring it to the attention of the Board, which, as it turned out, was not particularly true. Dr. Sofianos did not buy either explanation. The only other Greek Cypriot Board member present, Ourania Schiza, also expressed outrage. American Board member Richard Haber, a businessman, did not appreciate being put in the awkward position of having to possibly respond to questions should something leak out when he had not been informed. "Well, I am sure you guys have got your reasons, but I think if you are going to run the organization that you have to have faith in your Board," said Haber, "The Board has always been discreet."[14]

Dr. Sofianos was frustrated that Young and Baroody did not seem to understand his main point: "You could have brought the matter before us and said 'look, there are these allegations and we want to discreetly investigate,' then we, all of us, would authorize you to do that, but under what authority? Is he an American citizen? He is not. Is he employed by the Embassy? He is not. We are not anti-American in saying this. I am trying to protect you, but you don't seem to get it. In order for the Fulbright Commission to be fruitful and to be able to promote good relations between our two countries there has to be at least the appearance of being independent." He quoted a Greek proverb (Μας έγραψες στα παλιά σου τα παπούτσια) that suggested that the American Embassy had shown contempt for the Board.[15]

Dr. Baroody, as Board chairman, tried to lower the temperature in the room and stated "I have great faith in the staff as you do, and in Daniel as you do. Regardless of any things going on outside of the Commission, I know they will continue to do their jobs and do them well. I have complete faith in Daniel to control his staff and to continue to work with the discipline and effectiveness that he has shown these past years."[16] The meeting ended with the issue largely unresolved.

What the American Officers did not tell the Board members was that a team from the United States Information Agency's Office of Inspector General would be on the ground in Nicosia to audit the Commission in less than three weeks. However, in the meantime, the Board members reached out to members of the Greek lobby in the U.S. to try to limit the scope of any investigation, and a letter from Senator Paul Sarbanes soon arrived at the Department of State asking that any investigation be conducted in a "fair and professional manner."[17] There was also some outreach using Hadjittofi's own network of contacts. Dr. Susan Lazar, a prominent psychologist who had served on First Lady Hillary Rodham Clinton's healthcare taskforce, wrote letters to Senator Sarbanes and to Clinton. These efforts appeared to cause the investigation to be reoriented to the Commission's administrative procedures and not centered solely on Hadjittofi.[18]

The OIG team started its fieldwork in Nicosia on December 7, 1998 and concluded with exit interviews on December 15. It was an intense nine days. "We heard the auditors were coming," said Anna Argyrou, who ran the conflict resolution programs. "They would ask me how I was hired…if it was Daniel or someone else? Why did I keep all these files? Strange questions. They spent a lot of time with Kyp [accountant Kyproula Kyriakidou]. They had been told that Daniel was not treating people fairly and that some were given an advantage. And that he was not handling the money properly. We were a really efficient organization and we were good at what we did."[19]

For her part, Kyriakidou was not worried. Eighty percent of the CASP funds were in accounts in the U.S., overseen by Amideast and were not subject to the audit. Kyriakidou dealt with the accounts for the rest. "Because of the external accountant and the auditors I was not afraid," she said. "I didn't have any doubts about the money. I knew that Daniel was worried along with the rest of the staff. We did not do anything wrong so I was not worried. I had to stay in the office and help these people when they came. They were in the office for more than a week and I stayed late into the night. They checked all the accounts, everything, because we followed the Embassy rules and I kept everything in the files. I was not nervous about the size of the budget. It became routine. It was all broken down in categories and if I needed help there was the outside accountant and Daniel was very supportive."[20]

At the exit interview, the OIG team delivered its verdict: "The audit disclosed that the Commission adequately accounted for Federal funds. The Commission had supporting ledgers that contained sufficient detail to support receipts and expenditures. To further enhance accountability over Federal funds, the Commission contracted for annual audits of its traditional Fulbright and CASP operations."[21]

However, the Commission did not come away completely unscathed as the audit made 15 recommendations, calling on the Bureau of Educational and Cultural Affairs at the United States Information Agency to work with the Public Affairs Section of the Embassy to help the Commission tighten procedures. These included updating computer systems, personnel policies, and property inventories. Some of these changes had already been in the works for up to a year before the OIG team arrived.

The auditors also had a fundamental disagreement with both the Commission and the Embassy over the use of CASP funds for the Bicommunal Coordinator, for the funding of the Fulbright Center in the Buffer Zone (despite permission from USIA), the proposed use of $100,000 in CASP funds to create an Assistant Public Affairs Officer position at the Embassy that would, theoretically, provide oversight for the conflict resolution programs carried out by the Commission and Embassy, and the reserved positions at the Commission for American spouses. They did not feel the Commission had an adequate plan to spend residual funds despite the fact that the records showed that the residuals had been used to fund bicommunal programs and to boost the number of STTs to 60-65 grants a year. Yet most, if not all of these things, had been dictated to the Commission by the Embassy, which was not always reflected in the report. By the time the final report was issued 10 months later in September 1999, most – if not all – these issues had been resolved.

What was unexpected was that the OIG team would issue a second report that was critical of the Embassy. "The Office of Inspector General, Office of Audits, found that Embassy Nicosia's actions regarding the use of Economic Support Funds for bicommunal activities, despite the Embassy's best intentions, jeopardized the Commission's independence as a separate and distinct entity from the Embassy. This occurred primarily because the Embassy, in an effort to further U.S. diplomatic goals, took a leading role in the management of the Cyprus American Scholarship Program (CASP) funds. Embassy involvement increased tensions between the Embassy and the Cypriot Board members and offended both Greek and Turkish Cypriot Board members, including the Mayor of Nicosia, Lellos Demetriades, the Secretary of the Council of Ministers, Dr. Chrysotomos Sofianos, and the Director of Common Services for Education, Ali Cagansoy, all of whom we interviewed. OIG believes that the Bureau of Educational and Cultural Affairs, in coordination with the Bureau of European Affairs (EUR), the Embassy, and the Agency for International Development (AID), should restructure CASP funding and administrative procedures so that the Embassy could conduct bicommunal activities independent of the Commission, and ensure the Embassy relations with the Commission are consistent with the bilateral agreements with the Government of Cyprus."[22]

The OIG team wrote: "The Commission is well respected in both communities and is a principal contributor to promoting bicommunal activities. For these reasons, the Ambassador conducted bicommunal activities in the Commission's name, thereby reducing the appearance of any bias or misunderstanding of Embassy efforts. Further, the Ambassador recognized that the Commission had the experienced staff to administer these programs. The Ambassador's activism, however, was not free from criticism that it politicized these programs, but saw the possible damage to the Commission as a necessary risk given the high stakes of U.S. interests."[23]

For his part, Ambassador Brill rejected the findings of the second report and there was a disagreement between USIA and the Department of State. European Bureau Chief at USIA Brian Carlson argued that: "while every Ambassador would jump at the chance to augment a Mission's budget for policy goals, the CASP authorization was never meant for that purpose. To avert such usage, CASP expenditures are governed by a series of interagency agreements and require the concurrence of the Fulbright Board, precisely the controls which the Embassy has challenged by its greater involvement in the workings of the Board." He added: "Fulbright in Cyprus has operated with distinction since 1962 as an intrinsically bicommunal entity. To risk that tradition for immediate political gain is short-sighted at best." Of course, it was not just the redirecting of funds. Hadjittofi recalls receiving a phone call from Foreign Minister Ioannis Kasoulides, a former Fulbrighter, who asked Hadjittofi, "does your Ambassador want me to commit political suicide?" Hadjittofi had no idea what his friend was talking about. Kasoulides explained that he did not want to get crosswise with the Ambassador, but that Ambassador Brill had written letters to prominent political leaders on both sides of the dividing line, including Kasoulides's Turkish Cypriot counterpart, inviting them to meet off the island for a workshop. Brill invoked his title as honorary chairman of the Fulbright Commission, but did not inform Hadjittofi, the Board Chairman, or the Board.[24] Carlson noted the fact that the Cypriots on the Board had united against the Americans over several issues, which was undesirable.[25]

However, Assistant Secretary of State for European Affairs Marc Grossman wrote in response to the OIG report that "the draft report implies that the goal of achieving a negotiated end to the division of the island is an Embassy goal or a goal of the Ambassador. This impression is wrong. Resolving the Cyprus dispute is a top Administration priority. The Cyprus deadlock is a potential flash point for hostilities between NATO allies Greece and Turkey, blocks Turkey's further integration into Western Europe, and contributes to instability in the region. For those reasons, the overriding U.S. foreign policy goal in Cyprus is to achieve the reunification of the island through a negotiated settlement." Grossman argued that because of these interests the Embassy needed to play a "significant role" in determining how CASP funds were used and that the Embassy's role in overseeing bicommunal programs should not be reduced.[26]

USIA agreed to formalize the use of CASP funds for both the position of Bicommunal Coordinator and for the Assistant Public Affairs Officer (APAO) position, just months before USIA would disappear as an independent agency and its functions be incorporated into the State Department where State views would prevail. It would mean that the $5 million annual allocation for CASP that had been in place since 1982 would be reduced to $4.35 million in Fiscal Year 1999 and remain at that level for the next five years.[27]

The initial findings of the first report were shared with the Board orally at the February 5, 1999 Board meeting, but the second report remained only a rumor. Drs. Sofianos, Tahiroglu, and Phylactou expressed satisfaction with the audit, particularly because it focused on administrative procedures and not on an individual.[28] USIA was also satisfied. Roy Glover, who was the Fulbright program officer who covered Cyprus in Washington, noted that "the Board was furious and Daniel was very despondent about it, and rightly so, because he saw it as a challenge to his own integrity, as if he had done something wrong. However, it was clear to me that he was a professional and he was really, really good and loyal to the program and I certainly cheered when there was no problem at all. There were some small things, but I tried to make the case that this was Fulbright program money and that it was outside of Ambassador Brill's political purview. The feeling in the Fulbright office in Washington was that Daniel was a star."[29] From USIA's point of view what was then important was to clean up any loose ends and prepare the way for the arrival of a new Ambassador – Ambassador Michael Bandler – and a new Board Chairman, Walter Douglas, who would both arrive in the summer of 1999.

Still, at Board Chairman Baroody's last meeting on May 24, 1999, the issue of the not-yet issued OIG report and the aftermath of the events of the past eight months would not die. Board members asked that DCM Graze write a letter of apology to Executive Director Hadjittofi, something she ultimately refused to do. For his part, Hadjittofi asked that the past be set aside, that hatchets be buried, and that the Board and the Commission focus on the future. Dr. Baroody would write a brief letter on her way out the door that said: "On behalf of the Board of Directors of the Cyprus Fulbright Commission I hereby express regret to any and all individuals that may have been offended by the recent deliberations into the affairs of the Cyprus Fulbright Commission. This letter is written in line with the resolution of the Board at its special Board Meeting of May 24, 1999."[30] Baroody left Cyprus with some bitterness. Because she defended Hadjittofi to the Ambassador she did not receive the customary award at the end of her tour, which would do nothing to enhance her chances of promotion.

In August, Demetriades and Dr. Sofianos both wrote to Dr. Alan Schechter, the Chairman of the Board of Foreign Scholarships, decrying the reduction of $650,000 in the Commission budget, but pointing out that if the Embassy had the main responsibility for conflict resolution programs they would be seen as political and would have far less impact. Demetriades noted that "local bicommunal groups have expressed strong concerns about attending programs not under the aegis of Fulbright but under the aegis of the American Embassy, because of the real danger of being seen as agents of the U.S. State Department."[31]

When Douglas held his first Board meeting on September 21, 1999, Ambassador Bandler came to introduce himself to the Board. He noted that he had been briefed on the turmoil that had occurred over the previous year from every side and said that he hoped that the Commission could leave the past behind and focus on the future. He pledged that he would not micromanage the work of the Commission, and that he would do everything in his power to continue a fresh approach. As a mark of that independence, the Board resolved that the new Assistant Public Affairs Officer would not be allowed to attend Board meetings.

"The first Board meeting there was this attack on Brill," said Douglas. "So, the first thing I did was to institute some reforms. The first was to insulate it [the Commission] from political pressure from the Embassy or anywhere else. So, let's work by consensus. I think that reassured everyone. They were really tied into the Embassy administratively – retirement packages, health packages, so I broke them away from that. There is no reason you should be part of the Embassy, so then you are like employees. So, that was a bit of hardship. I remember I changed the vacation schedule...why are they taking American holidays? So they wanted the same number, so we added 4th of July and Thanksgiving to show the American connection. We made all these little changes to show that we were not so close to the Embassy. I am a big believer in an independent Fulbright Commission and it had been under attack."[32]

As the new millennium arrived, the $650,000 cut in CASP funds was going to reduce grants across the board. CASPs would fall to 50. STTs would be cut in half to 28. Ultimately, the conflict resolution programs would settle into about four a year, the most expensive being the summer camp for youths. The reduction in STT grants went down particularly badly with the Cypriot Planning Commission. The fully funded grants for up to three months training in the U.S. had become very useful and very popular.

Orcun Kamali, a professional football player in the Turkish Cypriot North for many years, had helped create a wheelchair basketball team. "I had a degree but did not know that much about wheelchair sports," said Kamali. "My STT was a one-month program and I worked with staff at

Orcun Kamali.

the University of Illinois, at the Wheelchair Sports Federation, and at the Roosevelt Rehabilitation Center in Atlanta. The quality was very good. I worked with coaches, made a lot of contacts that I still have today, so I think I got a good education and a vision about wheelchair basketball and all kinds of sports really."[33]

Kamali came back and coached the team in the North and as it got better it began to compete in Europe under the Turkish banner. Then they hosted some competitions, and that led to changes in Turkish Cypriot society. "There was no wheelchair lift at the airport. There were no parking spaces for the disabled or toilets for the disabled. Hotels did not have doors that allowed the passage of a wheelchair. All that had to change," noted Kamali. "We increased awareness."

"In about 2002, a young man came to me who had broken his back. He was very depressed. He had tried to kill himself. But after a year of playing basketball he decided to get a job and he got a job. Then he decided he wanted a family and so he married and he has had kids, all this because basketball helped him rediscover his life."[34]

Over the life of the Commission, it would grant 943 STTs. The largest number – 235 – went to individuals in the medical field with an additional 28 grants going to the Cyprus Institute of Neurology and Genetics (CING). The other large groups were in government – some 300 grants depending on what/how you counted, including 39 in information technology and 35 in agriculture and environment. Other major categories were education (161), business (88), law enforcement (40), and journalism (23). There was a hodgepodge of other specialties – architecture, air traffic control, town planning, antiquities, meteorology, engineering, and the fire service. Like scholarships, STTs were awarded to Greek Cypriots and Turkish Cypriots on a 4/1 ratio. As Hadjittofi observed, you learned a lot about a society from the applicants for the grants.

Dr. Eldem Albayrak would receive one of the last STTs in 2009. She had heard about them from colleagues who had applied in earlier years. She was seeking to learn more about forensic DNA, and with an STT she traveled to Texas to work in the Forensics Department at North Texas State University while she also attended classes there. She still maintains contacts with the people she worked with in the lab. That opportunity inspired her to seek a master's degree in forensics from the University of Florida on top of her first master's in molecular biology and genetics. "I am head of the molecular genetics lab at the Dr. Burhan Nalbantoglu State Hospital and I hope there will be more of a chance to do more forensic DNA work here, such as paternity testing, DNA analysis, STR analysis, etc."[35]

Dr. Antonis Jossif received one of the earlier STTs in 1992 to study fetal echocardiography. "Part of the training was at Children's Hospital in Boston, which was part of the Harvard Medical School, and part was at the SUNY Health Science Center in Syracuse, New York, where I trained in pediatric cardiology. It was a good experience. It met my expectations and gave me the opportunity to meet important colleagues." He continues to use those skills, and he encouraged colleagues to apply for STTs and several were successful.[36]

Dr. Panayiotis Hadjicostas ultimately received three STTs in 1993, 2004, and 2008. He had studied medicine in Greece, but then received a three-month grant to study at the Baylor College of Medicine in Texas. "It left me immensely impressed. The hospitals were very big in size, with state-of-the-art technology, and with highly advanced equipment. There I witnessed a very high standard of surgical practice with very well-known professionals. All the colleagues I worked with were very welcoming, the working environment was very friendly, warm, and educational. I felt that the U.S was tens of years ahead of Europe, to say the least, regarding surgical practice and patient care."

His STTs – at the Pittsburgh Transplant Institute at the University of Pittsburgh Medical Center; at the University of Colorado in Denver; and at Massachusetts General Hospital in Boston and the MD Anderson Cancer Center at the Houston Medical Center – focused on transplant techniques, particularly for the liver. "At that time I was a transplant surgeon in Cyprus and a staff member of the Paraskevaides Transplant Centre in Cyprus, which was the only center in the country," explained Dr. Hadjicostas. "At the time, the main procedures performed there were kidney transplants, and it was in our plan to start performing liver transplants, hence I found this as a great opportunity to enhance my skills and knowledge for this niche field."

"The training I received in the U.S via these STTs was beyond my expectations. There I observed very complicated and high-risk cases that in other centers or parts of the world would be considered as inoperable or palliative. I feel that during my time there, I witnessed patient care in a way that I did not even know existed." Hadjicostas maintains contacts with a large number of colleagues in the U.S. and they helped him to introduce new techniques in Cyprus. "We introduced and implemented new innovative techniques, most of them being performed for the first time in Cyprus, and managed to adopt these new methods as standard surgical practice, making the clinic up to date with the current surgical advances and latest evidence. For example, we managed to perform the first pancreatic resection for pancreatic cancer, the first 'bloodless' liver resection for cancer using energy devices such as RFA, the use of staplers in liver RFA destruction of tumors, open abdomen with secondary closure in severe and complex liver trauma and the early discharge of patient post-op." Of course, he encouraged other colleagues to take advantage of the same opportunities that the STTs had provided. Many did.[37]

Dr. Philippos Patsalis.

As noted, however, no organization benefited more from the STT program than the Cyprus Institute for Neurology and Genetics. Dr. Philippos Patsalis, who received his master's and Ph.D. degrees at the City University of New York, funded one of his four post-doctorates through an STT grant. It allowed him to study at NYU. His predecessor at CING initiated the relationship with Fulbright, and Patsalis pushed it hard when he became the Chief Executive and Medical Director. "I remember encouraging and sending people to get training in various fields at U.S. institutions. This was very good. These grants were very generous, very beneficial to the people of Cyprus," stressed Dr. Patsalis. "Well-educated scientists in Cyprus had the opportunity to go to various universities and hospitals to learn new technologies and new methodologies and experience how big centers in the U.S. do certain things and then transfer this knowledge to Cyprus and then beyond to the region. We had a lot of people from neighboring countries visiting us and learning from us. This training had a great impact on CING. It has a great impact because we had a unique opportunity provided by fully funded grants to go to the best places in the United States. Our scientists would go there, learn, make connections, create a network, and then bring it back in order to benefit the people of Cyprus. When the program ended, we did not have the means to do these kinds of programs financially or otherwise."[38] In 2011, Dr. Patsalis received a special award from Fulbright as a distinguished alumnus for his discovery of a non-invasive pre-natal test and the contribution it made to "maternal and fetal health." Today, this test is used all around the world.

After implementing the initial changes, Chairman Douglas had more alterations in mind. Under pressure from a dogmatic Washington, Douglas proposed to emphasize graduate over undergraduate CASP grants – two-year grants instead of four-year grants would stretch the dollars. Douglas argued it would enhance the prestige of Fulbright, but the Board would not have it. Particularly on the Turkish side, as almost all the grantees came from TMK and the availability of the CASP undergraduate grants compelled many Turkish Cypriots to enroll their children at TMK. Without that incentive many would go to Turkish-language schools and the quality of English in the community would deteriorate. That's something the American Embassy did not want to see because it would limit the number of people it could reach easily. In the end, undergraduate grants would remain, but were reduced by almost 50 percent. "I think we were the last program doing undergrad in the world but the Cypriot Board members were dug in – that is what we want to do," remembered Douglas. "Washington would push us but then we would say this is what the Board decided and I was fine with that."[39]

There were other pressures coming from Washington. Congressional staff delegations would come through and ask what CASP was doing to solve the Cyprus Problem. The implication was that if it was not helping to move toward that goal, then why was the U.S. spending the money? The Commission decided to fund an impact study. The Commission staff members, particularly Hadjittofi, were not all that pleased with the quality of the resulting product, but it did provide some ammunition. "Results of the Cyprus American Scholarship Program (CASP) Impact Study indicate that CASP alumni have risen to prominent positions primarily in the private sector. According to the study, CASP is clearly responsible for placing more than 1,000 highly talented, U.S.-educated young people in relatively high-level positions during a relatively short period of time. Self-reporting indicates that 73 percent of CASP alumni are in senior staff and management positions, 41 percent are decision-makers in their organizations, and 15 percent are already decision-makers for their country."[40] The study argued that CASP had helped tamp down the level of anti-Americanism on the island, and that the conflict resolution work funded by CASP dollars brought educated members of the two communities closer together. Hadjittofi even argued that CASP had contributed to a positive U.S. trade balance with Cyprus. He also pointed out that 93 percent of CASP funds were spent in the U.S. as tuition and fees and administrative costs.[41]

After January 2000, however, Greek Cypriot graduates of U.S. universities began to hit some obstacles in settling back into Cyprus. This was because the Cyprus Council for the Recognition of Higher Education

Qualifications, known by its Greek initials KYSATS, was established. Suddenly, Cypriots with degrees from U.S. universities who applied for government jobs, particularly secondary school teaching positions, found that their degrees were not accepted by KYSATS. The issue was both philosophical and parochial. KYSATS used the University of Cyprus or, if the university did not offer a particular degree, a Greek university as a benchmark. American universities, almost universally, believed in a liberal arts education. That meant that students would take a series of general education courses not in their major before concentrating on their majors and minors in the last several years of study. The University of Cyprus, like other European universities, particularly British, had students take the majority of their course work in their major. It was, from an American perspective, a narrower view of education.

Soon after KYSATS's founding, letters began to arrive at the Fulbright Commission from returning graduates who were being told that their degrees were not valid and they would be required to take additional courses – up to 10 for teachers – at the University of Cyprus. As Dr. Gregory Markides, the Director/Associate Dean of Enrollment Management at Intercollege wrote in an "urgent" letter to U.S. Ambassador Bandler in June 2001, there was a clear conflict of interest. The professors making the decisions at KYSATS also taught at the University of Cyprus and, according to Hadjittofi, had a very British point of view. Markides suggested these professors were using KYSATS to convince students that they were better off studying at UCY rather than an American university if they hoped to have a government position upon graduation.[42] In a February 12, 2002 letter from Executive Director Hadjittofi to Minister of Education Ouranios Ioannides, Hadjittofi called the decisions by KYSATS "haphazard" and noted that this was counterproductive since the University of Cyprus sought recognition for its graduates in the U.S.[43]

Some of the decisions by KYSATS did seem bizarre. A graduate of the medical schools at the University of Southern California and New York University was initially denied certification as a doctor because his American residency was three years rather than four. A graduate of the University of Kentucky in English Literature was asked to take five additional courses. When she pointed out that her transcript showed that she had already taken those courses in America, the KYSATS Board agreed, but told her to take five other courses, one of which was, insultingly, Introduction to English Grammar. A graduate of Florida State University with a degree in mathematics and a 3.8 GPA secured a job at the American Academy of Larnaca as a math teacher but KYSATS ruled that while she had earned a valid university degree it was not a degree in mathematics because she did not take as many math courses as math students did at the University of Cyprus. She lost her job. She wrote to the Commission: "I would like the Commission to be aware of this situation, and the fact that degrees from accredited American universities are not being accepted here in Cyprus. The aim of the Commission as I recall is to promote education in Cyprus by spending thousands of pounds on Cypriot citizens. It is a shame such a noble cause is not fulfilled."[44]

What the Commission asked was that the University of Cyprus not be used as a benchmark but instead, a degree be accepted as long as it was from an institution accredited by one of the six regional accrediting bodies in the U.S. or one of the subject specific accrediting bodies. KYSATS would not budge and said the issue could not be solved procedurally. It suggested that the U.S. and Cyprus sign an "Intercountry Educational Agreement." Yet over the next decade, despite occasional efforts by the American Ambassador, who even approached the Foreign Minister and President about the issue, it was not resolved. As the years went on, however, several factors reduced the number of cases. First, more American universities were added to the KYSATS list of accredited universities, a list that had been woefully small in the early years. Second, Hadjittofi was able to work with one of the KYSATS Directors, Marios Antoniades, to get cases resolved. "Marios told me what to write to get it to the Board to be approved." Finally, Hadjittofi noted that "throughout the civil service and at the universities you will find many of our scholars. Those that pushed on and earned their Ph.Ds. in America have all been hired at the universities and in the ministries in positions of influence."[45]

Harriet Fulbright (left), the widow of the late Senator J. William Fulbright, came to Cyprus for the Commissions 40th anniversary and was greeted by Ambassador Michael Bandler.

One of the Turkish Cypriot CASP scholars had dreams of leaving Cyprus and seeing the world. Gulsen Oztoprak was born in Canada and lived in Saudi Arabia because of the work of her engineer father, but returned to Cyprus in eighth grade and went to TMK. She earned a CASP and studied business at the University of North Carolina. She remembers the interview at the Commission was nerve-wracking and she thought Hadjittofi was intimidating: "He looked like a tough guy." Upon graduation, she tried a job in a Turkish bank but it did not feel right and she returned to Cyprus, where she taught English at Eastern Mediterranean University. Her grandfather saw a notice that the Fulbright Commission was looking for a Turkish Cypriot counselor and clipped it out and sent it to her while she was on her honeymoon. "I applied because I had benefitted so much from the opportunity and just wanted to help other students," said Oztoprak. "I was teaching at that point, but this just seemed so much more interesting." She joined in October 2001. She notes that as the years went on, the number of Turkish Cypriot applicants for scholarships dwindled. "It is a different demographic. It is expensive to study in the States and the application process is tedious. But we got students who were the children of alumni or risk-takers. As time went on the U.S. as an educational destination was less and less on the radars of the top Turkish Cypriot students."[46]

However, it was not just the Turkish Cypriot students. According to IIE figures, the number of Cypriot students studying in the U.S. hit a peak in the 2000-01 academic year at 2,217. By 2003-04, it fell to 1,582, and then, two years later, to 1,111 and by the end of the decade 470, similar to the number that existed just before the CASP was established in 1982.[47] It was not just because of a reduction in CASP grants. Many students found post-9/11 America less welcoming, more wary and paranoid. That was certainly true for the Muslim Turkish Cypriots. The University of Cyprus and Eastern Mediterranean University were growing and establishing themselves as viable alternatives to study in Greece, Turkey, the U.K. or America. They were joined by a growing list of universities in both communities. Soon, EU membership would offer wider opportunities and Turkey greatly expanded the number of grants it offered to Turkish Cypriot students. There was also an increasing number of Cypriots who did not want to be bound by the J-1 visa requirement to return to Cyprus for two years. If opportunities presented themselves, these very bright students wanted to seize them. Finally, the cost of a college education in the U.S. exploded. Over the first two decades of the new millennium, tuition, room and board, and fees at private universities grew 144 percent and 171 percent at public universities.[48] The Fulbright Commission's grants could not keep pace.

The year 2002 should have been a time when the Commission regained some momentum.   In the summer of that year, 800 alumni and dignitaries gathered at a reception for the 40th anniversary of the Commission and Harriett Fulbright, the widow of the late Senator, came to Cyprus to speak on the occasion.   She was feted at the Presidential Palace by President Clerides, whose administration had steadily increased the annual contribution from the RoC to the Fulbright Commission with a large push from Board member Dr. Sofianos, who was President of the Council of Ministers during this time.   The RoC contribution would peak at $600,000 in 2002, with 80 percent of that contribution still going into an endowment that had grown to nearly $4 million.   Then, in April 2003 the checkpoints opened and there was renewed momentum under UN Secretary General Kofi Annan for a settlement of the Cyprus Problem.   Could the Fulbright Commission, building on its conflict resolution work, play a role?

In the summer of 2002, a new team arrived in Nicosia – Ambassador Michael Klosson and Public Affairs Officer and Board Chairman Craig Kuehl.   Kuehl believed that the $15 million earmark, and thus the CASP program, was going to continue, though as Ambassador Klosson pointed out, "in the post-9/11 world, given the budgetary demands, that money should have disappeared in a nanosecond."[49]   When the checkpoints opened, the Fulbright Board held a special meeting to discuss how the Commission's role might change and if there was something it could do to foster cooperation between the two communities.   Ambassador Klosson thought ties that had been established by the Commission between professionals – for example, doctors and business leaders – held possibilities.   The Commission formed two subcommittees, one on education and one on federalism to kick around ideas.   At the same time, they encouraged the alumni to form a bicommunal association now that travel back and forth was possible.   Through the years hopes for a robust alumni association would rise and then crash on the issue of how money would be handled – if the association was registered in the Greek Cypriot South, the Turkish Cypriots would not participate, and vice versa.

The following autumn, Lellos Demetriades presented a one-page proposal for the establishment of a Greco-Turkish institute funded by the Commission to research issues pertaining to Greek-Turkish relations. Years earlier, in addition to Congressional ideas to fund a bicommunal university, Special Cyprus Coordinator Ambassador Nelson Ledsky, early in the Clinton Administration, had kicked around with Hadjittofi the idea of a Fulbright University in the Buffer Zone. "President Vassiliou was opposed because the University of Cyprus was just getting off the ground and he did not want the competition. Ledsky suggested the number $70 million to support such a venture," said Hadjittofi.[50] This idea, however, never went past the talking stage. Now, the Commission was looking for ways to create and fund some sort of permanent bicommunal institution, although any such efforts were soon overtaken by events – specifically the negotiation of the Annan Plan and the dual referenda. The political blowback after the vote by the Papadopoulos administration was largely focused on the American Embassy, but the Fulbright Commission would not be spared.

At the December 12, 2003 Board meeting, it was announced that the Congress had decided, for the first time since the late 1970s, to reduce its allocation to Cyprus from $15 million to $13.5 million after President Bush ordered that all federal department budgets should be reduced by 0.3 percent. A fight over who would take the bulk of the reduction ensued. At the Board meeting Kuehl said he thought the Ambassador's recommendation as to how the cuts would be apportioned would be decisive and that he would fight hard to preserve the CASP allocation and make the cuts fair. He also noted that they would have to overcome certain criticisms of CASP – that Turkish Cypriots do not return to Cyprus and that there are Greek Cypriot recipients who come from families wealthy enough to send their children on their own. The Turkish Cypriot Board members pushed back on the first, while Hadjittofi pushed back on the second, noting that there was an income criteria for the grants but that it was not within the Commission's power to make judgments about falsified tax statements.[51]

"I never looked at the actual Congressional language [concerning the Economic Support Funds]," said Ambassador Klosson 15 years later. "I just thought of it as funds that supported our activities and helped build bridges across the two communities…for me it was all together. I did not have the idea that you got a bigger bang for your buck with the scholarship money. That was not my thinking."[52]

"Ambassador Klosson had two strong-willed advisors who were locally engaged Americans arguing that the scholarships were not valuable and should not be sacrosanct as a priority. Yes, Kim Foukaris and Elizabeth Kassinis," remembered Kuehl. "And they were very articulate and persuasive and it was me against them and they had been there a long time. I knew the Congressional language and I am pretty sure I would have used it in one of the numerous meetings that we had. We had a bicommunal taskforce meeting and we would have the same argument over and over again. I was in favor of the scholarships and the kind of bicommunal programs that we ran, which were softer diplomacy in nature versus the kinds of bicommunal programs that they ran, which were more political."[53] This was a fight that would continue as long as the ESF continued to flow from Washington and each reduction would intensify that fight.

However, even as Cyprus moved closer to the Annan Plan vote, the Fulbright Commission Board was unable to meet because the Papadopoulos administration would not submit a list of Board members, as was done each new year. The rumor was that President Papadopoulos did not like the idea of appointing the Turkish Cypriot Board members, something that had been done by every other President of the Republic of Cyprus. There was a push from the American Embassy and Kuehl and Hadjittofi made decisions as necessary to keep things moving, but it was not until the end of March that the Board members were officially appointed. And when those names arrived, two were conspicuous by their absence – Lellos Demetriades and Dr. Chrysostomos Sofianos. In an act of political retribution, Papadopoulos removed them from the Board. Demetriades had served some 40 years and Sofianos 14. But more than their longevity, they had been the dominant force on the Board among the Cypriots, pushing the Commission into conflict resolution work and fighting for the Board's and the Commission's independence.

At the April 2, 2004 meeting – the first of the new year – Demetriades was accorded the privilege of addressing the new Board members, given his years of service. He was introduced with the words "as a distinguished ex-Board member you are invited to address the Board." Demetriades thanked the Board members and noted that that sentence was the first acknowledgement from anyone that his tenure on the Board had ended. "After so many years, more or less 40, of serving on the Fulbright Board the Republic of Cyprus did not have the decency to notify me of the end of my tenure to the Fulbright Board and the courtesy to thank me for my 40 years of service. I find this unacceptable," said Demetriades. Whatever bitterness he felt, Demetriades took the high road. "I am moved to read the words of Senator Fulbright – the aim of the Fulbright program is to bring a little more knowledge, a little more reason, and a little more compassion in world affairs so that people can live in peace and freedom. Whatever is happening in the rest of the world, the Cyprus Fulbright Commission has fulfilled all three of these objectives, and in particular the last one." He spoke more about the mission of the Commission, and then Dr. Mehmet Tahiroglu, as the senior Turkish Cypriot on the Board and now the longest-serving member, rose to praise Demetriades's contribution to the Board, his sensitivity to both communities, and his relentless efforts to preserve the integrity of the Commission. He said he would cherish their personal friendship. Hadjittofi joined the praise of his friends, but understood he had just lost his two most important confidants.[54]

Years later, Dr. Sofianos noted that many thought that the Commission was "radical" but "I was convinced about the quality of education in the United States. I consider this America's highest achievement – its system of higher education. It was not just the degrees that Cypriot students brought back, but the attitudes they achieved in the United States. How to think about things in front of you, to use logic, reason, to argue, to have respect, to express an opinion without oppression."[55]

Evie Sofianou.

Dr. Sofianos, who had not asked to serve on the Board, but had done so because he thought it was a way to give back, would leave one other exceptionally tragic legacy. His daughter Evie was a CASP scholar who had attended Georgetown and then went on to Cambridge for her Ph.D. in economics. "Evie was doing cutting edge research. She had an amazing collection of traits," said Hadjittofi. "She was intelligent, humble, dynamic, beautiful, and a natural born leader." Tragically, during her studies at Cambridge, she was diagnosed with cancer and passed all too quickly at age 26. Her parents founded the Evie Sofianou Foundation in her honor in 1994, and at the March 1995 Board meeting, the Commission decided to create a pair of supplemental scholarships in her name that would be given to the top Greek and Turkish Cypriot CASP grantees each year. "Lellos [Demetriades] got up at the Board meeting and said that there was really nothing to discuss. We were going to do this," said Hadjittofi, who spoke at Evie's funeral. "There were so many of her friends there from all over the world and they were all in tears," remembered Hadjittofi. "She was the kind of person who had helped so many of her friends through difficult times. They all said they did not know what they were going to do without her."[56]

As the years went on, the Embassy teamed up with the Commission to host an event to raise money for the scholarships and the Foundation, often a film premier in Cyprus. It was one of the few instances of alumni gathering to raise scholarship money for the program. However, that connection ended when the CASP program ended.

Three weeks after the April 2, 2004 Board meeting, the Annan Plan vote was held, and the rejection of the plan by Greek Cypriots would reverberate for some time. At the next Board meeting – on May 5 – members of the Board were still trying to figure out what it all meant. However, one thing was certain; there would be less money for CASP. It was argued that the Embassy would need more money for the post-Annan Plan vote transition and so the portion going to CASP would be cut from $4.3 to $2.8 million. In the end, given the rejection, that number would end up at $3.3 million. There was also new pressure from Washington to increase the grant amount of traditional Fulbright grants. The Commission, and Hadjittofi in particular, had always argued for smaller grants so that there could be more scholarship opportunities, relying on American universities to provide generous packages. That had generally worked. But there had been an increasing number of students who rejected the small grants in order to avoid the J-1 visa requirement that they return to Cyprus for two years. Washington argued that this situation was damaging the prestige of Fulbright in Cyprus. Kuehl and Hadjittofi said they would freeze salaries and cost of living adjustments for the staff, even as costs were rising in the wake of Cyprus's accession to the EU. They would negotiate lower administrative costs from Amideast and the Bureau of Educational and Cultural Affairs at State, and they would fold a much smaller STT program into the conflict resolution budget, issuing a handful of tandem grants. Six weeks later, at the June 18 Board meeting, the Board agreed to devote more of the contribution of the Government of Cyprus to traditional Fulbright grants, but to reject Washington's call for $18,000 annual grants, which would have reduced the total number of grants to six. Instead, they would set the size of the grants at $6,000 a year, which would allow for 12 undergraduate and six graduate Fulbright grants. The decision would be reviewed the following year.[57]

The rest of the June 18 meeting was business as usual – the Board approved the Commission's role in helping to administer a Department of Education program, co-hosted that summer by Cyprus and Turkey and by Greece and Cyprus the following summer; it approved the creation of a special program for Eastern Mediterranean University's new Rector, Dr. Halil Güven, a former Fulbright scholar (1979 – Mechanical Engineering/Mississippi State U.) in educational administration; the Board agreed to fund a Senior Specialist grant for Ms. Constantia Constantinou, the Chief Librarian at the State University of New York Maritime College, to work with staff at the University of Cyprus; they discussed how to bring a senior scholar from the U.S. Geological Survey to Cyprus; noted that several American Fulbright scholars and students had completed their programs in Cyprus; welcomed a new group of Americans; reported on ongoing bicommunal programs, including the orientation for the youth summer camps; and, at the traditional lunch held after every Board meeting, U.S. graduate student Sarah Harris, from the University of Texas and affiliated with CAARI, gave a presentation on her research.[58]

Ambassador Sotos Zackheos, the Permanent Secretary of the Ministry of Foreign Affairs, was not present at that meeting, so when the Board next met on September 2, he raised several issues. First, he was unhappy that the STT program had been reduced, judging it to be a particularly valuable program for the Cypriots. He charged that the Board had "rubber stamped" the decision too passively, like a "Soviet style" body. Second, he vehemently protested the directive from Washington that CASP grants were now to be equalized between Greek Cypriots and Turkish Cypriots. In the proposed program, Greek Cypriots would receive 17 scholarships and Turkish Cypriots 16 scholarships instead of the four-to-one ratio based on population that had always been used. Ambassador Zackheos charged that 57 percent of the budget would go to Turkish Cypriots and just 43 percent to Greek Cypriots. He charged that the U.S. Government was "punishing" Greek Cypriots for their "no" vote on the Annan Plan. One of the arguments made by Greek Cypriots opposed to the Annan Plan was that the Turkish Cypriots' economic development was too low and that the Greek Cypriots could not afford to absorb this poorer part of Cyprus as West Germany had done during the reunification with East Germany. As a result, the U.S. Congress had, in the wake of the referenda result, voted a special allocation of about $20 million for economic development in the Turkish Cypriot North and to ease their isolation. Kuehl argued that the Greek Cypriots were not being punished and that the Commission had no choice but to follow Washington's directive, which was all of a piece to foster Turkish Cypriot economic development. Ambassador Zackheos did not buy it. Several Board members expressed discomfort that the discussion had a political tone, which the Commission had always avoided.[59] "My impression is that it [the equalizing of scholarship numbers] was a reaction to the vote," said Kuehl. "Washington told us to change the ratio of the scholarships because that is what we told them we wanted to do."[60]

In the subsequent Board meetings that autumn, things grew more heated and uglier. Kuehl lamented the fact that he had served at the UN and in Geneva at the same time that Ambassador Zackheos was there and that they had developed a very cordial relationship. "But he was just carrying out the policy of the government," said Kuehl. For Hadjittofi, it was even more perplexing and disheartening. Zackheos was a former Ful-bright scholar who had attended Stanford and he thought he was a friend, but now they argued. "Zackheos decided that Fulbright had outlived its usefulness on Cyprus," said Hadjittofi. This was not about the education of Cypriots; this was about pure politics. "Papadopoulos felt he was not respected by the Americans and he took his anger out on the Commis-sion," said Dr. Sofianos years later.[61]

Ambassador Zackheos was not at the October 14 meeting, but alternate Demetris Hadjiargyrou picked up the baton. He inquired, and then com-plained about, the high administrative fees that the Department of State and Amideast charged for the CASP program. The 7.5 percent charge that the State Department took to transfer the money from USAID to the Fulbright Commission amounted to just over $300,000 when transferring $4.3 million. Amideast's were higher at more than $450,000. Kuehl noted they had protested many times, but the State Department would not yield. Hadjiargyrou said these costs raised questions as to the "aid" that was given to Cyprus. He added ominously that it raised questions whether it was worth having it and wanted to avert a negative decision by the RoC con-cerning aid to Cyprus. Hadjiargyrou also questioned the $269,000 in the program proposal allocated for bicommunal programs. He said he did not have anything against such programs, but thought scholarships should have the higher priority. Kuehl explained the Congressional mandate. Then Hadjiargyrou asked about the RoC contribution and how it was used, implying that there were "problems" that needed to be dealt with to prevent the RoC from "withdrawing its contribution."[62]

At the following meeting, on December 3, Hadjiargyrou began the discussion on the Commission's program plan by stating that the CASP program and the overall Fulbright program in Cyprus were under review by the RoC and that these discussions were an internal matter. He said the range of options ranged from "one extreme to the other" but that the question of whether or not there would be a Fulbright program in Cyprus the following year was dependent on how the government's questions about CASP would be solved. The first item discussed was finding a way to continue the STT program. On this, Greek Cypriots and Turkish Cypriots were united. However, the Greek Cypriots rejected various pro-posed compromises for the STT program and the issue had to be set aside for the next meeting. These were decisions that had always been made by the Board in times when larger budgets made such decisions easy. Now, it was a question that would be placed before the Council of Ministers.[63]

However, that next Board meeting would not take place until July 5,

2005 as the Papadopoulos government showed its displeasure with the situation surrounding the CASP program – in particular the ratios – and the Fulbright program in general.   Ambassador Klosson had written to Foreign Minister George Iacovou in December asking that the Board members be appointed early in the new year and followed that up with a second letter on January 27th.   He raised it again in a February 25th face-to-face meeting and followed that up with a letter to Iacovou on March 10.   He urged Iacovou to use his influence to "bring these matters to an early and successful conclusion so that the CFC and CASP can resume smooth functioning in full cooperation with the Government of Cyprus." He noted that an agreement on the future of the STT program had been reached with the Planning Commission but that they were already very much behind schedule in choosing American scholars and students who would come to Cyprus.   He also urged the RoC to renew its annual contribution.   That did not happen as the government chose to give nothing for that year, and it did not push the Papadopoulos administration to appoint Board members any more quickly.[64]   At the July 5th meeting, however, things largely settled into an uneasy truce and it was agreed that the falling number of CASPs would be awarded on the basis of merit and need.   At the end of the meeting, Kuehl bade farewell to the Board as he would depart Cyprus just days later for his next assignment.   A new Public Affairs Officer and Board Chairman, Tom Miller, and a new Ambassador Ronald Schlicher would soon arrive.[65]

Miller did not waste time proposing significant changes.   At his first Board meeting in September 2005 he noted the significant drop-off in CASP applications, from more than 100 Greek Cypriot undergraduate applicants a decade ago to just seven that past summer.   There had been a total of 43 CASP applications – seven Greek Cypriot undergraduate and 16 graduate versus 16 Turkish Cypriot undergraduate and four graduate. Moreover, the dropout rate for the less generous Fulbright grants had increased to 60 percent.   The growing number of universities in Cyprus, the availability of Erasmus grants now that Cyprus was in the European Union, free university education in Greece, an increasing number of scholarship opportunities in Turkey, the fact that an undergraduate degree in the UK was three years as opposed to four in the U.S., the cost of tests and application fees for U.S. universities, and rumors that the U.S. was a less welcoming place post-9/11 all were factors in the decline.   The fact that only 250 students and parents attended that year's university fair was a strong indication of the waning interest in U.S. education.   The Board held wide-ranging discussions and at the next meeting in November it was decided that CASP would continue to be both an undergraduate and graduate program – since there seemed to be more interest from the Cypriots in graduate education – and that there would no longer be full and partial grants, only full grants of $25,000 a year – $100,000 total for undergraduates and $50,000 total for graduate studies. The hope was that it would attract more applicants. As for Fulbright, only graduate scholarships would be given and they, too, would be $25,000 a year, while the number of grants, given the shrinking budget, would be reduced to a total of five. It is notable that there were, in comparison, 91 applications for STTs and 24 grants were awarded to 17 Greek Cypriots and seven Turkish Cypriots.[66]

Over the next couple of years, the budget picture was volatile. First the Commission was informed that there would be a significant cut and then it learned that extra money was found. During Miller's three years the CASP budgets were $3.3 million, $3.2 million and then $4.4 million. When Miller left, it dropped to $2.2 million. That said, Miller felt it was important to introduce a new program: English Language Teaching Assistants (ELTA). These were young Americans with master's degrees in teaching English as a foreign language who would be assigned to universities and secondary schools to assist with the teaching of English. Both the Embassy and the Commission had been concerned for years about the declining standard of English in Cyprus and this was a particular interest of Miller's, who had begun his Foreign Service career as an English Language Teaching Specialist.

"I was an English Language Officer at one time and I thought that English teaching was the thin edge of the wedge...everyone wants to have English, no matter their politics," explained Miller. "When you are teaching English it is student-centered so you empower the students and promote critical thinking because the basis of democracy is critical thinking and you can do all these things through English teaching. They end up reading about America and reading about American politics in their studies because you have to understand the culture and the institutions to understand the context. It is important because if you study any foreign language you are most likely going to end up more sympathetic to the culture that that language comes from. It just opens so many doors. Through the English language fellows we developed so many contacts."[67]

Not everyone was on board. One of the Greek Cypriot Board members did not want to see anything that reduced the number of scholarships or STT grants, but Miller was able to prevail. As he said: "It was money well spent. It was like a mini-Peace Corps. Generally, the positives outweighed the negatives."[68] It is a program that continues to this day.

Parallel to the ELTAs was a push to try to convince Cypriot universities to introduce programs in American Studies. The Embassy was also trying to set up what were called "American Corners" in several universities in both communities. The Corners were essentially a room with a collection of materials, increasingly digital, about the U.S. The American Library on Nechrou had been closed during Douglas's time as Board Chairman when USIA ceased to be a separate agency and all U.S. personnel moved into the new American Embassy on Metochiou. The Corners were supposed to try to make up for the closing of the library, to a small degree. One of the American scholars who came to Cyprus early in Miller's term to teach American Studies was Dr. Peter Rutkoff.

Rutkoff was standing in front of the Baseball Hall of Fame in Cooperstown, New York in 2004 when he received an email from Fulbright. They were looking for someone for whom "boundary crossing" was important. Dr. Rutkoff, with a sterling reputation as an American Studies professor, had studied many cultures and thought it sounded interesting, especially since he already had a sabbatical approved. That said, he admits he knew little about Cyprus – "I barely knew where it was." The turmoil at the Commission – the lack of a Board – delayed the process, but in the fall of 2005 he was on his way to Cyprus with his wife, D, also a professor of American Studies, to teach a course on American Studies for one semester in the English Department of the University of Cyprus.

His class was composed of 37 students, almost all young women, and at first all the Elenas and Irenes seemed so similar. At the end of the course, one of the students confessed "we took your course, some of us, because we wanted to keep an eye on the American." Dr. Rutkoff observed that some, apparently, expected him to deliver the party line at a time when the U.S. was not popular, accused by Greek Cypriots of meddling in the Annan Plan vote campaign. "When I taught them to sing 'We Shall Overcome' on the third day of class, they might have realized that I was not such a bad guy." The young women, in particular, threw themselves into the study of the American women's movement from the suffragettes to the feminists of the 1960s with great passion and understanding, which pleased Dr. Rutkoff to no end.

He also did a series of lectures at Eastern Mediterranean University in the Turkish Cypriot North, beginning with American jazz. There he found a diverse group of students that included "Africans, North Africans, Arabs, Turks, Turkish Cypriots with varied flavors of English." However, he soon learned to appreciate the diversity of his Greek Cypriot class – English and Greek parents, Greek and Palestinian, Russian and Cypriot,

Christian and Orthodox. Whichever side of the boundary, music was always an icebreaker.

Dr. Rutkoff and his wife, like so many American Fulbrighters before them, soon were drawn in by the warmth and hospitality of the Cypriot people on both sides of the divide as well as the beauty of the island, and the complexity of the culture and the politics. Two years later, D applied for the same job and they returned to Cyprus with Dr. Rutkoff as the trailing spouse. He threw himself into an oral history project. However, that was not the end. He and D organized more visits in 2011 and 2013. "It was hard to let go of the friendships we had made," he said. He praised the Fulbright Commission staff for their support and insights – "they were top notch" – that helped make the subsequent visits possible.

In the end, Dr. Rutkoff wrote a book – *Cyprus Portraits - 2005-2013*, which, with a keen eye for detail, recounted their journey – physical, intellectual, emotional, and political. It expanded a first, shorter book based on his initial visit. "The story that I was trying to figure out about this complicated place was worked out a bit better." So, what were the boundaries he crossed? "It is the literal boundary and the cultural boundary. I remember the first time that I went through the Ledra Palace crossing and it took my breath away because of how horrible it all looked but then we got to meet people and became friends with them and that was the human boundary crossing that enriched the whole spirit," said Dr. Rutkoff.[69]

While the Commission's program was still robust, particularly with a one-time infusion of CASP funds in fiscal year 2007, the financial pressures were growing. CASP funding was projected to drop to just over $2 million. The contribution for Fulbright proper, which had been as high as $400,000 in the 1980s, had fallen to $170,000. And the RoC contribution, which had peaked under the Clerides government at about $600,000 had been cut to a third of that. There came a point when a reduction in staff was inevitable and Hadjittofi made the difficult decision to let go the Commission's two longest-serving employees, Stella Zavallis and Hambis Koutlianos in the fall of 2006. Between the two of them, they had served 82 years. "The RIF was announced to me the same day I learned of my brother's death," said Zavallis. "I was devastated for my brother and disappointed by the RIF. My office was my second home and my second family for 41 years. It took me time to get over the shock."[70]

There were other pressures. Applications were continuing to fall and in January 2008, the RoC sent a diplomatic note to the Embassy informing it that it would no longer enforce the J-1 and J-2 home residency requirement for Cypriot CASP and Fulbright recipients. Amideast's Kate Archambeau had complained that after being quite strict in the early years, the GOC was handing out waivers "like candy," allowing the Cypriots to remain in the U.S., and contradicting the purpose of the program as a development tool. However, with EU membership giving Cypriots the right to work anywhere in the EU – particularly Greece and the U.K. – there was no way to keep track of these graduates anymore and, truth be told, the RoC was never insistent that Turkish Cypriots return. One student who was absolutely determined to stay in the U.S. was Margarita Constantinides Bradley, who had received a CASP to attend UC Berkeley in 1998 to study materials science and stayed to complete her Ph.D. She gives her parents credit for allowing her to dream big – to study at a top university in the United States and earn her doctorate. "I remember one of my father's classmates asking me why I didn't want to be like other girls and just be a teacher? He actually said that to me. Who says that? It was the environment," sighed Bradley.

However, the plan was always to be a professor, and then – mid-way through her Ph.D. – she had a crisis. If you are a professor, you are a researcher or a teacher. Suddenly, she did not want to do either. She could have worked as an engineer. That did not appeal either. She also received pressure from home. She had almost completed her Ph.D. and the University of Cyprus pushed hard for her to return and teach there. "I went for a visit and they showed me a lab and it was all new and it had the best labs and the best equipment but it was just sitting there because they did not have the people," said Bradley. "In the end, my heart was not there. I did not want to return."

The process to receive the visa waiver was fraught and the State Department rejected her request the first time but, by Bradley's own admission, she is stubborn. She asked her Congressman Nancy Pelosi to write a letter on her behalf arguing that Bradley could make more of a contribution in the United States. It worked. She is now working for her third tech company in the San Francisco Bay area – Google. "I really love my job at Google…it is a very values-driven company." She also married an American in 2011 and now has two children. "CASP was life-changing," said Bradley. "When I reflect on my life there were moments that were pivotal and that was one of them."[71]

Another Cypriot made his way to Google – on the other side of the country in New York – but Nektarios Paisios's path was far more unusual. Born prematurely, Paisios had lost his sight by age four. "If you are a child, you don't think about it…you create your life around your reality, you don't compare it to something else," said Paisios. With the strong sup-

Nektarios Paisos earned his Ph.D. and ended up with Google.

port of his parents he attended the English-language Falcon School. "My parents had high expectations for me."

Paisios went on to the University of Cyprus earning his bachelor's and master's degrees in computer science, and then Fulbright gave him a special opportunity. Emphasizing STEM (Science, Technology, Engineering and Math) education, Fulbright offered 25 special grants worldwide. The Commission pushed for Paisios. Anna Argyrou remembers sitting with Paisios reading the questions for the tests. "I was afraid I was mispronouncing the scientific terms, but Nektarios knew all the words," said Argyrou. "She was really good at reading...I don't remember her mispronouncing anything," grinned Paisios. The result was a full scholarship to pursue his Ph.D. at New York University.

"I finished in five years. The university was very helpful and found me a reader and computer software. The professors were understanding. I learned to appreciate the city and to move around," explained Paisios. With the financial crisis back in Cyprus and no opportunity there, Paisios received a pair of internships with Google and was able, with Google's help, to get a work visa and stay in the U.S. A J-1 waiver followed. "Fulbright was my ticket to the U.S. My impression is that in Cypriot society, Fulbright had a special place in people's hearts and minds," said Paisios.

"Now I work for Chrome Accessibility," said Paisios sitting in his office on 8th Avenue in the Chelsea Market area of the city. "It is really fulfilling because some of the things that I studied for my doctorate I can now apply to a product that is used by millions of people. I am sure many of those people have some sort of disability and I can try to make sure that the software works for these people and so that is really fulfilling. I am learning a lot here and working on software that is used by so many people and you get feedback from everywhere and that makes you learn a lot of different perspectives. If you only have five users in your circle you hear from just five people and their views might be similar to yours, but if you hear from millions of people you get a lot of perspectives."[72]

In the fall of 2008, a new Chairman came on board – Jim Ellickson-Brown – and an idea that had been lurking in the shadows for a decade appeared that it might provide a lifeline to the Commission. The Commission was only giving out four undergraduate grants and though it had funds for 16 graduate grants, there were only 10 because of a lack of applications. In the mid-1990s Hadjittofi and the head of the Planning Commission spoke with President Clerides and observed that Cyprus did not have a research foundation. Clerides offered 100,000 Cypriot Pounds, but Hadjittofi noted that would not do a lot. Washington, the Embassy, and the Board agreed that Hadjittofi could assume the position of honorary treasurer for a proposed Research Promotion Foundation (RPF), which remained largely talk. "Though," said Hadjittofi, "that pledged number reached 35 million Cypriot pounds, during the Papadopoulos administration." In the spring of 2008 the Board was assured that an agreement would be signed soon between RPF and the Commission. That agreement would provide substantial funds for scholarships to be administered by the Commission. But, in the fall of 2008 a more modest, but still substantial number of one million pounds ($2.2 million) was discussed. The Ambassador was on board and supportive. The Fulbright Commission would handle the administration – choosing the scholars for grants – and the RoC/RPF would provide the funding. "The Minister of Education was supporting it but he was undermined by the bureaucracy," said Hadjittofi. "Ultimately, the Commission was never involved beyond my position. But the foundation just involved itself with trivial matters."[73] The idea would linger and the Board would be updated, but eventually they were told that there was no money.

As the Commission approached its 50th anniversary one could argue that this was still an incredibly robust program relative to the population of the island, which was about 1.1 million in 2010. The Commission was still projecting $2 million a year in CASP funds for the foreseeable future. The RoC was contributing again and its full contribution was going toward scholarships. Fulbright money had settled into $170,000 a year and the Amideast fees had been greatly reduced to just $50,000 a year, given the decreased number of students it had to monitor. The Commission was receiving thousands of hits on its web site each month and was still conducting more than 10,000 counseling sessions in a calendar year. The University Fair, though down, still attracted 500 students with 20 universities represented. There was a full complement of quality U.S. scholars, such as Dr. Kimberly Anne Clausing of Reed College, who would go on to serve as a senior tax official in both the Obama and Biden administrations. Even when some Fulbrighters ultimately turned down their grants, it had a silver lining of sorts in that the residuals kept the STT and modest conflict resolution programs alive for another year. And the quality of the students had never been higher. The five Cypriot CASP grantees – two Greek Cypriots and three Turkish Cypriots – were headed to Cal Tech, MIT, Brandeis, and to American University. The Fulbrighters were similarly impressive – Dartmouth, NYU, the Pratt Institute, and Carnegie Mellon. Any Commission in the world would have been proud.

Still, Hadjittofi had a sense of foreboding. "Jim Ellickson Brown thought funds would continue...I knew they would not," he said. "You saw the darkness coming. What is my last act? I would offer the employees an average severance."[74] At the December 3, 2010 Board meeting a severance plan for Commission employees was presented to the Board. The rationale was "in the event the Commission needs to downsize because of the loss of a major funding stream such as CASP." Hadjittofi remembers a conversation with Ellickson-Brown and being asked to explore this contingency. Ellickson-Brown just remembers the item appearing on the agenda, with reference to a study that might have been conducted. What was presented to the Board was a severance plan for RIFed employees based on the model of a similar program at the Hellenic Bank. Benefits were based on final salary and years served. Included, too, was the projected cost of the program – $2.7 million – and it was stated clearly that the money would come from the endowment. The Board notes show the discussion was limited to an explanation of the mechanics. Then, a single entry: "The request for the retirement plan for the Commission employees was approved."[75] It would have been a unanimous vote with 12 of the 16 primary and alternate Board members present.

It was a decision that would, as the Commission faced severe downsizing just two years later, roil relations with the Embassy once again. There is an argument to be made that Hadjittofi should never have taken on the task or been asked to take on the task of presenting such a plan because the conflict of interest was absolutely clear. Potentially, Hadjittofi would benefit from the severance plan just as much as any other employee. Though as Hadjittofi said years later: "I guess I always thought I would be the last man standing."[76]

And yet, from the Board members' point of view they trusted Hadjittofi and believed they were doing the right thing. "My thoughts.... these people have spent a lot of years of their lives on this Commission and, yes, let's do the right thing for these people who have devoted so much of their lives to the Commission. It was more of a feeling," said Ellickson-Brown.[77] "I remember that I was supportive," said American Board member Chris Schabel. "It did not look like it [the Commission] was going to continue and we needed to do the best we could by the employees. People had an inkling of what was going to happen. We had the power to make decisions that impacted the employees' financial situation. I don't think I had any issues with it."[78] At the same meeting the Board stressed that it wanted to have a comprehensive discussion concerning both the CASP and Fulbright programs at the next Board meeting. That, however, would not occur for another seven months.

The government of Demetris Christofias was never going to be friendly toward an American institution given his party's communist/leftist proclivities. So it took half a year to name a Board despite prodding. At the June 3, 2011 Board meeting the RoC representatives did, however, express some concern that CASP might actually be eliminated, though the RoC's actions in Washington would make sure that is exactly what happened.

My first Board meeting as Chairman was September 23, 2011, and I did not bring good news. For the fiscal year that would begin in a week's time, there would be $8.5 million in Economic Support Funds. It would be apportioned by an eight-to-three ratio with the bulk of the funds going to the UNDP and the smaller portion divided between CASP and the Bicommunal Support Program (BSP). However, the following year the total amount of ESF would fall to $3.5 million; after that it was unknown, but zero was not out of the realm of possibility. If nothing else, the staff of 11 would face a significant reduction in force. Could the 8/3 ratio be changed? That was an Ambassadorial decision, but there was no new Ambassador on the horizon and the USAID staffers at the Embassy could be counted on to resist that mightily. With the 50th anniversary of the Commission coming in 2012, perhaps it could be leveraged for a fund-raising drive. Then there was the discovery of oil and natural gas in Cyprus's Exclusive Economic Zone (EEZ). Wouldn't Cyprus need more petroleum engineers? Perhaps the RoC could be persuaded to give more or perhaps Noble Energy of Houston, Texas, which was carrying out the exploratory work in the EEZ, might support a program of scholarships – but that would be the kind of approach that only someone at the level of the Ambassador could make.[79]

Just prior to that meeting, the selection panels had met to choose that year's CASP and Fulbright scholars – there were four CASP grantees, each receiving $100,000 to cover their four undergraduate years and eight Fulbrighters each receiving $50,000 for their two graduate years. They would be the last four undergraduate CASP grants the Commission would give.

Eliana Hadjiandreou received one, which took her to tiny Clark University in Wooster, Massachusetts where she studied psychology. She had

participated in one of the Commission's conflict resolution youth camps at 16 and that "made the idea of studying in the U.S. more real." A Ph.D. was always the goal and she followed the professor she wanted to work with – Dr. Daryl Cameron – to Penn State University where she is nearing completion of her doctorate. "The U.S. invests a lot in research and that is what pushes academia forward...anywhere you go in the world a U.S. degree is seen as something that is worth more than from anywhere else," said Hadjiandreou cradling a cup of coffee in a Penn State campus café. What the degree will lead to is a great – and somewhat stressful – quandary. Cyprus? "The opportunities in Cyprus are still very few."[80]

Doruk Unzunoglu also ended up in Wooster, but at the nearby Wooster Polytechnic Institute, to study computer science. There was culture shock. "I think the biggest game-changer was seeing how driven and how motivated most American students were...compared to the general group of Cypriots...where things are more relaxed," noted Uzunoglu. "But in the U.S. it just seemed that everyone was trying their best and trying to be very successful and that motivated me a lot." Unzunoglu moved on to the U.K., earning his master's degree in London. He has remained to work as

From top to bottom: Pinar Barlas, Doruk Uzunoglu, Aris Antoniades, and Eliana Hadjiandreou, the final four CASP grantees.

a programmer. "I could go back to Cyprus, but I don't think that I can in the early stages of my career because there is not that kind of opportunity in Cyprus given my skillset."[81]

Oddly enough, Pinar Barlas also ended up in Wooster at Clark University, which was particularly generous in giving grants to Cypriots. However, she had been inspired by her older sister Ceren, who – nine years earlier – had received a partial CASP to attend Washington College in Maryland and had gone on to earn a master's degree at Harvard's School of Public Health. "I had gone to her graduation at Harvard so I had some familiarity with Massachusetts," said Pinar. "It was either plunge into a pure physics program or go to an American liberal arts school and sample a little bit of everything. I understood the American system, so Clark was a choice." She started as a double major in physics and communications, but that became a degree in just communications. In 2020, she was trying out life in Cyprus after completing a master's degree program in Spain. Her sister tried the same path but admitted that Cyprus "broke" her. She felt she was being blocked no matter what she tried to do, so headed to the U.K. to study toward a Ph.D. in environmental science. Of course, the pandemic was rearranging both their plans. "If you want to make God laugh, show him your plans," said Ceren.[82]

However, if there was a star among the CASP interviewees it was clearly Aris Antoniades, whose enthusiasm and intelligence were both impressive and infectious. Antoniades wanted to study music in the United States and he brought a tape player to the interviews so that he could play one of his own compositions. "I wanted to be a composer as long as I could remember," said Antoniades. He remembers as a small child hearing the song "Walking in the Air" from the animated film *The Snowman* and the emotions it evoked. "It was such a powerful emotion and as a young kid I was trying to process this ...why is this so powerful and how could it make me feel this way and, of course, my parents said, well it is music ...it is magic and I still believe that ...that it is magic. I wanted to be able to do that magic, too." He applied at all the top schools – Julliard, the New England Conservatory, Curtis – but when he walked into the Manhattan School of Music he knew that was where he wanted to be. The application process was grueling and highly competitive and places were few. He did not quite believe it when he was accepted, and he felt he was not as qualified as others – one of his classmates had had a work performed at Carnegie Hall by age 16. But after four intense years, Antoniades received the award as the school's top student. "I felt that I worked 20 hours a day and slept four and so I wanted to take advantage of all the things that I could get in that place," said Antoniades. "Get film score credits and work with electronic music and the jazz department and there are only 24 hours in the day." The school and his mentor thought enough of him to give him a full scholarship for his master's. "Now I have written three symphony orchestra compositions and two of them have been performed in New York." More or less confined to Cyprus by the pandemic, Antoniades is pursuing a Ph.D. program in education remotely at St. Louis University, while also composing. His compositions have been performed and recorded, and he has created a theater orchestra of Cypriot musicians, also confined to Cyprus, that has played before sold-out houses.[83]

As those final CASP scholars were searching for schools in the fall of 2011, the Commission was grappling with its uncertain future. At the November 22, 2011 Board meeting, Hadjittofi presented two different budgets. The first assumed they would once again receive $1.67 million in CASP funds, and the second calculated that they would receive $900,000. Theoretically, a new Ambassador would decide how much the Commission would receive. Hadjittofi noted that both numbers were probably optimistic. At the same meeting, there was a brief discussion about possible staff lay-offs the following autumn. It was also noted that given the impending financial crisis in Cyprus that it was not the time to ask the RoC for more money. One Board member said: "Wait until we are an energy power!" There would be much to discuss at the next Board meeting in the new year.

That Board meeting, however, did not occur until August 3, 2012, as once again the Christofias government did not see fit to either reappoint or choose new members. When it did, two of the primary and two of the alternate Greek Cypriot Board members were new, meaning they would need to be educated quickly. In the interim, three important decisions, which would clarify the future of the Commission, were made.

The first was something I initiated. If all 11 staff members were to be laid off eventually, it was projected that their severance benefits would total at least $3 million, taking most of the endowment. I did not begrudge the employees their benefits, but wondered if it was possible to make an adjustment that would preserve a little more of the endowment by reducing some of the severance benefits. I was pretty sure the answer was no, but needed to do my due diligence. I was given permission to engage the Embassy lawyer – Polyvios Polyviou – and his verdict was swift: "Pay them." He said I could try to change the terms of the promised benefits, but I would be taken to court in Cyprus and I would lose. The staff members were, of course, unhappy I was even looking into this, but I felt that I had answered an important question that clarified matters.

Second, the financial future of the Commission became clearer during a spring 2012 meeting at the Embassy. USAID's staffers – Elizabeth Kassinis and Kim Foukaris – let us know that in the fiscal year beginning October 1, 2012 there would be $3.5 million in Economic Support Funds and then the following year $3.2 million. After that, in the fiscal year that would begin on October 1, 2014, the ESF would stop. Because we still did not have an Ambassador, the meeting was chaired by Deputy Chief of Mission and Chargé d'Affaires Andrew Schoffer. In the past, CASP would receive a third of the ESF, but that is not what USAID had in mind. After proposing a few hundred thousand dollars for the Bicommunal Support Program that would support the youth basketball program Peace Players and the American jazz musicians who worked with a group of Cypriot musicians on both sides of the island, there would also be a small amount for some grassroots bicommunal programs. Then, USAID proposed just $200,000 for CASP. I was stunned and turned to Schoffer and said: "If it is only $200,000 then I will walk out of this room right now and close the Commission." Schoffer asked me how much I needed to keep the Commission open and I said at least $500,000. "All right then," he said, "it will be $550,000 this year and $500,000 next year." USAID's staffers were not happy.

The $550,000 plus the $170,000 from Fulbright, a similar contribution from the RoC, and some residual funds would allow the Commission to cobble together a budget of about $1 million for the year. What I had in mind were four employees – a Greek-speaking counselor, a Turkish-speaking counselor, a combination alumni coordinator and backup, and a bookkeeper. Their combined salaries and other administrative costs could not total more than 30 percent or $300,000. It would mean laying off seven staff members and closing the offices in the South and the North of Cyprus and putting the four staffers in the Fulbright Center in the Buffer Zone, but it would mean that the Commission would remain open full time and would continue to provide counseling services to those Cypriots interested in study in the U.S. The Commission had also created a new program called "The College Club." It provided counseling and small amounts of money to students to pay for test and application fees, and had secured $1.7 million in scholarships for participating students in the previous year. The new Board, once it was named, would ultimately have to decide how the staff was to be reduced.

The third event was the brewing financial crisis in Cyprus as Greek banks tottered, fallout from the U.S. real estate crisis several years earlier. The Commission reaped the benefits in the run-up to the crisis, as Cypriot banks offered higher and higher rates on certificates of deposit to try to attract more and more deposits. Here Hadjittofi provided another important service to the Commission. He came to me in the summer of 2012 and told me that his contacts were telling him that the Bank of Cyprus and Laiki Bank, the two largest, were in trouble. The Commission had most of its funds, particularly the $4 million endowment, in those banks. Hadjittofi advised that as the various CDs matured, the Commission should move its money to safer banks. That is what we did, moving the money to Marfin Bank, the Cyprus Development Bank, and the church-owned Hellenic Bank. When the substantial (47.5 percent) "haircut" on deposits of more than $100,000 occurred in 2013, the Commission's funds were spared. That would be crucial as staff members were laid off and severance benefits paid out.

The day before the August 3, 2012 Board meeting, John Koenig was confirmed by the Senate as the new Ambassador to Cyprus, and he arrived in Nicosia two weeks later. Koenig had served on the Fulbright Board in 1994-97 when he was a political officer at the Embassy. In doing his consultations he tried to see if there was some way for the ESF to be restored. "Yes...I knew when I arrived that the money was scheduled to be eliminated," said Koenig. "It was portrayed as a fait accompli. I recall meeting several times on the issue. I went to meet the Deputy Secretary for Resources and I made a plea that the money be restored and I was politely ushered out. With regards to the level of concern in the Greek Cypriot community about this, it was zero. It had been overtaken by events...mainly the collapse of the Greek economy. They did not care about the earmark anymore. They had surrendered."[84]

"This is what I recall," said Nick Laragakis, the President and CEO of the American Hellenic Institute. "The money was a pittance and as it was reduced the Cyprus Government did not want to be held hostage by this money. There came a point when they were not interested in the money anymore. I remember that as the prevailing attitude coming out of Nicosia."[85]

"I got involved with the Cyprus Federation in 1989," noted Panicos Papanicolaou. "We worked with [lobbyist] Andy Manatos and Andy Athens, a leader of the Hellenic-American community. After 1974, every dollar counted. However, CASP is something that was brought up in Cyprus, but not in Washington. I did meet with Mrs. Fulbright on one occasion and she said that her husband wanted students to come to

America and get an excellent education. I think this is something that is in Greek culture, an emphasis on education. If you look at the first generation of Greek immigrants to America, this is their story. The first priority was to make sure their children received a good education. We worked with Andy Manatos. He knew how the Senate worked. And we worked with Senator Richard Shelby and Representative Anita Loy of New York. And, of course, the Greek-American community was relying on the advice of Senator Sarbanes (who would retire from the Senate in January 2007). I finished my tenure in 2011, but was not involved when the money stopped. If the community was willing to push we could get things done. I don't think the Government of Cyprus had it as a priority."[86]

"House Appropriations [where all spending bills originated] was the key," explained Manatos, who was in that meeting with Eugene Rossides all those years before and who became one of Washington's most powerful lobbyists. "We had to lobby hard. In the beginning it was Doc Long but then Representative David Obey. In the Senate it was Pat Leahy. CASP was not a selling point. It was the Government of Cyprus that stopped seeing it as a high priority. In the end I think it was a lack of enthusiasm. The Government of Cyprus said that the money was not being distributed properly." Then Manatos looked down, and with a wry smile that belied the confidence he felt in his ability to push amendments through the labyrinth that is Congress said: "We could have kept it going."[87]

Despite the Congressional language that always gave the scholarship program pride of place, the Greek lobby would rarely, if ever, bring it up. Indeed, the various Hellenic-American organizations never had programs that reached out to the CASP and Fulbright students from Cyprus when they arrived in America for their studies. Instead, in their eyes, the central focus was the violation of the Foreign Assistance Act as long as Turkish troops remained on the ground in Cyprus. "We spent a lot of time trying to prevent certain things from happening," said Papanicolaou, "like allowing flights into Tymbrou [Ercan] Airport." The American Embassy in Nicosia, too, had different priorities; the programs run by UNDP that built bridges between the communities and funding for confidence building measures were judged to be more important than the scholarship program. After the 2004 Annan Plan vote, it was the programs that sought to lift up the Turkish Cypriot community that drew the ire of the Greek Cypriot government and dampened their desire to push for the funding. Without a strong push from the Greek lobby, it was easy for Congress to eliminate the money, particularly after Cyprus became a member of the European Union.   When Eastern European countries, which had received some USAID funding after the collapse of the Soviet Union, joined the EU USAID funding stopped immediately.   It is testament to the power of the Greek lobby, its friends in Congress, and Cyprus's special circumstances that the USAID funding continued for a decade after Cyprus's accession to the EU.

So, when the Board finally met on August 3, 2012 there was an urgency. The new fiscal year was only eight weeks away.   There was also a group of new Board members who needed to be brought up to speed.   The initial proposal was to retain five staff members at 30 hours a week.   Executive Director Hadjittofi countered with a proposal to lay everyone off, paying them their severance benefits, and then hire back five at 20 hours a week.   It was up to the Board to decide, but there were problems with both proposals.   There were objections to the idea of paying people their severance benefits and then hiring them back: once they had received the benefits their employment with the Commission should end.   Also, the severance benefit for each employee was predicated on years served and the amount of their final salary.   When we asked Hadjittofi to consider taking a reduction in salary to stay on, he declined, noting that it would mean a substantial cut in the severance package that he would ultimately receive.   It was a lot to take in and a lot to consider.

The rest of the meeting had a strange, business-as-usual quality to it. Because there had not been a Board meeting in nine months, there was a lot of catching up to do. There was a proposed budget of a little more than $1 million, which would allow four American scholars to come to Cyprus, two American Ph.D. students, and three English teaching assistants. It would provide funds for seven Fulbrights for Cypriot graduate students, and one grant for a Cypriot senior scholar to go to the U.S. Almost lost in all of this was the fact that in June the Commission had marked its 50th anniversary with a reception for some 800 at the Hilton Park Hotel with a commemorative video, a web site, a photo exhibition, and other special events to mark the milestone.   However, behind the scenes the staff was in turmoil.[88]

"We all knew [the situation] because Daniel talked to us," said Anna Argyrou. "He had been fighting for years and he just could not do it anymore. It was a terrible atmosphere in the office because everyone wondered who would lose a job and who would stay on for a while and it was all that was discussed the last year or so." Hadjittofi noted that he was doing "psychological management."

"However, personally, I was okay with it," said Argyrou. "I had asked Daniel to lay me off two years earlier. I had been in that position for so long that I was tired and I wanted to do something different and Daniel said no, get back to your office and stay where you are. So, it was not stressful for me but for the others it was. It was terrible. We were left in the dark until the final Board meeting and then you sat down with all of us and told us."[89]

The Board agreed to meet five days later, on August 8, to decide what to do. Hadjittofi and I had agreed months earlier to renovate the Fulbright Center in the Buffer Zone to accommodate a small staff, and to prepare to close the office in the North near the Ledra Palace crossing and the long-time office in the South on Egypt Avenue. That building, and also the former American Center adjacent to the Fulbright offices, which had been rented for a pittance by the Commission, were owned by a Turkish Cypriot and were seized by the Greek Cypriot government as soon as the Commission vacated the two buildings.

When we informed the Board that Hadjittofi would not be one of the staffers staying on, Nancy Scudder, one of the longest serving American Board members, was clearly distressed. "I cannot imagine this Commission going forward without Daniel," she said and expressed the desire to resign her seat on the Board in protest. To be honest, I was both somewhat cold blooded and bloody minded about what I felt needed to be done. The Board was clearly having trouble coming to a decision but we just needed to decide. The plan that I had had in my head for a long time – four employees maintaining full-time hours – was what I ultimately pushed through. Seven employees, including Executive Director Daniel Hadjittofi, would be laid off by October 13 and the Commission would move into the Fulbright Center by October 15.

"Everyone wanted the Commission to be gone," said Hadjittofi. "The Embassy decided the CASP should end. The Ministry of Foreign Affairs said it had outlived its usefulness. The Greek lobby said, under the circumstances, we cannot support this. At that point I knew that it was only going to be a couple of more years. I needed to get out and find a way to make a living. It made no sense to stay."[90]

We asked Anna Argyrou to be the Greek Cypriot counselor and the nominal Executive Director, though she could not hold the title because if there was such a position with that title the previous occupant, under Cypriot labor law, had the right to claim it. We knew Hadjittofi would not do so, but we decided to call Argyrou the Senior Counselor. Ioli Kythreotou had been Daniel's deputy, but because of health issues had rarely been in the office the previous year. So the position fell to Argyrou.

"I was annoyed," said Argyrou. "I felt I was put in a corner. But then I thought, okay, this will be a challenge and I learned more in those two and a half years about the accounts and I learned to deal with officials in the government and with the Board. Daniel disappeared. I asked a couple of questions at the beginning but it was clear he was done. He felt he had done his time. My husband Sol said to me 'you cannot take Daniel's job...that is his job.' Daniel was godfather to my youngest son. But I explained that I did not have a choice. I had people on my case from all sides but Daniel said: 'I am not needed here anymore.' I had to be the one to tell Revy [Payiata-Chishios] that she was not going to stay. I think the staff had a sense of why the money was disappearing. Daniel talked to us. But it is one thing to have a sense of it and another when it actually happens. It is sad."[91]

The Board met next on October 5, which would be Hadjittofi's last Board meeting as Executive Director. A revised program plan had to be approved and it was interesting that certain Greek Cypriot Board members wanted to see fewer American scholars come and more American students. Their reasons were revealing: they felt the Ph.D. students would be a longer-term investment in a Cypriot-American relationship; that some of the American scholars in their final reports had expressed disappointments with their placements, or the level of the students in their classes, or the chilly "welcome" they had received from Cypriot colleagues on the faculties. He noted that Cypriots who went to the U.S. received a warmer welcome. He also noted that, increasingly, the Commission had to "beg" Cypriot universities to take American scholars. Hadjittofi did his best to counter these arguments, as there was no evidence that this was true. It might have been the case, at that point, of Greek Cypriot Board members wanting to paint a picture of a Commission that no longer worked well in order to justify the withdrawal of their support. Was it a "fox and the grapes" scenario?

At the end of the meeting, Hadjittofi made brief remarks in which he thanked the Board for its support, noting that a talented staff had made him look good, and that he was proud that the Cyprus Commission was seen as a model for other Commissions. A few nights earlier, at a reception to honor the seven departing employees, Hadjittofi's more extended remarks were perceived to be far less gracious, particularly by Embassy officers. When I told him this later in the evening he was shocked that his remarks had been perceived this way and that he meant no offense. My sense of it is that he allowed his deep emotions to get the best of him. It was unfortunate. It soured relations with the Embassy, particularly with the newly arrived Ambassador, but what would happen in the coming weeks would cause an almost irrevocable breach.

The process for distributing the severance benefits was that accountant Kyproula Kyriakidou would prepare the vouchers for the payment of the benefits. The seven checks would total a little more than $2.3 million. Then, I, as Board Chairman, and Economic Officer Susan Delja, as Commission Treasurer, would sign the vouchers. I signed those vouchers on a Friday and left the folder on Delja's desk as she was away from the office. I waited for her to sign, but she did not.

Initially, Delja did not return my emails or phone messages. What eventually became clear is that she found the paperwork she was given inadequate. So, what did she need? That remained a mystery. At the recent Board meeting she had not raised any issues. Would it help to speak to Kyriakidou? No. Would it help to speak to the outside accountant? No. Meanwhile, Hadjittofi was asking me daily what was going on and I did not have a good answer, but I asked him to be patient while I figured it out. However, that was not something he was willing to do and he reached out to his contacts in the United States for help. After five days letters arrived via email to Ambassador Koenig, to Delja, to me, and to all the Board members from a Washington, D.C. law firm threatening legal action if the checks to the staff were not forthcoming. That created a whole new situation. In view of the threatened legal action, Hadjittofi said he could not speak to me, though he was somewhat apologetic about that stance. Despite cutting off contact with the Embassy, Hadjittofi knew the state of play at the Embassy because the Fulbright desk officer at the State Department gave him daily updates. A decade later his decision still gnaws at him. "My guilt feelings for having to do this go beyond anything I would think of as normal and continue to bother me every so often when I feel that I had bitten the hand that helped me, protected me, and allowed me to fulfill an ideal," said Hadjittofi.[92]

The Ambassador did not appreciate being threatened and efforts to find a solution ground to a halt. The Board members were blindsided. "It was clear to me that there were no choices to be made," said Board member Claire Georghiou. "Then we got the letters that we were being sued. That was very unpleasant and I had to explain it all to my husband. But we wondered. I woke up in the middle of the night and wondered if this is how 14 years of voluntary service is going to end? At the end there was the door now get out...it was very upsetting."[93]

Dr. Chris Schabel remembered how he felt at the time. "I did not appreciate the letter. Americans don't threaten very well. It makes you want to reconsider granting the benefits," he said. "But then I talked to a few people and they said it was not going to actually amount to anything and that this just had to be done to get things resolved and then I guess I kind of calmed down. It was an unpleasant ending."[94] "I kind of laughed off being sued," said Dr. Andrew McCarthy of CAARI. "I thought that I could show them what I am paid and they would not be impressed. But when I spoke to you I felt that this was going to be a matter that was going to be resolved and I did not take great offense. It seemed a little impatient to me...which was irritating."[95]

"It was a nightmare for me though I had several layers of insulation," noted Ambassador Koenig. "I think that Susan (Delja) was just afraid... afraid of the liability. I don't blame Susan. She got extremely emotional at times about this and was very worried but I think that she believed that she had some sort of fiduciary responsibility that would come back to haunt her."[96]

Delja might have sought advice from the Embassy's Administrative Officer Tracy Harding. In a conference call with a senior Fulbright official in Washington that included myself, Ambassador Koenig, and Harding, Harding's mouth literally dropped open when the Fulbright official said that it was their position that once U.S. Government funds were given to the Fulbright Commission that those funds ceased to be U.S. Government funds and became Commission funds under the control of the Board. It was clear that Harding thought this was nonsense. The thing was, all of the funds used to pay out the severance benefits came from the endowment, which, in turn, came from the contributions made by the RoC and accrued interest and not from USG funds. Yet, like Cyprus itself, this was a conflict between the Commission and the Embassy that seemed frozen.

"It was not completely clear where it was coming from," said Ambassador Koenig, "but it was understood that Daniel had engineered it. His behavior was not what I would have hoped. He did lose a job that he had invested so much in and it shook him up but he thought that he could intimidate the Embassy and U.S. Government. I think that he overplayed his hand. I think if he had been more cooperative that we could have worked things out. This desire to drive the situation to a conclusion with the letter from the lawyers was a horrible miscalculation.

"I said we had to get this "over with"...there was no legal basis to not sign the checks. I think it was a disaster to get into this disagreement."[97]

When Ambassador Koenig reached that conclusion, the issue was solved. The vouchers would be signed. The checks would be issued. The one new requirement was that each employee would have to sign a one-sentence letter that said they would make no further claims on the U.S. Government. It was that simple. And so they gathered at the Fulbright Center and one by one they stepped forward, signed their names and received their checks: Deputy Executive Director Ioli Kythreotou, Executive Secretary Voula Michael; Messenger and Caretaker Stelios Christoforou; Secretary Yiannoula Panteli; Counselor and Web Editor Rebecca Payiata, Cleaner Maria Antoniou, and last Executive Director Daniel Hadjittofi. All together, they had devoted 128 years to the Commission. The mood was solemn. Almost no one spoke. They took their checks and departed and then it was up to the remaining four employees – Anna Argyrou, Kyproula Kyiakidou, Gulsen Oztoprak, and Dr. Sondra Sainsbury – to move forward.

Ambassador Koenig, in his role as Honorary Chairman, made a point of coming to the next Board meeting on November 9. Almost all the Board members attended except the two most senior Greek Cypriots, which was common. The Ambassador said all the right

Gulsen Oztoprak (top) was a CASP grantee and returned to be the Turkish Cypriot counselor at the Commission. Kyproula Kyriakidou (center) rose from secretary to the primary accountant for the Commission, handling millions of dollars. Anna Argyrou (bottom) was asked to take on the conflict resolution programs soon after she joined the Commission and became its last Executive Director.

words. He noted that it had not been an easy year for the Commission; that he believed that everyone was still adhering to the principal of supporting the spirit of Senator Fulbright; that all were keeping with the tradition of intensive academic exchange between the U.S. and Cyprus. He urged that there be a rebirth of Fulbright but acknowledged that it would be without the substantial funds provided by CASP. Nevertheless, he still believed that Fulbright would have a bright future in Cyprus, built upon the foundation that had been created over many years. He pledged his help in this endeavor.[98]

During the rest of the brief meeting, the process by which the retirement benefits were ultimately disbursed to the seven employees was explained, and then I noted that in the process of downsizing the Embassy found certain aspects of Fulbright operations that did not square with diplomatic rules and regulations. Without a legal identity of its own, the Commission was intertwined with the Embassy and had not had to pay VAT. That would now change, increasing costs 17 percent. Also, in the process of downsizing, the Commission got rid of three cars. All had diplomatic plates to which they were not entitled. Why was this so? Because all the cars had been acquired prior to 2003 – i.e., before the Green Line was open – and only with the diplomatic plates could Fulbright staff move back and forth and conduct its work as a bicommunal organization. It never occurred to anyone to change it after 2003. It was one of those "look the other way" arrangements, with which the Ministry of Foreign Affairs agreed, that allowed the Commission to function, but would give Embassy Administrative Officers a case of indigestion.

There was one other item brought before the Board that the Commission would, ultimately, ignore. It received a letter from the RoC asking it to cease cooperating with Turkish Cypriot universities. It was the kind of letter sent to others to try to intimidate them and prevent them from working with Turkish Cypriots but it was not the kind of letter the Commission would have received. After all, senior officials from the Ministry of Foreign Affairs had sat on the Commission Board for decades even as the Commission worked closely with Turkish Cypriot universities, scholars, and students. One had to suspect that the arrival of such a letter was connected to the departure of Hadjittofi, who would have quickly seen to it that it be rescinded. The Board would meet briefly in early December to approve a program, but then would not meet again for nearly a year.[99]

This time it was not the animus of AKEL, but the February 2013 election of Nicos Anastasiades as RoC President that led to uncertainty about the relationship between the RoC and the new Fulbright program once the Commission was closed.   There were discussions between Ambassador Koenig and Foreign Minister Kasoulides about the possibility of a new bilateral agreement to replace the one signed in January 1962. Still, it would take until November 2013 before another Board, with a completely new cast of Greek Cypriot members, would meet.   I remember the look on the face of one of the new Greek Cypriot alternate Board members when I explained that we had gathered to decide how to shutter the Commission.   She apparently had not been briefed and she had the most shocked expression on her face.

During the 11-month interim, there had been another dispute with USAID over the final year of CASP funds.   Instead of $3.2 million in Economic Support Funds (ESF), we learned it would be $2.9 million and rather than designating $500,000 for the CASP program, as Chargé Schoffer had decided, Foukaris and Kassinis decided the Commission should have zero dollars.   I refused to clear the document going to Washington and complained bitterly to the Ambassador.   In the end, the final year of ESF saw $360,000 devoted to CASP.   However, with no contribution from the RoC, the Commission funding was less than $600,000 in its final year.   More than half of that was allotted to salaries and administrative costs.

In 2013, a class of nine Fulbrighters was chosen, each receiving a $50,000 grant for graduate studies. The quality of the students continued to be extraordinary.   Melina Philippou went to MIT and Demitris Venizelos to Harvard, both to study architecture.   Christodoulos Savva went to Penn and Michelle Pinharry to the University of Minnesota, both to study mathematics.   Michalis Yerou went to study software engineering at USC and Michaella Georgiou neurobiology at Northwestern.   Marios Hadjitonis would go the University of Michigan and stay for his Ph.D. in physics.   Michalis Skitsas would also study architecture at Pratt, and Ioanna Michail would study law at NYU.   Six years later, three were back in Cyprus, one in Greece, one in London, one in Stockholm and three still in America.

Michail was one of those who returned to Cyprus to practice law in Limassol.   She had grown up in Limassol, where her father drove a taxi and her mother was a homemaker.   She earned her law degree at the University of Cyprus and was called to the bar.   By chance she heard about the Fulbright program from friends, and applied and was accepted at NYU. "When I was waiting for a response from Fulbright I had also applied to the United Kingdom and everything happened very fast," remembered Michail.   "I was quite convinced that I had failed the interview at Fulbright, so I wanted to have a Plan B, and so I had everything ready to go to the UK. But it is not the same…the master's program in the United States is so different from the programs in the United Kingdom. They are more practical. They prepare you for your practice when your studies are done. They are not so academic. They give you extra professional experience. Most of my modules were mock trials, practical problems… we had so many networking events, which was another advantage. We had so many opportunities in New York. The firm where I work now just does international commercial law. We deal with international cases every day, and many are multi-jurisdictional, so some of them deal with the U.S. Many involve arbitration and my master's degree also dealt with international arbitration so what I learned in New York I use every day. A U.S. degree is very, very prestigious, especially from NYU because I came back as a Fulbright Scholar and that has so much value. People recognize it and know it. You are part of this very special group, a circle of international people."[100]

In the final year with little money, no real program plan, and no Board until November 2013, the Commission gave just three student grants, though one student withdrew at the last moment. Chrysovalantis Anastasiou is working on his Ph.D. in computer science at USC and met and married an American and plans to stay in the U.S. He is also the Chief Technology Officer at a tech start-up. Despo Thoma earned her degree in architecture and urban planning at Columbia and obtained an O Visa, granted to individuals with extraordinary ability in science, the arts, education, business or athletics, and has also remained in the United States as a designer at a New York architectural firm.

In that final year there were a handful of English Teaching Assistants and American scholars and Ph.D. students who had been in the pipeline as the remaining four staff members tried to figure out how one closes a Commission. Clinical psychologist Loretta Brady came to Cyprus with her five children and worked on substance abuse issues at the University of Nicosia. Rita Axford consulted on graduate nursing studies. James and Paula Buck taught American studies and literature in both communities. Patricia Marie Martin worked on domestic violence issues, and Daniela Donno studied the peace movement.

We were all trying to figure out how the Commission's work might be carried out once the doors were closed. It was clear that one person would run the grant program out of the Embassy Public Affairs Section and I had decided in my own mind that that person should be Dr. Sondra Sainsbury, who was also the Commission's Alumni Coordinator. Sainsbury had come to Cyprus indirectly because of CASP. Her eventual husband, Dr. Spyros Spyrou, came to the U.S. on a CASP and both would eventually earn their doctorates in cultural anthropology. It seemed that whatever the future of the Fulbright program in Cyprus, the thousands of alumni could – potentially – play an important role. As such, Argyrou told Sainsbury that she might as well start taking over the Fulbright portfolio. "I remember when a couple of the newly arrived English Teaching Assistants came in for their orientation to a fairly empty Fulbright Center in the Buffer Zone," recalled Sainsbury. "I said 'well, we are going through a bit of a transition' and tried to be upbeat."[101] But it was a far cry from the bustling office that had existed just 18 months earlier.

In the meantime, there was the issue of the counseling services. Given the tight security at the Embassy, the new Fulbright Coordinator in the Public Affairs Section could not be expected to carry out that role. Students could not just walk into the Embassy, and the security measures could be off-putting [you mean I have to leave my phone?]. The Commission was still fielding more than 6,000 inquiries a year even though the number of Cypriot students in the U.S. had dropped to under 500. Argyrou and Oztoprak decided to form a non-profit that would provide counseling services and be connected to the State Department's StudyUSA program. Even with a declining number of Cypriot students studying in the U.S., there were still hundreds who inquired, took the tests, and made applications. Even with the Internet, a guide through the process was incredibly valuable and given that Ambassador Koenig had decreed that the Embassy needed to hold on to the Fulbright Center in the Buffer Zone they would have a place from which to operate. So, they set about founding AG StudyUSA Higher Education Consultants, Ltd.

The Board met twice in the first half of 2014, its last two meetings. At the first, on Valentines' Day, I told the Board there were two main issues. What should we do with the Commission's funds when the Commission closed? Our best estimate was that there would be about €370,000 from the endowment and $700,000 in CASP residuals remaining. Second, how would the funds be managed? The Embassy was making it clear that it did not want to manage these funds. Connected to this was the idea of a non-binding Memorandum of Understanding (MOU) that laid out how the Fulbright program and its counseling program would be structured. I had written a draft MOU and submitted it to the lawyers in Washington. However, what this was really about was how the RoC would continue to have a say in the way that Fulbright program money would be spent.

Given that the Cypriot government had gone nearly a year without appointing a Board and that it had not made its promised donations to the program two years running, not to mention that it was rare for the most senior Greek Cypriot officials to find the time to attend the Board meetings, it seemed that they were displaying a good deal of cheek in essentially threatening to withhold their contribution unless there was an MOU that gave them a more formal role. The Turkish Cypriot representative made no such request, but then the Turkish Cypriots could not make a donation to the program because if they did it would have caused the Greek Cypriots to withdraw.

Argyrou made a presentation on the new non-profit counseling service she was forming with Oztoprak, and pointed out their success in finding scholarships for Cypriot students. For example, Oztoprak had just helped to secure a $250,000 four-year undergraduate grant for Elgin Gulpinar Korkmazhan to study physics at Harvard.[102] Some Board members questioned how we could provide financial support for this non-profit without a formal bidding process, but we explained this would be a grant, and not a contract. I thought it should be self-evident that we would not find any other counselors on the island with their experience, expertise, and contacts. One Cypriot Board member changed the subject and raised the issue of graduate versus undergraduate grants. I was incredulous. Didn't they understand that we were entering a new era with a very small program? It was a good time to end the meeting.

The final Board meeting – the 253rd – was on April 11, 2014. It was much the same discussion. Iacovos Georgiou of the Ministry of Foreign Affairs said without an MOU laying out the mechanism by which the RoC would have input there could be no contribution from his government. There were also questions about the endowment funds and, at the time, I did not fully grasp what they were getting at. My successor, Ingrid Larson, would find out soon enough. Georgiou suggested that the Board needed options, including keeping the Commission going. It seemed to me that any options had to be realistic, but the State Department and its lawyers would soon make decisions that would render Board action moot. There would be no MOU, Board, or advisory panel. The new Coordinator could consult with officials at the Ministry of Education as necessary. StudyUSA would sign a contract with Argyrou and Oztoprak. I would write a position description for a combined Fulbright and Alumni Coordinator, and, ultimately, there would be a call for applications. However, there could be no Coordinator until the beginning of the new fiscal year on October 1, and the Embassy would not allow me to do the interviewing prior to my mid-August departure because they believed I would be biased toward Dr. Sainsbury. Well, they were right about that. "We interviewed a couple of candidates," explained Larson, who arrived in Cyprus in mid-August to take up the position of Public Affairs Officer, "and we picked the best one and Sondra [Sainsbury] was obviously the best one so to me I did not have to take on board the stuff that had happened before I got there."[103]

At the Fulbright Center in the Buffer Zone, Argyrou and Oztoprak were mentally and physically exhausted, but Larson asked them to keep the Commission offices and the counseling services running through August and September. "We did not take one day off," said Argyrou. "One day we were the Fulbright Commission and the next we were the Study-USA non-profit, though we were sitting in the same offices."[104] Sainsbury had to wait for her security background check so for a couple of weeks the English Teaching Assistants and the American scholars in Cyprus were pretty much on their own.

So, on October 1, 2014, after 52 years and nine months, the Cyprus Fulbright Commission ceased to function as one of the only bicommunal institutions on that divided island. What had been for decades – on a per capita basis – the largest Fulbright Commission in the world, quietly slipped away. A few months later, the Embassy and Ministry of Foreign Affairs exchanged diplomatic notes ending the bi-national agreement that had created the Commission in January 1962. In inflation-adjusted dollars, more than $250 million in U.S. funding had flowed through the Commission, which does not count the contributions by the RoC or the millions of dollars that Commission, Amideast, and IIE counselors secured from American universities. It was an institution that made little sense when it was founded in 1962, but one that pursued its mission with a seriousness of purpose and a commitment to the ideals of Senator Fulbright that was unmatched. More importantly, its Board members and staff members refused to be infected by the poisonous politics that kept that island nation divided. In its wake, it left thousands of Cypriots scattered throughout Cyprus and the world who had first-class educations or training and who were making invaluable contributions to science, the arts, education, media, business, and politics. In addition, thanks to its commitment to conflict resolution, there were thousands of Cypriots on the island who had participated in training programs that taught them skills that still might prove instrumental if leaders in the two communities ever decide to make a serious effort to end one of the world's longest running frozen conflicts. Of course, America profited immensely as well, and not just because the vast majority of funds expended by the Commission paid for tuition and fees at American universities or training facilities. There are literally hundreds of Cypriots who decided to pursue their dreams in America where there were opportunities for brilliant and motivated Cypriots, and the contributions they have made to their adopted country are incalculable. It was not the aim of the program to "poach" many of Cyprus's best and brightest, and the tug of family and the island's beaches, mountains, and Mediterranean lifestyle eventually brought many of these Cypriots back home after many years in America. On the other side of the ledger, hundreds of American scholars and students came to Cyprus and built life-long relationships and were changed and enriched by their Fulbright experiences just as Cypriots were changed by their encounters with America and Americans.

Senator Fulbright wrote: "In our quest for world peace, the alteration of attitudes is no less important, perhaps more important, than the resolution of issues. It is in the minds of men, after all, that wars are spawned; to act upon the human mind, regardless of the issue or occasion for doing so, is to act upon the course of conflict and a potential source of redemption and reconciliation."[105] To the extent that Cyprus has evolved into a more civil and prosperous island nation in the last half century, the ideals of Senator Fulbright as put into practice by the determined efforts of the Cyprus Fulbright Commission surely played an outsized role. The Commission gave thousands of Cypriots the chance to dream what seemed, at first blush, to be both an impossible American dream to study at some of the world's great universities and, through bicommunal conflict resolution training, to explore the dream of a united and peaceful Cyprus. In the video produced for the 50th anniversary of the Commission, Sarper Ince, who received a pair of Fulbrights, relates how he suddenly found himself in America and not just America but New York City as a young student. The sense of wonder and astonishment that spread across his face was just as vibrant 40 years on. That is what a dream come true looks like, and thanks to the Cyprus Fulbright Commission it was shared by generations of Cypriots.

EPILOGUE/ACKNOWLEDGEMENTS

Clearly, it is impossible to measure the impact of the Cyprus Fulbright Commission's work over 52 years. One can cite numbers – the tens of millions of dollars expended or the 1,754 CASP and the 574 Fulbright scholarships, the 943 STTs, and the 170 American scholars and students who came to Cyprus to share their expertise as well as the hundreds of short-term specialists who came to the island to speak at conferences or consult under the auspices of the Commission. One must add the several thousand Cypriots who participated in conflict resolution training, the hundreds who received USAID grants to attend the American University in Beirut, received Humphrey grants, participated in the teacher exchange and summer institutes, benefited from the English Language Teaching Assistants and the various training programs for social workers, the alumni, and – going back to the beginning of the Commission – the American Farm School in Thessaloniki. How many young people did the Commission's counselors encourage and then, using their expertise, illuminate the path that would ultimately change their lives? But that does not tell you much about the knowledge gained, the minds enriched, the attitudes influenced, or the hearts turned in a more hopeful direction.

Washington likes to measure the impact of Fulbright programs by listing the names of grantees who have gone on to positions of prominence. The U.S. Embassy in Nicosia did the same. A March 1996 cable was typical, listing Alecos Michaelides from the Ministry of Foreign Affairs, Panayiotis Hadjipavlou from the Planning Bureau, Demetrios Lazarides from the Higher Technical Institute and, from the Turkish Cypriot community, Kenan Atakol, Osman Ertug, Salih Djoshar and Mustafa Olgun and many others.[1] One could put together a similar list today, many of whom are featured in this book. Records show that more than 400 of the Fulbright and CASP grantees from Cyprus went on to complete their Ph.D. degrees. Dr. Leondios Kostrikis noted that many of his colleagues at the University of Cyprus were educated in America on CASP or Fulbright grants just as he was. However, it is the cumulative impact of so many individuals – making policy, educating young people, creating businesses and jobs – that is immeasurable. Take Sofoklis Vlassides, a third-generation winemaker from Limassol, who sought a CASP grant to pursue a master's degree in oenology at the University of California Davis in 1996.

"I knew quite a lot about UC Davis and I had a clear idea of what I wanted to do," said Vlassides. "I think the panel was impressed that I had a very strong sense of purpose. UC Davis provides a very strong course in the basics of wine and did not venture into certain modern ideas. It was about the fundamentals." Today, he runs Vlassides Winery in the hills above Limassol, producing more than 175,000 bottles a year with the grapes he inherited from his parents. On the winery's web page, Vlassides states: "My studies at Davis defined the way I make my wines."[2]

***

As Dr. Sondra Sainsbury settled into her new office at the American Embassy with a budget of roughly $160,000 from the Bureau of Educational and Cultural Affairs at the State Department, she had to decide – with Public Affairs Officer Ingrid Larson – what the Fulbright program in Cyprus would look like. "Sondra had a very clear vision for the program when she came in," noted Larson and that vision did not include graduate scholarships.[3] "It was a practical decision," explained Sainsbury. "Each Fulbright student degree program cost us $50,000 per year. With our Fulbright annual allocation, we could either fund two Cypriot master's degree students, or we could have a whole slate of Cypriot scholars going to the U.S. to teach and do research, as well as incoming American Fulbright ETA's, researchers, and student researchers, all for the same money."[4]

It is interesting to note that when the Cyprus Fulbright Commission was founded in 1962 it received $100,000 annually from Washington. If that allocation had kept pace with inflation it would be just under $1 million today. The RoC showed no interest in renewing its contribution. Indeed, the Cypriot government demanded that Fulbright give back the remaining funds that it had donated, the roughly $400,000 that remained in the endowment account. "Yes, the government wanted the money back and the Ambassador decided that because it had become an irritant we should just give it back," said Larson. "They said that the money was given for the Fulbright Commission and since there was no longer a Commission they wanted the money back. My arguments about how many (smaller) countries don't have Commissions but still have Fulbright programs and contributions from the host governments fell on deaf ears," said Larson. "I felt as if they did not understand what Fulbright is...that they had this conception based on how it had been, which is understandable. I did not think that they had any appetite for looking creatively at a program that benefits both sides – both sides in Cyprus and both sides in the U.S.-Cypriot relationship. They showed no interest, no creativity, no interest in hearing about other models. They said we want CASP back or we want Fulbrights back. They showed an unwillingness to discuss other models or examine other ways. So, we decided to give them a cooling-off period. I found them to be willfully ignorant about the value of exchange in a society that has an educated class that has largely gotten their education elsewhere."[5]

The RoC demands also meant that there would not be as much money to support the non-profit that Anna Argyrou and Gulsen Oztoprak had founded. The government kept demanding audits to insure that they had received back all the money they had donated, and that Argyrou's and Oztoprak's non-profit was not somehow making a profit. As Larson related, the RoC was not supportive of their new venture. One senior Foreign Ministry official said – insultingly –"we are not giving money to two secretaries." Larson knew that she and Dr. Sainsbury had to decide how much to preserve to support the Fulbright program and how much of the residual funds could support Argyrou and Oztoprak.

"I thought they [Argyrou and Oztoprak] were quite brave," said Larson. "But perhaps not realistic about how much the Embassy was going to be able to help, given our own financial constraints...but not unrealistic over all. They were really focused on making things work. Promises had been made to them and I was going to keep those promises for the time that I was there [two years]. They had to have time to find their footing and figure out a model that would work. We valued the services that they were providing but eventually we were going to have to taper our support."[6] Their model tried to remain affordable to Cypriot students, charging half what the British Council was charging for similar support. The goal was still to get as many Cypriots to the United States as possible. Until the COVID pandemic brought educational exchange to a screeching halt, Argyrou and Oztoprak helped dozens of Cypriots from both communities pursue their studies in America. On average, the "two secretaries" found $3 million in scholarship offers every year for those students – which was duly reported to StudyUSA officials in Washington. However, the struggle to generate enough revenue, as the number of Cypriot students interested in studying in America continued to fall and the Embassy contribution diminished, meant something had to eventually give. The pandemic gave a final push. Argyrou left the partnership and now consults privately. Oztoprak continues to run the StudyUSA program in Cyprus part-time with Embassy and Washington help. As

Oztoprak noted, Cypriot students have so many more choices today but children of alumni or students with a particularly adventuresome streak still seek to study in the U.S.

Dr. Sainsbury has used the remaining residual funds to top up the current program, sometimes giving a third research grant instead of just two. To the extent there are problems they are bureaucratic. KYSATS can still bedevil Cypriots with American degrees. And while Cypriot scholars traveling on American grants have their fees waived, American scholars and students have to provide myriad documents and pay fees in order to receive long-term visas to Cyprus, which had not been an issue when the Commission was still functioning. One reason appears to be that the European Union is pressuring Cyprus to improve its border security, but Sainsbury hopes that tougher rules will not impede the exchange of scholars. Of course, the Washington bureaucracy does not always make things easy, either. Then there is the matter of the alumni.

"So, you know I have tried several times to start an alumni organization," explained Sainsbury. "Washington would like to see us have an alumni organization and when I was still at the Commission we tried and it always turned into a mini-Cyprus Problem. So when I became Alumni Coordinator I tried to create something more informal and that was the Cyprus American Alumni Network (CAAN). There are a number of alumni organizations with varying degrees of activity, and so CAAN tried to be an umbrella organization. We sent a lot of alumni on training and to conferences hoping that they would take a more active administrative and creative role in the organization. When Glen Davis came in (as Public Affairs Officer following Ingrid Larson) we decided to try an advisory board that would advise the Ambassador. We thought that it would give them some status and a connection to the Embassy and hoped there would be a shared passion to try to help continue the tradition of sending Cypriot students to the U.S. for their education without the support of the Fulbright program. They talked about starting a scholarship program. There were legalities concerning what an Ambassador could and couldn't do. Of course, the pandemic made it impossible to host a fund-raising event, even if the advisory board wanted to."[7] In the end, Ambassador Garber – with her departure from Cyprus approaching – sent a letter to the members dissolving the board. It is still the fervent hope that an active alumni network in Cyprus will, in the future, be able to assist Cypriot students who want to study in America.

One of the alumni who served on the advisory board was Maria Tsiakka. She received a Fulbright in 1983 to attend MIT. "I completed both my bachelor's and my master's degrees in chemical engineering at MIT, because at the time I got some credits for my A Levels and so I was able to do both," explained Tsiakka. "Then I decided that I really did not want to be an engineer, so I went over to the Harvard Business School and did something completely different and earned my MBA. I very much enjoyed my time at both schools." The J-1 visa requirement drew her back to Cyprus, where she worked at the Bank of Cyprus, met her husband and decided to stay. Ultimately she ran the company her father had founded. "When I came back I attended some alumni events and there is an effort to bring together alumni. There is a Harvard Club and an MIT Club. There is an advisory council at the Embassy and the aim is to get young people to think about studying in the U.S., particularly as undergraduates. So I am part of that effort. It is such a shame the program stopped. The program allowed a lot of people to get to know the U.S. and they became sort of U.S. supporters ...people who have actually lived there for a couple of years and appreciate the people and the culture. I think most of the people who went really had a good experience...you really get a very positive view of the United States by studying there. Look at our universities. There are so many professors who studied in America and the way they started was through these scholarships. Now they are the top academic elite of Cyprus. So, many people benefited."[8]

It is a bit astonishing how many alumni organizations there are in Cyprus formed by graduates of American universities. The Turkish Cypriots have their own, and another long-standing group has formed in the Paralimni area. As Tsiakka noted, there is a Harvard Club and an MIT Club and clubs connected to schools such as Macalester in Minnesota and SUNY Albany and its Cypriot Studies program. University clubs, like the Harvard Club, are bicommunal, and Turkish Cypriot members say that they feel welcome as school ties nudge aside ethnic considerations. All these graduates can be found throughout Cypriot society in positions of influence, although the first CASP students are now nearing retirement.

At a reception in May 1992, Education Minister Christoforos Christofides praised the contribution that a group of newly arrived American academics were making to Cyprus. But then he went on:

> *"These scholars are only the tip of the iceberg of Fulbright's contribution to Cyprus. The 25th anniversary publication of the Fulbright Commission includes an impressive list of Cypriots who have been educated through the Commission and are now*

leading figures in the economic, political and social life of Cyprus. It is perhaps the most far reaching of all the U.S. government's contributions to Cyprus. The visionary Senator, Senator Fulbright, who once saw this program as a way to turn the spoils of war into the instruments of peace could not have done his country and Cyprus a greater service. The program inspires me and gives me courage for one other reason. It is virtually the only bicommunal organization functioning on the island at present. It is our hope for approaching the Turkish Cypriot community, and a bridge that could bring about inter-communal understanding and cooperation."9

The Fulbright program will continue to make its contribution to Cyprus, but it will never be on the scale of that provided by the Fulbright Commission that existed between January 1962 and September 2014. That was, in so many ways, an aberration, an accident of history and geopolitical forces, and, as that Washington official noted, a "miracle." Perhaps, in the future, another American Senator or President will come to the realization that investing in educational exchange – in human infrastructure – pays great dividends and helps the people come closer to Senator Fulbright's goal of a world governed by reason. The most appropriate way to close is with a quote from Senator Fulbright:

> *"The essence of intercultural education is the acquisition of empathy-the ability to see the world as others see it, and to allow for the possibility that others may see something we have failed to see, or may see it more accurately. The simple purpose of the exchange program...is to erode the culturally rooted mistrust that sets nations against one another. The exchange program is not a panacea but an avenue of hope."10*

***

It was Anna Argyrou who said "someone needs to write a history of this Commission" and in the waning days of the Commission we tested the waters by putting out a tender that received a couple of bids from Cypriots who expressed an interest in writing the history of the Cyprus Fulbright Commission. But my sense was that the incentive would be to do something quickly and that an outsider would not have the understanding or feel for the subject. As my retirement from the diplomatic service

The majority of the staff of the Fulbright Commission in pictured in 2022.
They ran the Commission between 2001 and 2012 when the staff was downsized
from 11 to four. Left to right they are Voula Michael, Yiannoula Panteli, Kyproula
Kyriakides, Daniel Hadjittofi, Anna Argyrou, Gulsen Oztoprak, and Ioli Kythreotou.
Not pictured are Rebecca (Revy) Payiata, Dr. Sondra Sainsbury, Maria Antoniou,
and the late Stelios Christoforou.

loomed, it seemed logical that this was something that I needed to take on. And for the past seven years I have done just that.

However, one never takes on such a project alone. When I met Haris Ioannides of Armida Books in the summer of 2014, just a few months prior to my departure from Cyprus, he was encouraging and said "I like books about Cyprus." Subsequent meetings provided more encouragement, and I am grateful for that initial push. As this project neared its end, Haris assigned Kathleen Stephanides to edit the manuscript. I am immensely grateful for her keen eye, indefatigable diligence, and her many astute suggestions that greatly improved the text.

Prior to my departure Anna handed me a disc with the minutes of the 253 Board meetings and some 50,000 pages of documents related to the Commission. That provided a start.

As the manuscript took shape I asked several individuals to read the chapters and make edits and suggestions. In particular, Ambassador John Koenig, who, like me, served twice in Cyprus, made invaluable comments and corrections that greatly strengthened the first two chapters.

In like manner, Stuart and Laina Swiny read the chapter on the Cyprus American Archaeological Research Institute and their comments made it a much stronger and more accurate chapter. Of course, Laina also served on the Fulbright Commission staff at the time of the transition from Renos Kamenos to Daniel Hadjittofi and, thus, her recollections were particularly valuable. My Foreign Service colleague Mary Jeffers deserves special thanks for reading the chapter on CASP. She was on the staff of Amideast when it took on the task of helping the Commission launch the CASP program. And while Amideast's Kate Archambault, who supervised the CASP program for its entire 30-year run, would not sit for an on-the-record interview, she generously provided space at Amideast where I could review every quarterly report for the program. For the chapter on conflict resolution I am indebted to Dr. John Ungerleider, who read and improved that chapter. He spent a year in Cyprus as a Fulbright scholar and, as Director of the School for International Training (SIT), ran the majority of the youth camps sponsored by the Commission. Needless to say, Anna Argyrou, Gulsen Oztoprak, Dr. Sondra Sainsbury, and Daniel Hadjittofi have read each chapter as it was completed and provided ideas and corrections that were essential.

I have relied on several institutions to help me assemble material for the book. As such, I am grateful to the staff of the National Archives in College Park, Maryland, the staff of the Special Fulbright Collection at the University of Arkansas, the staff of the Law Library at the Library of Congress, the Freedom of Information Office at the Department of State, and the staffs at the Northern Illinois University Library, New York University Library, George Mason University Library, the Ronald Reagan Presidential Library, the Richard Nixon Presidential Library and Museum, and the Office of the Historian at the Department of State. I am also grateful to the founders of Zoom, which allowed me to conduct face-to-face interviews during the pandemic.

At the end of the bibliography I include a list of the nearly 170 interviews conducted for this book. As I wrote in the Author's Note, the story of the Commission is a story about people – people who oversaw the Commission, people who ran the Commission and, most certainly, people who benefitted from the Commission. I am grateful to everyone on that list of interviewees who took the time to relate their experiences and provide a piece of the story of the Commission. Obviously, there are thousands of grantees who I did not interview, but it is my hope that the stories in this history are representative of the experiences of the vast majority of the grantees, whether Fulbright scholars and students, CASP scholars, STT grantees, or participants in the more than 200 conflict resolution programs.

Clearly, however, some individuals' contributions were absolutely essential to the telling of this story. First, Stella Zavallis, the widow of the first Cypriot Executive Director of the Commission Renos Kamenos, who guided the Commission through its first 24 years. Stella was always incredibly responsive and she provided invaluable insight into the workings of what was a small but aggressive Commission in the early years. Of course, as this book explains, Stella was also a senior staff member of the Commission for 41 years, and particularly in the early years when the small staff had to do everything – counseling, administration, logistics, and organization. She was described as the "brass tacks" person who got things done and so many of those interviewed expressed their great affection for Stella and the contribution she made to a successful program in Cyprus for America scholars or for Cypriot students about to begin their great educational adventure in America. As she said herself, the Commission was her second family.

Next, my thanks go to Anna Argyrou, who was hired to run the conflict resolution programs that provided some of the most remarkable stories of the Commission's work. This effort, which saw some of the most important scholars in conflict resolution in the world come to Cyprus under the auspices of the Commission, made the Commission completely unique in comparison to other Fulbright Commissions around the world. Of course, she was also the last "Executive Director" of the Commission, even if one could not bestow that title formally. It was a thankless job, but her intelligence, grit, and great judgment made my final months as Chairman much, much easier. For the past six or seven years, Anna was my "go-to" person for the many questions I had about conflict resolution and about grantees who might have some very important stories to tell. Joining Anna was her partner in the launch of a Study USA non-profit Gulsen Oztoprak, who provided the invaluable Turkish Cypriot perspective, and her many contacts in that community helped me tell the story of the Commission from the viewpoint of both communities on the island. In addition, I must thank Ipek Uzunoglu, my Embassy colleague, who made numerous introductions and arranged a number of contacts in the Turkish Cypriot community. Anna and Gulsen are brilliant counselors and hundreds of Cypriots have benefited from their wise counsel and tireless efforts. So have I.

Of course, Dr. Sondra Sainsbury, who now runs the Fulbright program in Cyprus, has been essential, both as a keeper of records but also as someone who worked for years with the alumni to try to build a community in Cyprus, something that was never easy. Even Cypriot alumni groups can be a bit tribal. Her insights about the final days of the Commission and the transition to the Fulbright program in Cyprus today were crucial. My successor, Ingrid Larson, praised Sondra's astute decisions that provided a sound foundation for the new program.

Finally, I give my greatest and most heartfelt thanks to Daniel Hadjittofi, the Executive Director who guided the Commission for 26 years. The bibliography lists a dozen formal interviews with him, but my files include hundreds of email exchanges, while he also opened his personal files to me.   As one of the Washington desk officers noted, officials in the Fulbright office at USIA and, ultimately, the State Department, saw Daniel as a star.   When he attended Fulbright conferences, other Executive Directors always sought him out. The Commission's insistence on providing both undergraduate and graduate grants provoked resistance from Washington for years, but now is often the rule and not the exception. His dogged determination to provide more grants by keeping them small and then seeking aid packages from universities meant much more work, but many more students ultimately benefited from the program. Hadjittofi himself is an excellent example. He ran a multi-million dollar scholarship program skillfully and fairly and his championing of conflict resolution work, despite a personal story that would not have predicted such an outcome, meant taking on risks to both the Commission and to himself. He held steady even when some would call him traitor, while others would accuse the Commission of "brainwashing" an entire population of Cypriots. This book would not exist without his steadfast support, encyclopedic memory, and unwavering friendship.

No book is perfect nor can hope to tell the complete story of an institution such as the Cyprus Fulbright Commission, given the vast number of characters, the complicated political cross-currents, and the many issues surrounding a Commission that was a multi-million-dollar enterprise on a small, politically divided island. Omissions, mischaracterizations, and other flaws are my fault and mine alone. I hope they will not detract from what is a remarkable story about a group of remarkable people.

***

ENDNOTES

Preface

1. Walter Johnson and Francis J. Colligan, *The Fulbright Program: A History* (University of Chicago Press, 1965), p. 12.
2. Ibid.
3. Randall Bennett Woods, *Fulbright: A Biography* (Cambridge University Press, 1995), p. 87-91.
4. Ibid. p. 131.

A Little History

1. Remarks made by Mustafa Akinci, Turkish Cypriot political leader, at a seminar at the University of Cyprus, *The Cyprus Problem: 40 Years On*, Nicosia, Cyprus, July 2014 (attended by the Author).
2. George W. Ball, *The Past Has Another Pattern* (W.W. Norton & Company, New York, 1982) p. 337.
3. Ted Gup, *The Book of Honor: The Secret Lives and Deaths of CIA Operatives* (Anchor Books, New York, 2000), p. 92.
4. Harold MacMillan, *Riding the Storm 1956-1959* (Harper & Row, New York, 1971) p. 663.
5. Ibid., p. 660.
6. Ibid., p. 696.
7. Claire Palley, *An International Relations Debacle: the UN Secretary-General's Mission of Good Offices in Cyprus: 1999 – 2004* (Hart Publishers), p. 350.

Cyprus and America

1. Message from the President of the United States to the two Houses of Congress at the Commencement of the Third Session of the Twenty-Fifth Congress, December 4, 1838, pp. 31-32.
2. Elizabeth McFadden, *The Glitter and the Gold* (The Dial Press, New York, 1971), p. 98.
3. Ibid., pp. 117-118. Note that Cesnola also served as the Greek Consul, and perhaps one other undisclosed sinecure.
4. David Lavender, *The Story of the Cyprus Mines Corporation* (The Huntington Library, San Marino, California, 1962), p. 56.
5. Ibid., p. 216.
6. Ibid., p. 249.

7. Ibid., pp. 251-255.

8. Central Intelligence Agency, Staff Memorandum 44-61, August 10, 1961, *The Current Situation in Cyprus* (Declassified June 22, 2005).

9. Memorandum, Central Intelligence Agency, Dated March 28, 1947 (Declassified on June 6, 2009).

10. Memorandum, Central Intelligence Agency, Dated July 2, 1948 (Declassified September 12, 2008).

11. *Giorgos Georgiou, "British Bases in Cyprus and Signals Intelligence"* (Cryptone.org,, 2012).

12. Fraser Wilkins, Gift of Personal Statement to the John F. Kennedy Library, March 1972 (General Services Administration National Archives and Records Service), p. 18.

13. Ambassador William R. Crawford, Jr., Foreign Affairs Oral History Project, October 24, 1988; interviewed by Charles Stuart Kennedy.

14. U.S. Consulate Nicosia, Telegram classified secret from Consulate General Nicosia to Secretary of State, October 20, 1959 (Department of State Central Files).

15. Letter from President Eisenhower to King Paul I, transmitted by telegram 1048 to Athens, September 30, 1958.

16. Eisenhower-Dulles phone conversation, June 14, 1958 (Eisenhower Library, Dulles Papers, White House Telephone Conversations), transcribed by Phyllis D. Bernau. This was not the only time that U.S. officials proposed moving Turkish Cypriots off the island. In 1964, Senator J. William Fulbright visited Cyprus in his capacity as Chairman of the Senate Foreign Relations Committee and suggested that Turkish Cypriots be moved en masse from the island, a suggestion that was immediately rejected by Turkish Cypriot leaders.

17. Statement of U.S. Policy Toward Cyprus; National Security Council Report 6003, Washington, D.C., February 9, 1960.

18. Ibid.

19. Taylor Belcher, Telegram 391 from U.S. Consulate Nicosia to the Department of State (Secret), March 6, 1959 (Note: $20 million in 1960 is equivalent to $175 million in 2020 dollars.)

20. Editorial Note, Foreign Relations Series of the U.S. No. 336, 424th meeting of the National Security Council, November 11, 1959, and Memorandum of Discussion, 434th meeting of the National Security Council, February 4, 1960.

21. Fraser Wilkins, Gift of Personal Statement to the John F. Kennedy Library, March 1972 (General Services Administration National Archives and Records Service), pp. 9-10.

22. Memorandum from the Executive Secretary of the Department of State to the President's Special Assistant for National Security Affairs, Washington, July 13, 1962.

23. Letter from Vice President Fazil Kutchuk to Vice President Lyndon Johnson, August 28, 1962. The Turkish Cypriots complained that agitation for enosis continued; that the constitution was not being implemented; that the physical security of Turkish Cypriots was threatened; that the communist danger (AKEL) was growing; that they disagreed with a non-aligned orientation in foreign policy; that the London-Zurich accords recognized two separate communities; asked for a "fair" apportionment of U.S. aid (Rauf Denktash asked that aid be funneled through the communal chambers as opposed to the central government).

24. George W. Ball, Op. Cit., p. 338.

25. Ibid., pp. 350-351.

26. Memorandum of Conversation, *U.S. Position on the Cyprus Problem*; meeting between Acting Secretary of State George Ball and Cypriot Foreign Minister Spyros Kyprianou, Washington, D.C., February 4, 1965.

27. Cyrus R. Vance, Interview with Paige E. Mulhollan (LBJ Library, Foreign Affairs Oral History Project), pp. 31-38.   Vance shuttled between Athens and Ankara in November 1967 to hammer out a four-point agreement that defused a conflict between Greece and Turkey over Cyprus.   Vance was assisted by representatives of the U.N. Secretary General and an envoy from NATO as well as the American Ambassadors in Athens, Ankara and Nicosia.

28. CIA Analysis of Cyprus situation, Foreign Relations Series of the United States, (Department of State Historian), September 24, 1973.   The CIA concluded that the best that could be hoped for was maintaining the status quo.

29. Thomas Boyatt and Richard Erman, National Security Council Contingency Plans: Cyprus (Secret), Foreign Relations Series of the U.S., Document No. 76, May 5, 1974.

30. Thomas Boyatt, Foreign Affairs Oral History Project, Presentation at the Foreign Service Institute, Washington, D.C., September 30, 1992, p. 8.

31. The most prominent book in this genre is Brendan O'Malley's and Ian Craig's *The Cyprus Conspiracy* published in 1999, which did not spare the British in its condemnation.   There is also *The United States, Cyprus, and the Rule of Law, 1974-1994: Twenty Years of Turkish Aggression and Occupation*, published in 1996, written by Eugene Rossides, a prominent member of the Greek lobby in the United States.   Historian Niall Ferguson, who is working on the second volume of Henry Kissinger's biography, told the author in 2019 that that volume would have a section on Cyprus and 1974.

32. James Ker-Lindsay, *The Cyprus Problem: What Everyone Needs to Know* (Oxford University Press, 2011), pp. 45-46.

33. Author interview with Ambassador James Williams and Ambassador Ray Ewing, March 25, 2019 at Mamma Lucci's Restaurant, Leesburg, Virginia.

34. There are a number of first-hand accounts of the killing of Ambassador Davies.   Ambassador James Williams, who was a political officer at the Embassy, tells the story as part of the Foreign Affairs Oral History Project.   Assistant

Public Affairs Officer David Grimland told the story in chapter 10 of his memoir *Journey to Ithaka*. In the charged atmosphere, there were no arrests for the murders. However, years of sustained pressure from the American government and Makarios's desire to patch up relations with the U.S. led to the arrest of Ioannis Ktimatias and Neoptolemos Leftis, who were convicted of weapons charges and sentenced to prison in 1977. After 18 months, a court threw out their convictions and they were released. Today, the American Ambassador's residence in Nicosia is known as the Rodger Davies House, and a room in the Embassy is dedicated to the memory of Antoinette Varnavas. Clerides and Kissinger spoke for the first time the day after the killing and Clerides assured Kissinger that he had made a statement that the invasion had not been the fault of the United States.

35. David Grimland, *Journey to Ithaka* (Lulu Publishing Services, 2015) p. 76.

36. Matthew Nimitz, *"The Cyprus Problem Revisited," The Mediterranean Quarterly*, entered into the record April 17, 1991 during a hearing before the Subcommittee on European Affairs of the Committee on Foreign Relations of the U.S. Senate entitled: "Cyprus: International Law and the Prospects for Settlement," p. 27.

37. In recent years, Turkish and Turkish Cypriot officials have opened stretches of the beach at Varosha and the RoC has said that this is unacceptable.

38. Richard Boucher, interview with author, January 26, 2017, Washington, D.C.

39. See American Diplomacy website for former Cyprus Desk Officer David Jones's appreciation of Reginald Bartholomew, November 2012. See also "The State Department Oral Histories" by Christian Chapman and Nelson Ledsky for detailed discussions of their time as Special Cyprus Coordinators. The authorization for a $250 million "peace and reconstruction fund" was contained in PL99-83.

40. Thomas Weston, Oral interview by Charles Stuart Kennedy. Foreign Affairs Oral History Project; Association for Diplomatic Studies and Training (May 19, 2005), pp. 130-148.

41. Ambassador Michael Klosson; Interview by Author; Washington, D.C. June 21, 2017.

42. Ambassador John Koenig, Interview by Author (by video) Bellingham, Washington, April 17, 2020 and exchange of emails, November 10-11, 2020.

43. Ambassador John Koenig; Interview by Author (by video) Bellingham, Washington, April 17, 2020.

Renos and Stella

1. Dr. Michael Sarris; Interview by Author, Nicosia, Cyprus, November 21, 2018.

2. Memorandum of Conversation from a meeting between Secretary of State Dean Rusk and Cyprus Ambassador to the United States Zenon Rossides,

March 3, 1961, Washington, D.C.   Foreign Relations Series of the United States, Document 247.

3. National Security Action Memorandum No. 71, August 23, 1961, from Present John F. Kennedy to Secretary of State Dean Rusk. Foreign Relations Series of the United States, Document No. 248.

4. Memorandum from the Executive Secretary of the Department of State (L.D. Battle) to the President's Special Assistant for National Security Affairs (McGeorge Bundy), September 7, 1961, Washington, D.C. "Proposals for U.S. Action in Cyprus," Foreign Relations Series of the United States, Document No. 249.

5. Telegram from Consulate General Nicosia to the Department of State, "Annual Educational Exchange Report, August 3, 1959.   Signed by Consul General Taylor Belcher. Telegram notes that the Consulate General Nicosia would send four Cypriots to the U.S. on "leader grants" – two in education and two in labor relations.

6. Letter from Wilfred "Bill" Mauck, Chief Education Officer at USAID/State Department to the USAID Mission in Nicosia, December 1962. National Archives, College Park, Maryland.

7. Letter from American University of Beirut President Samuel Kirkwood to U.S. Ambassador Taylor Belcher, July 3, 1966, National Archives, College Park, Maryland. Belcher had planned a trip to Beirut to lobby for a university branch but decided against it after receiving Kirkwood's letter.

8. Kyriacos Markides; *The Rise and Fall of the Cyprus Republic* (Yale University Press, 1977), p. 98.

9. In the office of the Public Affairs Officer at the American Embassy Nicosia, there hung a photograph of the opening of the USIS American Library that shows President Makarios making remarks while Vice President Kuchuk and a beaming Ambassador Wilkins look on.   When I visited the Embassy in 2022, the photo had disappeared.

10. Fraser Wilkins, Gift of Personal Statement to the John F. Kennedy Library, March 1972, General Services Administration National Archives and Records Service, p. 10. Note: $40 million in 1961 translates to approximately $340 million in 2020 dollars.

11. Joseph Toner, USAID Director in Nicosia, Cyprus. Interview with the Cyprus News Agency on March 13, 1963. Transcript in the National Archives, College Park, Maryland. Toner outlined the number of American experts working in the Water Department, the Planning Department, the Cyprus Development Bank, the Ministry of Labor and the Ministry of Agriculture.

12. Agreement between the Government of the Republic of Cyprus and the Government of the United States of America for financing certain educational exchange programs, January 18, 1962, Nicosia, Cyprus.   Signed by Cyprus Foreign Minister Spyros Kyprianou and U.S. Ambassador to Cyprus Fraser Wilkins.

13. Ibid.

14. Interview with Dr. Andreas Kamenos by Author, December 6, 2019.

15. Interview with Stella Zavallis by Author, December 5, 2017, Nicosia, Cyprus.

16. Ibid.

17. Ibid.

18. Minutes of the fourth and fifth board meetings of the Commission for Educational Exchange between the Republic of Cyprus and the United States of America, July 19, 1962 and October 10, 1962, held at the American Center, Nicosia, Cyprus.

19. Interview with Sophocles Michaelides by Author, November 18, 2019, Nicosia, Cyprus.

20. Ibid.

21. Minutes of the fifth Board Meeting of the Commission for Educational Exchange between the Republic of Cyprus and the United States of America, January 18, 1963.

22. Interview with Dr. Sokrates Pantelides by Author via Zoom, August 28, 2020, Nashville, Tennessee.

23. Kenan Atakol, *Turkish & Greek Cypriots; Is Their Separation Permanent?* (METU Press; June 2012), pp. 37-43; Interview by Author with Kenan Atakol, June 20, 2016, Kyrenia/Girne, Cyprus.

24. Interview with Telemachos Mouschovias by Author, August 10, 2020.

25. Ibid.

26. Open Doors, International Institute of Education, Washington, D.C. Special request from the IIE database.

27. Minutes of the 43rd and 47th Board Meetings of the Commission for Educational Exchange between the Republic of Cyprus and the United States of America, July 10, 1967 and November 6, 1967. Ioannis Kyriacou was found by Greek police in Emvia, Greece and returned to Cyprus with his father.

28. Original Certificate of Death, Department of Health and Social Services, State of Wisconsin. The certificate states that Christodoulos Mouzakis died by suicide (hanging) on January 10, 1968 at the University of Wisconsin.

29. Minutes of the 62nd Board Meeting of the Commission for Educational Exchange between the Republic of Cyprus and the United States of America, February 17, 1969.

30. Minutes of the 63rd Board Meeting of the Commission for Educational Exchange between the Republic of Cyprus and the United States of America, March 3, 1969.

31. Minutes of the 64th Board Meeting of the Commission for Educational Exchange between the Republic of Cyprus and the United States of America, April 7, 1969.

32. Lonnie R. Johnson, *The Making of the Fulbright Program, 1945-61: Architecture, Philosophy and Narrative*, pp. 23-25.   Paper presented at the Blair

Center at a conference at the University of Arkansas, Fayetteville; September 1-2, 2015. The conference was entitled "J. William Fulbright in International Perspective: Liberal Internationalism and U.S. Global Influence."

33. USIS Press Release, January 19, 1972. Ambassador David Popper hosted a small lunch to mark the 10th anniversary of the Fulbright program in Cyprus attended by Foreign Minister Sypros Kyprianou and Education Minister Frixos Petrides and past and present members of the Commission. Ambassador Popper and Foreign Minister Kyprianou made remarks in praise of the program and its staff.
34. Ibid.
35. Minutes of the 73rd Board Meeting of the Commission for Educational Exchange between the Republic of Cyprus and the United States of America, September 14, 1970.
36. Email exchange between Author and Stella Zavallis on August 19, 2020.
37. Interview with Dr. Jack Balswick by Author, April 15, 2019 via telephone. Balwick published a number of academic articles about Cyprus, including *The Effect of Urbanization Upon Household Structures in Cyprus,* with C. Paschalis, *International Journal of Sociology and the Family* (4/1 Spring 1974), pp. 101-108; *Comparative Earnings of Greek Cypriot Women and Men* (*Sex Roles* 4, 1978) pp. 877-885; a study on the dowry system in *The International Journal of the Family* in 1975; a study entitled *The Greek Cypriot Family in a Changing Society*, published by the Ministry of Labor and Social Insurance, Nicosia, Cyprus.
38. Interview with Dr. Donald Reeb by Author via telephone, February 28, 2018.
39. Interview with Kerri Ballantyne by Author via Zoom, August 28, 2020.
40. Minutes of the 95th Board Meeting of the Commission for Educational Exchange between the Republic of Cyprus and the United States of America, December 10, 1973.
41. 1976 Annual Program Plan for the Commission for Educational Exchange between the United States and Cyprus, p. 4 (adopted June 10, 1975).
42. Interview with Michael Tringides by the Author via telephone February 26, 2018. Tringides went on from Yale to do his Ph.D. at the University of Chicago and was granted a waiver for his J-1 visa requirement, allowing him to stay in the U.S. and pursue his academic career. His specialty is materials sciences.
43. Interview with Sarper Ince by the Author in Nicosia, Cyprus, November 8, 2017.
44. Interview with Stella Zavallis by Author in Nicosia, Cyprus, December 5, 2017.
45. Interview with Sheila Austrian by the Author via telephone, April 5, 2019.
46. Interview with Rea Yiordamlis by the Author in Nicosia, Cyprus, November 11, 2019.

The Board

1. Minutes of the 99th Board Meeting of the Commission for Educational Exchange between the Republic of Cyprus and the United States of America, October 3, 1974.
2. Minutes of the 100th Board Meeting of the Commission for Educational Exchange between the Republic of Cyprus and the United States of America, December 13, 1974. (Italics added to the word "all.")
3. Memo from Executive Director of the Fulbright Commission, Daniel Hadjittofi to Board Chairman Thomas Miller, February 25, 2008. Hadjittofi characterized the situation as a "can of worms" because Dr. Akbil had already been informed of his impending appointment to the Board. Hadjittofi had to use his diplomatic skills to smooth over relations with the Turkish Cypriots and held out hope they might offer Dr. Akbil a place on the Board later, but they never did. Hadjittofi asked the Embassy to consider an intervention with the Ministry of Foreign Affairs.
4. Interview with Daniel Hadjittofi by Author in Nicosia, Cyprus, June 2016.
5. Interview with Dr. Hüseyin Yaratan by Author in Nicosia, Cyprus, November 2019.
6. Post-World War II, public diplomacy efforts, including the management of the Fulbright program, were part of the Department of State. President Eisenhower believed that foreign audiences would be more receptive to the Cold War messaging if it came from an independent agency and so USIA was created in August 1953. The public diplomacy function was merged back into the Department of State on October 1, 1999 along with the Arms Control and Disarmament Agency and, partially, the United States Agency for International Development (USAID) in a move orchestrated by Senator Jesse Helms (R-NC), the chairman of the Senate Foreign Relations Committee. Helms sought cost savings and argued that all instruments of foreign policy should be under the control of the Secretary of State.
7. Kristine Konold, *Backstage at the Big War: A Memoir of World War II* (Brunswick Publishing Corporation, Lawrenceville, Virginia, 1991), pp. 1-5.
8. Email from Nicolas Sparsis in Nicosia, Cyprus to the Author, October 21, 2020.
9. Email from Stella Zavallis in Nicosia, Cyprus to the Author, August 19, 2020.
10. Interview with Lellos Demetriades by Author in Nicosia, Cyprus, June 2016.
11. Interview with Achilleas Demetriades by Author in Nicosia, Cyprus, November 18, 2019.
12. Ibid.
13. Interview with Ambassador John Koenig.
14. Interview with Mustafa Raif by Author in Nicosia, Cyprus, July 16, 2016.
15. Minutes of the 103rd Board Meeting of the Commission for Educational Exchange between the Republic of Cyprus and the United States of America, June 29, 1976.

16. Interview with Mustafa Raif by Author in Nicosia, Cyprus, July 16, 2016.

17. Interview with Esat Hilmi by Author in Nicosia, Cyprus, July 16, 2016.

18. Interviews with Dogan Yavuz by Author in Kyrenia/Girne, Cyprus, July 16, 2016 and November 18, 2019.

19. Minutes of the 101st and 102nd Board Meetings of the Commission for Educational Exchange between the Republic of Cyprus and the United States of America, June 17, 1975 and October 14, 1975.

20. Memo from Fulbright Commission Executive Director Daniel Hadjittofi to Roy Glover, Cyprus Program Officer at the United States Information Agency, July 21, 1999. Hadjittofi, in the course of discussing the Embassy's post of bicommunal coordinator and the feelings of the Commission Board, explained Board "dynamics" before Glover briefed newly appointed Ambassador Donald Bandler.

21. Minutes of the 94th Board Meeting of the Commission for Educational Exchange between the Republic of Cyprus and the United States of America, December 3, 1973. Excerpts of a report were read from the September 19-21, 1973 meeting of the Board of Foreign Scholarships. It was noted that two of the smallest commissions in the Near East Asia region – Cyprus and Afghanistan – had initiated some of the most interesting projects.

22. Minutes of the 104th Board Meeting of the Commission for Educational Exchange between the Republic of Cyprus and the United States of America, June 9, 1977.

23. Foreign Minister Spyros Kyrianou made his speech in praise of the Commission on March 15, 1969 at a lunch at the Hilton Hotel.

24. Interview with Lellos Demetriades by Author in Nicosia, Cyprus, June 2016.

25. Interview with Dr. Chryssostomos Sofianos by Author in Nicosia, Cyprus, June 2016.

26. Ibid.

27. Interview with Dr. Cem Tanova by Author November 21, 2018, Nicosia, Cyprus.

28. Interview with Gunfer Erkman by Author November 18, 2019, Nicosia Cyprus.

29. Interview with Dr. Chris Schabel by Author (via Zoom) July 3, 2020, Paris, France.

30. Interview with Board member Claire Georghiou by Author in Nicosia, Cyprus, November 15, 2017.

31. Ibid.

32. Ibid.

CAARI - Cyprus American Archaeological Research Institute

1. Ellen Herscher, *Lapithos 1931: An Unofficial ASCSA Excavation in Cyprus*, American School of Classical Studies at Athens Newsletter, May 2007.

2. Ibid.

3. Interview with Dr. Ellen Herscher by Author in Georgetown, Washington, D.C., June 8, 2016

4. Ibid.

5. Ibid

6. Ibid

7. Stuart Swiny, *CAARI – The House of the Dancing Bird; A History of the Cyprus American Archaeological Research Institute, Nicosia Cyprus, 1978-2000* in *An ASOR Mosaic: A Centennial History of the American Schools of Oriental Research*, edited by Joe D. Seger (Boston, Massachusetts, 2001), p. 322 Note: ASOR changed its name from the American Society of Oriental Research to the more politically correct American Society of Overseas Research in 2021, thus retaining the acronym ASOR.

8. Ibid., p. 323.

9. Ibid., p. 324.

10. Interview with Stuart and Laina Swiny by Author via Zoom in Dover, Massachusetts, June 18, 2020.

11. Swiny, *CAARI – The House of the Dancing Bird*, p. 325.

12. Minutes of the 104th Board Meeting of the Commission for Educational Exchange between the Republic of Cyprus and the United States of America, June 9, 1977, Nicosia, Cyprus.

13. Interview with Dr. Anita Walker by Author via Zoom, March 20, 2020 in Concord, New Hampshire.

14. Ibid.

15. Ibid. Note: A.G. Leventis would die in October 1978.

16. Ibid.

17. Interview with Stuart and Laina Swiny by Author via Zoom in Dover, Massachusetts, June 18, 2020. Note: Stuart Swiny became a U.S. citizen in 2020.

18. Ibid.

19. Swiny, *CAARI – The House of the Dancing Bird*, p. 335. The purchase and transport of the nearly 10,000 items in the collection was supported by a grant from USIA and a second substantial grant from Board Trustee Patricia Plum Wylde in remembrance of her father-in-law John I. Wylde, who passed away in 1982, the same year as Schaeffer.

20. Interview with Ronald Ungaro by Author via telephone, January 5, 2021, West Palm Beach, Florida.

21. Interview with Gustave Feissel by Author via telephone, August 28, 2018, San Francisco, California.

22. Interview with Dr. Julie Hansen by Author via telephone, January 16, 2021, Atlanta, Georgia.

23. Email exchange between Dan Howard and the Author, December 31, 2020 and January 1, 2021.

24. Draft USIA response to the Cyprus Fulbright Commission program plan for fiscal year 1989/90, undated.

25. Interview with Vathoulla Moustoukki by Author via Zoom, January 4, 2021, Nicosia, Cyprus.
26. Swiny, *CAARI – The House of the Dancing Bird*, p. 333.
27. Interview with Dr. Pamela Gaber by Author, November 17, 2018, Denver, Colorado.
28. Ibid.
29. Minutes of the 135th Board Meeting of the Commission for Educational Exchange between the Republic of Cyprus and the United States of America, April 27, 1987, Nicosia, Cyprus.
30. Interview with Dr. Tom Davis by Author, November 25, 2019, San Diego, California.
31. Ibid.
32. Ibid.
33. Ibid.
34. Interview with Dr. Andrew McCarthy by Author, November 25, 2019, San Diego, California.
35. Ibid.
36. As CAARI continues to be seen as one of the only American institutions on Cyprus, the Embassy's Public Affairs Section continues to support CAARI. One of my last acts as Public Affairs Officer in the summer of 2014 was to give CAARI a $5,000 grant for the publication of the proceedings of a conference. There was also support for CAARI's 40th anniversary celebration, which took place in June 2018. I currently serve on CAARI's Board.
37. Interview with Hannah Gaber by Author, November 2017, Nicosia, Cyprus.
38. Ibid.

CASP - Cyprus American Scholarship Program

1. Interview with Eugene Rossides by Author, October 11, 2017, Washington, D.C. Rossides had a remarkable biography. He was a college (American) football star at Columbia during its "golden age" of football and helped end Army's 32-game win streak. He was drafted by the New York Giants of the National Football League in 1949 but chose to go to law school instead. He moved back and forth between private law practice and government positions and was the Assistant Secretary of the Treasury for Enforcement when the war in Cyprus occurred in 1974. It was at that point that he founded the Hellenic American Institute. He died in May 2020 at the age of 92.
2. Ibid.
3. U.S. Assistance to Cyprus: Report to the Subcommittee on Europe and the Middle East; House Committee on Foreign Affairs, by the U.S. General Accounting Office, November 30, 1981, signed by Frank C. Conahan, Director, pp i-iii.
4. Ibid.

5. Interview with Dan Howard by Author, June 6, 2016, Centerville, Virginia.
6. Interview with Ambassador Galen Stone by Author via telephone, July 14, 2016, Boston, Massachusetts.
7. David Grimland, *Journey to Ithaka*, p. 91.
8. Interview with Tim Kernan by Author via telephone June 1, 2018, Washington, D.C.
9. U.S. Assistance to Cyprus: Report to the Subcommittee, p. 7 and p. 35.
10. Interview with Michael Van Dusen by Author via telephone, May 18, 2020, Washington, D.C.
11. Interview with Tim Kernan.
12. Interview with Diana Ohlbaum by Author via telephone June 3, 2020, Washington, D.C.
13. Interview with Marx Sterne by Author, Washington, D.C., May 7, 2018.
14. Interview with Eugene Rossides.
15. Congressional Record, Senate Committee on Foreign Relations, February-March hearings on "International Development and Security Assistance Act."
16. Ibid.
17. Interview with Ambassador Galen Stone.
18. Interview with Senator Chris Van Hollen by Author, March 27, 2019, Washington, D.C. Van Hollen travelled to the region in1988-89 and produced a report entitled *New Opportunities for U.S. Policy in the Eastern Mediterranean*, which was presented to the Senate Committee on Foreign Relations in April 1989. He argued that the emergence of the Davos process, the election of President Vassiliou, and his subsequent re-launching of talks with Rauf Denktash (August 24, 1988) provided new opportunities for the U.S. to strengthen the southern flank of NATO. That said, he noted that all sides, including Greece and Turkey, would not accept the U.S. as a direct mediator. He argued that the CASP program could be structured to promote more interaction between Greek and Turkish Cypriots, noting that an entire generation was growing up in the two communities with no contact between them.
19. Interview with Ambassador Andrew Jacovides by Author, January 29, 2017, New York City, N.Y.
20. Interview with Christina Hadjiparaskeva by Author in Nicosia, Cyprus, November 18, 2019.
21. Ibid.
22. HR 4473. Foreign Assistance and Related Programs Appropriations Act 1980. Conference report filed February 27, 1980.
23. Amideast was founded in 1951 as the American Friends of the Middle East as a cultural exchange organization that was, at one point, partially funded by the CIA. In 1967, the CIA funding was exposed and the organization cut its ties to the CIA, restructured and became Amideast. In 2018, Amideast had a portfolio of $66 million, a staff of 1,200 and 20 offices in 11

Middle Eastern and North African countries as well as the United States. In 2018, its grants serviced 2,350 exchange and scholarship students, 15,500 youth and women through special programs, 57,000 students and professional trainees, 100,000 recipients of academic guidance, and oversaw 210,000 test-takers. A senior Amideast official declined to be interviewed on the record for this book.

24. Diplomatic Note from the Government of Cyprus to the American Embassy dated November 9, 1981 detailing decision 20,9 by the Council of Ministers.

25. Interview with Stella Zavallis by Author.

26. Minutes of the 116th, 118th, and 119th Board Meetings of the Commission for Educational Exchange between the Republic of Cyprus and the United States of America, April 3, 1981, September 24, 1981 and October 7, 1981, Nicosia, Cyprus

27. Interview with Katharine Redmond by Author via phone, April 1, 2019, Washington, D.C.

28. Cyprus Project Paper: Cyprus Scholarship Program; Project No. 233-0002. U.S. Agency for International Development, Washington, D.C., June 24, 1981, Annex C, p. 1, written by Antoinette Ford on September 4, 1981.

29. Interview with Steve Brattain by Author in Washington, D.C., July 18, 2018.

30. Report by Amideast on the CASP program September 25, 1981 through January 31, 1982, Washington, D.C.

31. Personal Letter from Kate Archambault to Betsy Fenhagen, October 18, 1982, Washington, D.C.

32. Letter from Kate Archambault (in Washington, D.C.) to Mary Howard (in Nicosia, Cyprus), March 18, 1985.

33. Ibid.

34. Interview with Chrysanthos Panayiotou by Author via phone, May 5, 2020, Ft. Pierce, Florida.

35. Ibid.

36. Interview with Olcay Firinciogullari by Author via Zoom, February 5, 2021, Nicosia, Cyprus.

37. Ibid.

38. Ibid.

39. Interview with Alexandros Josephides by Author, November 7, 2019, Limassol, Cyprus.

40. Ibid.

41. Exchange of emails with Laina Swiny and the Author, January 25, 2021.

42. Exchange of emails with Dan Howard and the Author, January 24, 2021.

43. Interview with Dr. Leondios Kostrikis by Author at the University of Cyprus, Nicosia, November 7, 2017.

44. Ibid.

45. Ibid.

46. Ibid.

47. Interview with Fehmi Tokay by Author via telephone, December 6, 2019, Nicosia, Cyprus.

48. Ibid.

49. Interview with Walter Douglas by Author, January 2017, Washington, D.C.

50. National Center for Educational Statistics, Table 330.10: Average undergraduate tuition and fees and room and board rates charged for full-time students in degree-granting postsecondary institutions, by level and control of institution: Selected years, 1963-64 through 2018-19.

51. CASP Program 1983 Annual Report by Amideast, January 1984, Washington, D.C.

52. Exchange of emails between Stella Zavallis and Author, January 28, 2021, Nicosia, Cyprus.

53. Exchange of emails between Dan and Mary Howard and Author, January 24, 2021, Clifton, Virginia.

54. Interview with Mehmet Ali Yukselen by Author, November 8, 2019, Lefke, Cyprus.

55. Ibid.

56. Ibid.

57. Interview with Ambassador Richard Boucher by Author, January 26, 2017, Washington, D.C.

58. Open Doors – International Educational Exchange between the United States and Cyprus 1970/71 to 2018/19, the Institute of International Education, Washington, D.C.

Daniel

1. Interview with Daniel Hadjittofi by Author, November 21, 2017, Nicosia, Cyprus. Note: The remains of Tofis Hadjittofi, his brother and brothers-in-law were eventually found and identified via DNA testing.

2. Interview with Daniel Hadjittofi.

3. Interviews with Stella Zavallis and Daniel Hadjittofi.

4. Interview with Daniel Hadjittofi.

5. Exchange of emails with Dr. Michael Granof, University of Texas at Austin, September 20, 2018.

6. Interview with Daniel Hadjittofi.

7. Exchange of emails between Dan Howard and the Author, February 18-19, 2021.

8. Interview with Stuart and Laina Swiny by Author via Zoom, June 18, 2020, Dover Massachusetts.

9. Interview with Stella Zavallis by Author, December 5, 2017, Nicosia, Cyprus

10. Minutes of the 133rd Board Meeting of the Commission for Educational Exchange between the Republic of Cyprus and the United States of America, September 19, 1986, Nicosia, Cyprus.

11. Nora Boustany, *Two Cypriot Hostages Released*, special to the *Washington Post*, June 22, 1986.

12. Interview with Sonuc Demililer by Author, November 14, 2019, Nicosia, Cyprus.

13. Ibid.

14. Interview with Dr. Stelios Georgiou by Author, April 26, 2021 via Zoom, Nicosia, Cyprus.

15. Interview with Ioli Kythreotou by Author, November 5, 2019, Nicosia, Cyprus.

16. Interview with Daniel Hadjittofi by Author, November 23, 2017, Nicosia, Cyprus.

17. Interview with Achilleas Demetriades.

18. Minutes of the 162nd Board Meeting of the Commission for Educational Exchange between the Republic of Cyprus and the United States of America, October 14, 1994, Nicosia, Cyprus.

19. Interview with Daniel Hadjittofi by Author via Zoom, April 1, 2021, Nicosia, Cyprus.

20. Interview with Constantinos Pitris by Author, November 22, 2017, Nicosia, Cyprus.

21. Ibid.

22. Ibid. The technique that Pitris worked on is called optical coherence tomography and has earned him other patents. One at MIT earned him $25,000, which meant a new laptop and moving expenses back to Cyprus. He has now earned his first patent in Cyprus.

23. Ibid.

24. Commentary on the FY-1989/90 Program Plan for the Cyprus Fulbright Commission by the USIA Desk Officer responsible for Fulbright in Washington, D.C. (Undated).

25. Minutes of the 134th Board Meeting of the Commission for Educational Exchange between the Republic of Cyprus and the United States of America, November 28, 1986, Nicosia, Cyprus. It took a couple of years, but the Commission raised just over $10,000 (about $22,000 in current dollars) and presented books on both sides of the island in 1988. Newspaper clippings show then-Board Chairman Lane Cubstead presenting 250 books at the Greek Cypriot Pedagogical Academy.

26. Interview with Daniel Hadjittofi by Author, November 23, 2017, Nicosia, Cyprus.

27. Interview with Idil Akcal by Author via Zoom, December 23, 2020, Nicosia, Cyprus.

28. Vassos Phtohopoulos, *Scandalous propaganda in favor of the 'TRNC' by an American Fulbright scholar*, *Kyrikas*, May 21, 1989. The conversation with Daniel Hadjittofi occurred on May 16, 1989. The Commission kept a memorandum of the conversation and when the article appeared, Hadjittofi

wrote a memo to the Board Chairman, noting that the article was "ignorant" and that the Commission could issue a brief statement, or do nothing. It did nothing.

29. Interview with Daniel Hadjittofi, April 1, 2021.

30. Interview with Kyproula Kyriakidou by Author, November 20, 2017, Nicosia, Cyprus.

31. The first cable was in response to the initial changes proposed by Amideast on January 21, 1989. In a January 27, 1989 response via an unclassified cable approved by Ambassador William Perrin, the post argued that it "strongly opposes proposed change assigning Amideast principle authority for hiring and supervising the CASP Coordinator in Cyprus." In an April 24th cable it further argued that: "The Amideast-drafted revision is unacceptable to the Mission because it would drastically reverse the roles between, on the one hand, the Embassy and Fulbright Commission in Cyprus, and, on the other, the contractor in Washington. It would cast the Mission and Fulbright Commission as secondary and ineffectual players in the daily on-the-ground administration of a politically sensitive and costly USG scholarship program."

32. Memorandum from Executive Director Daniel Hadjittofi to Board Chairman Lane Cubstead. Subject: My visit to Washington, D.C. August 29-September 10, 1989. Memo dated September 25, 1989.

33. Interview with Daniel Hadjittofi, November 21, 2017. The contract language in the paragraph comes from his September 28, 2001 contract, which had been amended with minor changes seven times since the original contract on September 19, 1986.

34. House Foreign Affairs Subcommittee on Europe and the Middle East Authorization for Fiscal Years 1990-1991, June 20, 1989, Washington, D.C., pp. 74-75. Note: The State Department had requested $8 million for each of those fiscal years and the subcommittee authorized $15 million for each of those years. It also instructed that $5 million of the money (not going to the CASP program) be used for bicommunal activities.

35. Minutes of the 143rd Board Meeting of the Commission for Educational Exchange between the Republic of Cyprus and the United States of America, September 15, 1989, Nicosia, Cyprus; Minutes of the 147th Board Meeting of the Commission for Educational Exchange between the Republic of Cyprus and the United States of America, October 19, 1990, Nicosia, Cyprus. These decisions were made as the RoC was raising the level of its representation on the Board. The primary members were Dr. Jacovos Aristidou, the Minister of Labor and Social Insurance, and Ambassador Andreas Jacovides, the Director General of the Ministry of Foreign Affairs.

36. Interview with Daniel Hadjittofi, November 23, 2017. In 1990, Hadjittofi's second son, Andrew, was born.

37. Interview with Ozdil Nami by Author, November 13, 2019, Nicosia, Cyprus.

38. Interview with Ahmet Sözen by Author, November 6, 2019, Famagusta, Cyprus.
39. Interview with Ozdil Nami.
40. Ibid.
41. Interview with Ahmet Sözen.
42. Interview with Sevina Floridou by Author, November 7, 2019, Limassol, Cyprus.
43. Interview with Nicolas Philippou by Author, November 11, 2019, Nicosia, Cyprus.
44. Hearing Before the Subcommittee on European Affairs of the Senate Foreign Relations Committee, First Session, April 17, 1991. Chaired by Senator Joseph Biden (D-DE). Biden went on in the hearing to explore the idea of using the withholding of the $15 million in aid as leverage to get the Cypriots to accept more confidence-building measures, but doubted that the amount was enough to create real leverage.
45. Marvine Howe, *Cyprus Needs A University, But Gets Talk*, *The New York Times*, March 13, 1983, Section 1, p. 11.
46. Exchange of emails between Daniel Hadjittofi and the Author, April 10, 2021.
47. Interview with Dr. Fred Hicks by Author, via Zoom, February 19, 2021, Sarasota, Florida.
48. Interview with Dr. Marla Stone by Author via telephone, May 19, 2020, Nairobi, Kenya, and exchange of emails between Kypros Kyprianou and the Author, June 14, 2020.
49. Ibid.
50. Ibid.
51. Interview with Dr. Allan Felsot by Author via Zoom, November 23, 2020 in Pullman, Washington.
52. Interview with Dr. Jacqueline Robeck by Author via telephone, March 9, 2021, in Atlanta, Georgia.
53. The annual program proposals listed the number of Cypriots studying in the U.S., numbers that came from the Ministry of Education. IIE also kept track of the number of foreign students studying in the U.S. under its "Open Doors" reports and listed lower numbers for Cyprus than the Ministry.
54. Interview with Dr. Giorgos Zacharias by Author, April 28, 2017, Boston, Massachusetts
55. Ibid.
56. Address of Dr. John Brademas, President, New York University to the Cyprus American Association at the American Center, May 28, 1990, Nicosia, Cyprus.
57. Ibid.

Conflict Resolution/Peace Building

1. During my brief time as Assistant Public Affairs Officer (1989-90) and with the strong support of Public Affairs Officer Lane Cubstead, I created two programs aimed at bringing Greek Cypriots and Turkish Cypriots together in the same room. One was relatively simple. We used the visit of an editor from *The Christian Science Monitor* to bring together Greek Cypriot and Turkish Cypriot editors in the ballroom of the Ledra Palace. Our Political Officer, Eric Tunis, walked up behind me at the reception as the guests from the two communities chatted amiably and whispered: "This is sooo great." The second was more dramatic. We wanted to do a video conference with an expert in Washington on the issue of drug abuse, a growing issue for both societies. As such, it had to be held at the American Center Library on the Greek side given the technology of the day. That meant getting permission to bring 15 Turkish Cypriots across the Green Line, some of them officials with the TRNC Department of Public Health. A diplomatic note was prepared by the Consular Section at the Embassy (the Public Affairs Section was still under a separate federal agency, the United States Information Service, and so relied on the Embassy to produce diplomatic notes) and delivered to the Ministry of Foreign Affairs. That's when all hell broke loose. The diplomatic note listing the names of the Turkish Cypriot participants included some of their official titles, which implied recognition by the Embassy of the TRNC. Public Affairs Officer Cubstead was summoned to the MFA and screamed at for a good long time, a humiliating experience for any diplomat. Quickly, a second diplomatic note was produced listing only names and no titles. Personally, I always had the suspicion that the Greek Cypriot employee who had produced the original note could not have been oblivious to the political implications of the titles and left them in intentionally to try to sabotage the program, though I have no proof. Once the program was allowed to proceed we did not look back. There was one memorable moment in that program. The Greek Cypriots and Turkish Cypriots were seated in separate groups and while we waited for the program to start it was very quiet. Then a Greek Cypriot doctor suddenly got up and walked over to the Turkish Cypriots and shook the hand of a woman doctor and said "nice to see you again" and then returned to his seat. It had been at least 16 years since they had seen each other. No one else said a word.

2. Marcelle Wahba entered the Foreign Service with USIA in the summer of 1986 and trained with my class. She rose to become the United States Ambassador to the United Arab Emirates (2001-2004) and was the founding president of the think tank The Arab Gulf States Institute, in Washington.

3. Richard Boucher, interview with author, January 26, 2017, Washington, D.C.

4. Interview with Marcelle Wahba by Author, July 8, 2016, Washington, D.C.

5. Given that the Greek Cypriots regarded the territory beyond the Green Line as occupied territory, they have never recognized it as a "border." Particularly after the 1983 declaration of the Turkish Republic of Northern Cyprus, Turkish Cypriots regarded the Green Line as a border with passport and customs controls. This was one of many barriers prior to 2003 that prevented Greek Cypriots and Turkish Cypriots from meeting. In the case of the Brushstrokes exhibition, Denktash deputy Ergün Olgun was particularly insistent that Greek Cypriots present their passports and sign papers, something the Embassy deflected and worked around.

6. Interview with Marcelle Wahba.

7. Interview with Christina Hadjiparaskeva by Author, November 10, 2019, Strovolos, Cyprus.

8. Interview with Marcelle Wahba.

9. Interview with Christina Hadjiparaskeva.

10. Ronald J. Fisher, *Interactive Conflict Resolution* (Syracuse University Press, 1997), p. 6.

11. Ibid., p. 26.

12. Leonard Doob, A Cyprus Workshop: An Exercise in Intervention Methodology, *The Journal of Social Psychology*, 94 (1974), p. 166.

13. Ibid., pp. 161-178.

14. Ibid., pp. 175-177.

15. Interview with Dr. Herbert Kelman by Julian Portilla, for BeyondIntractability.org, 2003; Ronald J. Fisher, pp. 56-74.

16. Kyriacos C. Markides, *The Accidental Immigrant: A Quest for Spirit in a Skeptical Age* (Hamilton Books, London, 2021), pp. 97-99.

17. Interview with Drs. Kyriacos and Emily Markides by Author, via Zoom, Orono, Maine, August 11, 2021.

18. Interview with Dr. Lennox Joseph by Author, via Zoom, Sifnos, Greece, July 13, 2021.

19. Dr. Louise Diamond and Ambassador John McDonald, *Multi-track Diplomacy: A Systems Approach to Peace* (Kumarian Press, Third Edition, 1996).

20. Interview with Daniel Hadjittofi by Author via Zoom, Nicosia, Cyprus, October 6, 2021.

21. Interview with Jamie Notter by Author, Chevy Chase, Maryland, October 3, 2017.

22. Interview with Ambassador Richard Boucher.

23. Interview with Diana Chigas by Author, Cambridge, Massachusetts, September 26, 2017.

24. Email exchange between Dr. Ahmet Sözen and Author, October 14-16, 2021.

25. Interview with Dr. Eleni Kyza by Author via Zoom, Limassol, Cyprus, November 10, 2021. For more information on the initial 1993 program at Harvard, see: Sibel Erduran, *Reflections on Turkish Cypriot and Greek*

Cypriot Students's Perceptions of the Cyprus Conflict: Implications for Peace Education, presented at the annual meeting of the American Educational Research Association, New York N.Y., April 8-12-1996. https://scholar.google.com/citations?view_op=view_citation&hl=en&user=_YOxIKQAAAAJ&cstart=300&pagesize=100&sortby=pubdate&citation_for_view=_YOxIKQAAAAJ:8moDcb_GFzgC

26. Unclassifed USIA Cable No. 04865 from AmEmbassy Nicosia to SecState Washington, D.C., October 13, 1993.   Note that when the cable speaks about a new anthem, this refers to the fact that the Greek Cypriots/Republic of Cyprus use the Greek National Anthem as their own and do not have a separate Cypriot National Anthem.

27. Interview with Douglas Stone by Author, Cambridge, Massachusetts, September 29, 2017.

28. Interview with John Ungerleider by Author, Brattleboro, Vermont, April 30, 2017.

29. Interview with Margarita Constantinides Bradley by Author, Berkeley, California, May 2, 2020 via Zoom.

30. Interview with Serder Denktash by Author, Nicosia, Cyprus, November 14, 2019.

31. Interview with Katie Clerides and Costas Shammas, Nicosia, Cyprus, November 16, 2017.

32. Interview with Costas Shammas and Katie Clerides by Author via Zoom, Nicosia, Cyprus, July 5, 2021.

33. Marion Peters Angelica, *A Report: Evaluation of the Conflict Resolution Training Efforts Sponsored by the Cyprus Fulbright Commission, 1993-1998*, July 1999, Nicosia, Cyprus, p. 31.   The cover letter to the proposal was dated November 21, 1991, 18 months before the Commission would launch its efforts.

34. Interview with Anna Argyrou by Author, Nicosia, Cyprus, November 17, 2017.

35. Ibid.

36. Ibid.

37. Interview with Katie Economidou by Author (via Zoom) Nicosia, Cyprus December 7, 2021.

38. Ibid.

39. Marion Peters Angelica, "Report," p. 14.

40. Interview with Anna Argyrou. An article in the Friday, June 24, 1994 issue of the Greek Cypriot newspaper *Phileleftheros* written by Andrea Hadjikyriakou reported that 40 VIPs from both communities were participating in a workshop conducted by two American professors in the U.S. and that they were guests of the American Embassy and they were invited in their personal capacities in order to avoid problems stemming from the fact that individuals from the "pseudo-parliament" and "pseudo-government" would

be attending. After listing the general skills that would be taught, the article listed some of the participants: Nicosia Mayor Lellos Demetriades, Chairman of the Chamber of Commerce, Phanos Epiphaniou, and the Chairman of the Cyprus Telecommunications Authority Michalakis Zivanaris. From the Turkish side, YKP Party Leader Alpay Durduran, Vedat Celik, Chairman of the Chamber of Industry, businessman Ozdil Nami, the "so-called Attorney General" Nail Atalay, and pseudo parliamentarians Omer Kalyoncu and Gulsen Bozgurt. It listed other party members who would attend, but also those who turned down the invitation.

41. Interview with Daniel Hadjittofi, October 6, 2021.

42. Interview with Richard Moon, Chris Thorson, and Douglas Stone by Author via Zoom, September 20, 2021.

43. Ibid. To learn more about Richard Moon's philosophy see his video *Aikido the Way of Harmony: Life in Three Easy Lessons*, January 30, 2013; www. moonsensei.com or (https://www.youtube.com/watch?v=DxyMZtA452k)

44. The first VIP group included a mixture of politicians, businessmen, a number of journalists, lawyers and judges, and mayors. The Greek Cypriot contingent included two Ministers and a Permanent Secretary as well as several Members of Parliament. The Turkish Cypriot contingent included an advisor to Rauf Denktash, three mayors and several Members of Parliament.

45. Interview with Anna Argyrou.

46. Board meeting notes from the 163rd and 165th meeting of the Board of the Commission for the Educational Exchange between the United States and Cyprus, November 30, 1994 and June 22, 1995. The Fulbright Center would bedevil the State Department's Office of Building Operations (OBO) over the question of who "owned" the structure and who had responsibility for its maintenance. When the Commission existed, that was somewhat clear, though the Commission had no legal identity of its own and was not really capable of "owning" anything. After the Commission closed, it became murkier still. The U.S. Embassy wanted to keep it as a space where bicommunal meetings could take place, but the questions of maintenance costs, liability, and other issues – not to mention how the structure might appear in OBO records – were not completely resolved. The UN, the Church and the Foreign Ministry were willing to let the original agreement stay in place, but Washington's bureaucracy would have been happy if the building had just gone away.

47. Benjamin J. Broome, *Designing a Collective Approach to Peace: Interactive Design and Problem-Solving Workshops with Greek-Cypriot and Turkish-Cypriot Communities in Cyprus, International Negotiations* 2, p. 385.

48. Interview with Diana Chigas.

49. Broome, *Designing a Collective Approach to Peace*, p. 400.

50. Broome, *Reaching Across the Dividing Line: Building a Collective Vision for Peace in Cyprus, Journal of Peace Research*, 41/2 (March 2004), p. 194.

51. Kutlu Adali was a columnist with the Turkish Cypriot newspaper *Yeni Dûzen*, where he wrote daily under the title "From Blue Cyprus." He was machine-gunned to death in front of his house on July 6, 1996. The crime was never solved. Some blamed the ultra-nationalist Grey Wolves while others blamed the Turkish Revenge Brigade, which was responsible for killing hundreds of hundreds of those thought to have "insulted" Turkey. The deaths of Isaac and Solomou came in the wake of a planned protest to mark the 22nd anniversary of the Turkish invasion. It grew to such proportions – including the transport by Turkey of several thousand members of the Grey Wolves to confront the Greek Cypriot protestors – that the UN Secretary General urged that the event be canceled. However, a large group of protestors decided to march and were met with counter-protestors at Deryneia in the Buffer Zone. Isaac was beaten to death on August 11, 1996. Three days later, the funeral of Isaac led to a second protest during which Solomou attempted to climb a flagpole in the Buffer Zone to take down a Turkish flag. He was shot and killed by Turkish troops. If one goes to the Ledra Palace crossing today, there are large posters displaying photos of Isaac being beaten to death. In late January 1996 a dispute over the uninhabited islet known as Imia to the Greeks and Kardak to Turkey became part of the long-running dispute concerning islands belonging to Greece, but close to the Turkish coast. Special forces from both countries landed on the islet before furious work by diplomats, particularly America's Richard Holbrooke, defused the crisis. However, not before the Greek Cypriot National Guard was put on high alert. John Ungerleider was working with a group of CASP students in the U.S. the week of the Deryneia protests and he noted that all the young men in the group wondered if they were going to be called back to serve.

52. Interview with Anna Argyrou.

53. Interview with Dr. Benjamin Broome by Author, Tempe, Arizona, March 1, 2018.

54. Ibid.

55. Ibid.

56. Broome, *Reaching Across the Dividing Line*, p. 202.

57. Interview with Marion and Emil Angelica by Author, February 15, 2018, Minneapolis, Minnesota.

58. Interview with Anna Argyrou.

59. Interview with Douglas Stone.

60. Interview with Valentina Toumaniou by Author, November 21, 2017, Nicosia, Cyprus.

61. Interview with Daniel Hadjittofi and Anna Argyrou by Author, via Zoom, Nicosia, Cyprus, November 17, 2021.

62. Interview with Burcu Barin by Author, November 21, 2017, Nicosia, Cyprus.

63. Interview with Valentina Toumaniou.

64. Interview with Anna Argyrou by Author, (via Zoom) November 17, 2021, Nicosia, Cyprus.

65. Interview with Walter Douglas by Author, January 2017, Washington, D.C.

66. Interview with Michael Donahue by Author (via phone) July 20, 2020, Denver, Colorado. One can learn more about the program at boldleaders.org.

67. Interview with Birkan Uzun by Author (via Zoom) July 7, 2020, Seattle, Washington.

68. Ibid.

69. Interview with Costas Georgiades by Author via Zoom, August 13, 2020, Maastricht, The Netherlands.

70. Interview with John Ungerleider.

71. Ibid.

72. Email from USIS North (in the north of Cyprus) to the American Embassy Public Affairs Section in Nicosia, July 30, 1996. Email contained a translation of an article from the monthly magazine *Kibrisli* with a notation "please pass to Daniel."

73. Interview with Lazaros Lazarou by Author November 13, 2019, Nicosia, Cyprus.

74. Interview with Dr. Judith Baroody by Author via phone, July 16, 2016, Arlington, Virginia.

75. Notes from the 171st Board meeting of the Commission for Educational Exchange between the United States of America and Cyprus, December 6, 1996, Nicosia, Cyprus.

76. Notes from the 175th Board meeting of the Commission for Educational Exchange between the United States of America and Cyprus, September 11, 1997, Nicosia, Cyprus. Baroody noted that some of the BSP programs were geared toward the simple task of getting Greek and Turkish Cypriots to just talk to one another. "The other thing that we did that was important was to set up Internet cafes on both sides....we called it 'Technology for Peace.' People started to be able to communicate. We also set up tours where we would take Greek Cypriots to the North and they could go to Kyrenia and Famagusta and different places and see Turkish Cypriots and get away from this 'otherness.'" The Fulbright Commission also organized some bus tours to the North and Anna Argyrou remembered after one of the first tours a representative of the Ministry of Foreign Affairs called to chew her out and charge that she had put people's lives in danger. "I just played dumb and said I had no idea," said Argyrou.

77. Interview with Fatma Azgin by Author, November 18, 2017, Nicosia, Cyprus.

78. Interview with Marco Turk by Author, February 28, 2018, Los Angeles, California.

79. Ibid.

80. A. Marco Turk, *Cyprus Reunification Is Long Overdue: The Time is Right*

for Track III Diplomacy as the Best Approach for Successful Negotiation of this Ethnic Conflict, Loyola of Los Angeles International and Comparative Law Review, 28/205, 2006, pp. 205-255. The 46-page final report was broken into six sections with subsections: (1) Bicommunal Movement; (2) Structure of Government; (3) Human Rights, (A) Missing Persons, (B) Settlers, (C) Refugees and Property, (D) Freedom of Movement, (E) Identity; (4) Social Issues, (A) Education, (B) Language, (C) Environment, (D) Health Services, (E) Public Relations, (F) Cultural Heritage, (G) Reconstruction of the Society; (5) Security, (A) Guarantees, (B) Demilitarization, (C) Extremists, (D) Trust, (E) Territory; (6) Economic Issues, (A) Compensation, (B) European Union, (C) Embargoes, (D) Fiscal Issues.

81. Ibid. p. 243.
82. Interview with Marco Turk
83. Turk, *Cyprus Reunification is Long Overdue*, p. 255.
84. Interview with Marion and Emil Angelica.
85. USIA Cable 12260, July 22, 1999; Subject: Fulbright Commission, CASP X Agreement, and Precedence (Unclassified). A copy of the cable was sent via email by Roy Glover at USIA to Daniel Hadjittofi for his information. Dr. William Bader, a former Fulbright grantee and the former Staff Director of the Senate Foreign Relations Committee, had been appointed to the position of Associate Director of USIA by President Clinton the previous year.
86. USIA was created in 1953 when the public diplomacy functions were taken from the State Department. USIA was very much a Cold War agency. In 1997, President Clinton wanted the Senate to pass the Chemical Weapons Convention, which had already been ratified by 65 countries, and wanted an increase in the State Department budget to fund, among other things, back dues to the United Nations. Standing in the way was Senate Foreign Relations Committee Chairman Jesse Helms (R-NC) who New York Times columnist Thomas Friedman referred to as Dr. No. Helms never met a foreign affairs program he did not want to defund (except for the military). He referred to diplomats as "striped pants cookie pushers." What Helms wanted was to consolidate USIA, the Arms Control and Disarmament Agency, and USAID into the State Department. It was argued that the Secretary of State should have all the tools of foreign policy under their control. The real reason is that Helms believed that there would be cost savings in consolidation (see Tom Friedman in *The New York Times* "The Big Deal of the Day," March 27, 1997, p. 29). I was in the Bureau of Near Eastern Affairs at USIA in 1997 when my Director, Kenton Keith, was chosen to be part of a senior leadership team tasked to begin discussions with State Department officials on how a merger might be structured. When I asked him how it was going, he noted that some State Department officers, for whom diplomacy was a quiet, behind-closed-doors activity and then said, with tongue slightly in cheek: "You

mean you talk about our foreign policy in public? To people? Well, we have to put a stop to that."

87. Interview with Diana Chigas.

88. Cyprus Fulbright Commission Financial Audit Report for the fiscal year ending September 30, 1999.

89. Interview with Daniel Hadjittofi and Anna Argyrou, November 17, 2021.

90. Interview with Peter Sulski by Author, April 29, 2017, Lexington, Massachusetts.

91. Interview with Roxanne Kibben by Author, August 27, 2017, Schaumburg, Illinois.

92. Interview with Daniel Hadjittofi and Anna Argyrou, November 17, 2021.

93. Ibid.

94. The remainder of the Economic Support Funds not given to the CASP program that began in fiscal year 1975 and continued until the end of the 2014 fiscal year totaled roughly $1 billion in constant, inflation-adjusted dollars. Restoring churches, besides their cultural significance, attempted to address an issue the Church in Cyprus uses to illustrate the barbarity of the Turks, though many churches, such as the ones in Asha, remain just shells. Delegations from Christian organizations in the U.S. would come to the American Embassy in Nicosia regularly to press for more to be done to support the restoration of the churches. The Cyprus Institute of Neurology and Genetics received millions from the USAID funds and played an important role in identifying remains from the 1974 conflict. Indeed, the remains of Daniel Hadjittofi's father and uncles were found and identified through genetic testing.

95. Louise Diamond, *For a Short-Term Training Grant from the Fulbright Commission for a Bicommunal Training Program in Conflict Resolution and Inter-Group Relations Skills on behalf of the PeaceWorks Consortium*, November 22, 1991.

96. Interview with Diana Chigas.

97. Interview with Ambassador John Koenig.

98. Interview with Gustave Feisel by Author (via phone) August 24, 2018, Petaluma, California.

99. Interview with Ambassador Richard Boucher.

100. Interview with Katie Economidou.

101. Interview with Marion Angelica.

102. Interview with Huseyin Gursan by Author, November 17, 2017, Nicosia, Cyprus.

103. Interview with Dr. Benjamin Broome.

104. Interview with Dr. Ron Fisher by Author via telephone, May 30, 2018, Washington, D.C.

105. Interview with Dr. Harry Anastastiou and Dr. Birol Yesilada by Author, February 22, 2018, Portland, Oregon.

106. Interview with Diana Chigas.
107. Interview with Katie Clerides and Costas Shammas.
108. Interview with Dr. Maria Hadjipavlou.
109. English translation in the U.S. Embassy prepared press summary of October 3, 1994 quoting a lead article from the newspaper *Kibris*.
110. Interview with Serder Denktash.
111. Interview with Katie Economidou.
112. Interview with Daniel Hadjittofi and exchange of emails between the Author and Daniel Hadjittofi, January 3, 2022.
113. Interview with Dr. Lennox Joseph.

The Long Goodbye

1. Audit Report USIA-99-CG-017, Cyprus Fulbright Commission, September 1999 (Sensitive but Unclassified), p. 25. Employment for the spouses of Embassy officers was always a sensitive issue for all Embassies. In some countries, spouses – who were often highly educated and had set aside their careers for their spouses' – could not obtain work permits because there was no bilateral agreement. Language and other barriers also prevented employment. Finding jobs for spouses helped with morale and the Fulbright Commission had been a source of employment ever since the launching of the CASP program when Betsy Fenhagen, the wife of Public Affairs Officer Wes Fenhagen, came on board.
2. Open Doors – International Educational Exchange between the United States and Cyprus, 1970/71 to 2018/19, Institute for International Education, New York, New York.
3. Interview with Ron Ungaro by Author via Zoom, January 5, 2021, Palm Beach, Florida.
4. Memorandum from Cyprus Fulbright Commission Executive Director Daniel Hadjittofi to Embassy Public Affairs Officer and Commission Board Chairman Judith Baroody, Subject: The Traditional Fulbright Program, dated May 22, 1996. Hadjittofi wrote: "The Traditional Fulbright Program has allowed the Commission to raise significant financial aid from American institutions – approximately $1 million annually." The Amideast number comes from the Amideast quarterly reports on the CASP program.
5. Minutes of the 175th Board Meeting for the Commission for Educational Exchange between the United States of America and Cyprus, September 11, 1997, Nicosia, Cyprus
6. Minutes of the 180th Board Meeting for the Commission for Educational Exchange between the United States of America and Cyprus, September 18, 1998, Nicosia, Cyprus
7. Ibid.
8. Minutes of the 181st Board Meeting for the Commission for Educational Ex-

change between the United States of America and Cyprus, September 25, 1998, Nicosia, Cyprus

9. Ibid.

10. Interview with Daniel Hadjittofi by Author, November 2017, Nicosia Cyprus.

11. Interview with Dr. Judith Baroody by Author, July 16, 2016, Arlington, Virginia. Dr. Baroody did reveal the name of this person in the interview, but I have made the decision to withhold the name. Both Dr. Baroody and members of the Fulbright staff commented on this person in ways that were not particularly flattering, but the description by Dr. Baroody suffices to paint a picture of the situation.

12. Minutes of the 182ⁿᵈ Board Meeting for the Commission for Educational Exchange between the United States of America and Cyprus, November 20, 1998, Nicosia, Cyprus, Annex A., pp. 13-14.

13. Normally, there were a minimum of two American Embassy officials on the Board– the Chairman, who was the Public Affairs Officer, and one other who served as Treasurer. The normal procedure for all Commission expenditures was for both officers to sign off on all vouchers. The Fulbright office at USIA and later at the State Department made a distinction concerning both the Fulbright funds from ECA and the CASP funds that came from USAID. Yes, they were U.S. tax dollars. However, once transferred to the Commission, they were Commission dollars. A number of Administrative Officers at the American Embassy did not agree.

14. Minutes of the 182ⁿᵈ Board Meeting for the Commission for Educational Exchange between the United States of America and Cyprus, November 20, 1998, Nicosia, Cyprus, Annex A., pp. 19-20.

15. Ibid.

16. Ibid.

17. Letter dated January 22, 1999 from Senator Paul Sarbanes to Assistant Secretary of State for Legislative Affairs Barbara Larkin.

18. Dr. Susan Lazar's sister was one of the CAARI archaeologists, but Dr. Lazar had also read Dr. Kyriacos Markides's book *The Magus of Strovolos* and had come to Cyprus to meet the mysterious healer Daskalos, who was featured in the book. Hadjittofi became her contact and guide. Lazar, in Hadjittofi's words, "fell in love with Cyprus" and talked to Hadjittofi about setting up a peace center. "When I was in Washington, she always invited me to her house and introduced me to very prominent people," remembered Hadjittofi. She wrote a pair of letters to Senator Paul Sarbanes and to First Lady Hillary Rodham Clinton on December 14, 1998 in support of Hadjittofi. According to Lellos Demetriades, the First Lady's staff intervened with certain members of Congress friendly to the Greek Lobby.

19. Interview with Anna Argyrou by Author, November 17, 2017, Nicosia, Cyprus.

20. Interview with Kyproula Kyriakidou by Author, November 20, 2017, Nicosia, Cyprus.

21. Report of Audit, Cyprus Fulbright Commission, USIA 99-CG-017, September 1999 (Sensitive but Unclassified), p. 3.

22. Report of Audit, Embassy Nicosia Interaction with the Cyprus Fulbright Commission, 99-CG-020 (Sensitive but Unclassified), September 1999, p.1.

23. Ibid., p. 2.

24. Interview with Daniel Hadjittofi by Author (via Zoom), May 20, 2022, Nicosia, Cyprus.

25. Report of Audit, Embassy Nicosia Interaction with the Cyprus Fulbright Commission, 99-CG-020 (Sensitive but Unclassified), September 1999, Attachment B.

26. Ibid., Attachment C.

27. Chart on U.S. Government and Government of Cyprus contributions produced by the Cyprus Fulbright Commission, January 12, 2011. Incoming Ambassador signed a Memorandum of Understanding with USIA to use $100,000 in CASP funds for an Assistant Public Affairs Officer position in the summer of 1999, shortly after he arrived at post to succeed Ambassador Kenneth Brill. The post had not had an APAO since budget cuts eliminated the position (of the Author) in the spring of 1990.

28. Minutes of the 183rd Board Meeting for the Commission for Educational Exchange between the United States of America and Cyprus, February 5, Nicosia, Cyprus. The second report would never be shared with the Board. Executive Director Hadjittofi first saw that report in 2019 after the Author obtained a copy via a Freedom of Information Act request to the Department of State.

29. Interview with Roy Glover by Author via Zoom, July 19, 2020, Christchurch, New Zealand.

30. Letter from Board Chairman Dr. Judith Baroody to the Fulbright Board and Executive Director dated June 17, 1999.

31. August 13, 1999 letter from Lellos Demetriades to Dr. Alan Schecter, Chairman of the Board of Foreign Scholarships, and September 1, 1999 letter from Dr. Chrysotomos Sofianos to Dr. Schecter.

32. Interview with Walter Douglas by Author, January 23, 2017, Washington, D.C.

33. Interview with Orcun Kamali by Author, November 18, 2019, Kyrenia/Girne, Cyprus.

34. Ibid.

35. Interview via email with Dr. Eldem Albayrak by Author, May 11, 2022, Famagusta, Cyprus.

36. Interview via email with Dr. Antonis Jossif, by Author, June 5-6, Nicosia, Cyprus.

37. Exchange of Emails between Dr. Panayiotis Hadjicostas and the Author, May 17-June 8, 2022, Nicosia, Cyprus.

38. Interview with Dr. Philippos Patsalis by Author via Zoom, August 24, 2022, Nicosia, Cyprus.

39. Interview with Walter Douglas.

40. Memorandum to Board Chairman Walter Douglas from Commission Executive Director Daniel Hadjittofi, November 10, 2000.

41. Ibid.

42. Letter from Dr. Gregory Markides, Director/Associate Dean of Enrollment Management at Intercollege, to U.S. Ambassador Michael Bandler, June 11, 2001, Nicosia Cyprus.

43. Letter from Cyprus Fulbright Commission Executive Director Daniel Hadjittofi to the Minister of Education, H.E. Ouranios Ioannides, February 12, 2002, Nicosia, Cyprus.

44. Letter from Litsa-Evlambia Theophylou to the Cyprus Fulbright Commission, June 26, 2002, Nicosia, Cyprus. The other examples cited were part of a collection of letters maintained by the Commission as examples of the problems U.S. graduates were having with KYSATS.

45. Interview with Daniel Hadjittofi by Author (via Zoom) May 20, 2022, Nicosia, Cyprus.

46. Interview with Gulsen Oztoprak by Author, November 7, 2019, Nicosia, Cyprus.

47. Open Doors: International Educational Exchange between the United States and Cyprus 1970/71 and 2018/19, International Institute of Education, Washington, D.C.

48. Briana Bovington, Emma Kerr, and Sarah Wood, "Twenty Years of Tuition Growth at U.S. Universities," *U.S. News and World Report*, September 17, 2021: https://www.usnews.com/education/best-colleges/paying-for-college/articles/2017-09-20/see-20-years-of-tuition-growth-at-national-universities

49. Interview with Ambassador Michael Klosson by Author, June 21, 2017, Washington, D.C.

50. Interview with Daniel Hadjittofi by Author (via Zoom), May 20, 2022, Nicosia, Cyprus. Hadjittofi had been given a mandate by the Board to explore the idea of a Fulbright University in Cyprus that would be small, English-language and bicommunal. In his private capacity he looked at other ideas for creating a more American-style university in Cyprus with formal ties to one or more American universities. Some of the ideas included "upgrading" the American Academies in Larnaca and Limassol. "If the ideas had ever gotten past the talking stage, I would have brought it to the Board's attention," said Hadjittofi.

51. Minutes of the 211th Board Meeting of the Commission for Educational Exchange between the United States of America and Cyprus, December 12, 2003, Nicosia, Cyprus

52. Interview with Ambassador Michael Klosson.

53. Interview with Craig Kuehl by Author (via Zoom), June 26, 2020, New York, New York. The Congressional language had only changed to emphasize more bicommunal programs, but still read: "For scholarships, administrative support of the scholarship program, bicommunal programs and the administration of scholarships and measures aimed at the reunification of the island and designed to reduce tensions and promote peace and cooperation between the two communities on Cyprus."

54. Minutes of the 212th Board meeting of the Commission for Educational Exchange between the United States of America and Cyprus, April 2, 2004, Nicosia, Cyprus. Note: The primary Turkish Cypriot members of the Board always came from the Turkish Cypriot Education Office, which was enshrined in the original 1960 constitution. As a result, there should have been no issue for the Papadopoulos administration in appointing the members. There were no so-called recognition issues involved.

55. Interview with Dr. Chrysostomos Sofianos by Author, November 2016, Nicosia, Cyprus.

56. Exchange of emails/voice messages with Daniel Hadjittofi, January 11, 2023, Nicosia, Cyprus.

57. Minutes of the 213th and 214th Board meetings of the Commission for Educational Exchange between the United States of America and Cyprus, May 5, 2004 and June 18, 2004, Nicosia, Cyprus.

58. Ibid.

59. Minutes of the 215th Board meeting of the Commission for Educational Exchange between the United States of America and Cyprus, September 2, 2004.

60. Interview with Craig Kuehl, June 26, 2020.

61. Minutes of the 216th Board meeting of the Commission for Educational Exchange between the United States of America and Cyprus, October 14, 2004.

62. Minutes of the 217th Board meeting of the Commission for Educational Exchange between the United States of America and Cyprus, December 3, 2004.

63. Interview with Dr. Chrysostomos Sofianos by Author, November 2016, Nicosia, Cyprus.

64. Letter dated March 10, 2005 from U.S. Ambassador Michael Klosson to Republic of Cyprus Foreign Minister George Iacovou, Nicosia, Cyprus.

65. Minutes of the 218th Board meeting of the Commission for Educational Exchange between the United States of America and Cyprus, July 5, 2005.

66. Minutes of the 219th and 220th Board meeting of the Commission for Educational Exchange between the United States of America and Cyprus, September 23, 2005 and November 11, 2005.

67. Interview with Tom Miller by Author (via Zoom), April 23, 2020, Washington, D.C.

68. Ibid.

69. Interview with Dr. Peter Rutkoff by Author via telephone, June 6, 2022, Cooperstown, New York; see Peter Rutkoff, *Cyprus Portraits – 2005-2013* (XOXOX Press, Gambier, Ohio, 2007 and 2013), pp. 29, 45-47, 93.

70. Exchange of emails between Stella Zavallis and the Author, July 12, 2022.

71. Interview with Margarita Constantinides Bradley by Author via Zoom, May 2, 2020, Belmont, California.

72. Interview with Nektarios Paisios by Author, February 26, 2020, New York, N.Y.

73. Interview with Daniel Hadjittofi by Author, November 2017, Nicosia, Cyprus.

74. Ibid.

75. Minutes of the 243rd Board meeting of the Commission for Educational Exchange between the United States of America and Cyprus, December 3, 2010. In addition to Chairman Jim Ellickson-Brown, Treasurer Jessica Adams from the Embassy was present as well as Andreas Charalambous.

76. Interview with Daniel Hadjittofi, November 2017, Nicosia, Cyprus.

77. Interview with Jim Ellickson-Brown by Author (via phone), April 29, 2020, California.

78. Interview with Dr. Chris Schabel by Author (via Zoom), July 3, 2020, Paris, France.

79. Minutes of the 245th Board meeting of the Commission for Educational Exchange between the United States of America and Cyprus, September 23, 2011, Nicosia, Cyprus. The idea of Nobel Energy funding a large scholarship program was seductive, but unrealistic until Nobel – or if they were bought out by another company – would recover its investment and start to make a profit from the Aphrodite site.

80. Interview with Eliana Hadjiandreou by Author, February 29, 2020, College Park, Pennsylvania.

81. Interview with Doruk Uzunoglu by Author (via Zoom), May 4, 2020, London, U.K.

82. Interview with Pinar Barlas by Author (via Zoom), May 15, 2020, Kyrenia, Cyprus, and interview with Ceren Barlas by Author, (via Zoom), May 25, 2020, Kyrenia, Cyprus.

83. Interview with Aris Antoniades by Author, November 7, 2019, Limassol, Cyprus. Exchange of emails between Aris Antoniades and the Author, July 20-22, 2022.

84. Interview with Ambassador John Koenig by Author, February 20, 2018, Seattle, Washington.

85. Interview with Nick Laragakis by Author, April 2, 2019, Washington, D.C.

86. Interview with Panicos Papanicolaou by Author, November 13, 2019, Limassol, Cyprus.

87. Interview with Andrew Manatos by Author, May 9, 2018, Washington, D.C.

88. Minutes of the 247th Board meeting of the Commission for Educational Ex-

change between the United States of America and Cyprus, August 3, 2012, Nicosia, Cyprus.

89. Interview with Anna Argyrou by Author, November 17, 2017, Nicosia, Cyprus.

90. Interview with Daniel Hadjittofi by Author, November 2017, Nicosia, Cyprus.

91. Interview with Anna Argyrou by Author, November 17, 2017, Nicosia, Cyprus.

92. Exchange of emails between the Author and Daniel Hadjittofi, October 12, 2022.

93. Interview with Board Member Claire Georghiou by Author, November 15, 2017, Nicosia, Cyprus.

94. Interview with Dr. Chris Schabel, by Author July 3, 2020 (Via Zoom), Paris, France.

95. Interview with Dr. Andrew McCarthy by Author, November 25, 2019, Denver, Colorado.

96. Interview with Ambassador John Koenig by Author, February 20, 2018, Seattle, Washington.

97. Ibid.

98. Minutes of the 249th Board meeting of the Commission for Educational Exchange between the United States of America and Cyprus, November 9, 2012, Nicosia, Cyprus.

99. Ibid.

100. Interview with Ioanna Michael by Author, November 12, 2019, Limassol, Cyprus.

101. Interview with Dr. Sondra Sainsbury by Author (via Zoom), September 27, 2022, Nicosia, Cyprus

102. Minutes of the 252nd Board meeting of the Commission for Educational Exchange between the United States of America and Cyprus, February 14, 2014 Nicosia, Cyprus. Elgin Gulpinar Korkmazhan completed his bachelor's and master's degrees at Harvard and is currently pursuing his Ph.D. at Stanford.

103. Interview with Ingrid Larson by Author (via phone), May 3, 2019, Washington, D.C.

104. Interview with Anna Argyrou by Author (via Zoom), September 27, 2022, Nicosia, Cyprus.

105. Walter Johnson and Francis J. Colligan, *The Fulbright Program: A History* (University of Chicago Press, 1965), p. 312.

Epilogue/Acknowledgements

1. Unclassified cable from American Embassy Nicosia to USIA, Washington, D.C., March 6, 1996. Drafted by Daniel Hadjittofi.

2. Interview with Sofoklis Vlassides by Author (via phone), December 12, 2019, Koloni, Cyprus; (https://vlassideswinery.com/about/)

3. Interview with Ingrid Larson by Author (via phone) May 3, 2019, Washington, D.C.

4. Interview with Dr. Sondra Sainsbury (via Zoom), September 27, 2022, Nicosia, Cyprus.

5. Interview with Ingrid Larson.

6. Ibid.

7. Interview with Dr. Sondra Sainsbury.

8. Interview with Maria Tsiakka by Author (via Zoom), November 16, 2020, Nicosia, Cyprus.

9. "Minister of Education Honors Fulbright Scholars in Cyprus," Unclassified Cable from American Embassy Nicosia to USIA Washington, DC, May 28, 1992; drafted by Daniel Hadjittofi.

10. Fulbright, J. William; "The Price of Empire," address to a lunch hosted by The American Bar Association in Honolulu, Hawaii, August 8, 1967.

BIBLIOGRAPHY

BOOKS

Adams, Thomas W. and Cottrell, Alvin J.; *Cyprus Between East and West;* The Washington Center of Foreign Policy Research of the Johns Hopkins University, School of Advanced International Studies; Johns Hopkins University Press, Baltimore, Maryland, 1968

Anastasiou, Harry; *The Broken Olive Branch: Nationalism, Ethnic Conflict, and the Quest for Peace in Cyprus, Volume One;* Syracuse University Press, 2008

Anastasiou, Harry; *The Broken Olive Branch: Nationalism, Ethnic Conflict, and the Quest for Peace in Cyprus, Volume Two;* Syracuse University Press, 2008

Atakol, Kenan; *Turkish & Greek Cypriots: Is Their Separation Permanent?;* METU Press, 2012

Ball, George W.; *The Past Has Another Pattern*; W.W. Norton & Company, New York, 1982

Bamford, James; *Body of Secrets: A History of the Ultra-Secret National Security Agency*; Random House, New York, 2001

Bartlett, Charles and Weintal, Edward; *Facing the Brink: An Intimate Study of Crisis Diplomacy;* Charles Scribner Sons, New York, 1967

Chigas, Diana; *The Harvard Study Group on Cyprus; Contributions to an Unfulfilled Peace Process*; Chapter Seven from *Across the Lines of Conflict*; Columbia University Press, 2015

Craig, Ian and O'Malley, Brendan; *The Cyprus Conspiracy: America, Espionage and the Turkish Invasion*; I.B. Tauris & Company Ltd., London, 1999

Denktash, R.R.; *The Cyprus Triangle*; K. Rustem and Brothers and George Allen & Unwin, London, 1982

Diamond, Dr. Louise; *The Courage for Peace*; Conari Press, Berkeley, California; 2004

Diamond, Dr. Louise and McDonald, Ambassador John; *Multi-Track Diplomacy: A Systems Approach to Peace*; Kumarian Press, 1996

Ertekün, N.M.; *The Cyprus Dispute: The Birth of the Turkish Republic of Northern Cyprus;* K. Rustem and Brothers, 1984

Fisher, Roger and Ury, William; *Getting to Yes: Negotiating Agreement Without Giving In;* Houghton Mifflin Company, New York, 1981

Fisher, Ronald J.; *Interactive Conflict Resolution*; Syracuse University Press, 1997

Grimland, Dave; *Journey to Ithaka: Memoirs of an American Diplomat;* Lulu Publishing Services, 2015

Gup, Ted; *The Book of Honor: The Secret Lives and Deaths of CIA Operatives;* First Anchor Books, 2001

Johnson, Walter and Colligan, Francis J.; *The Fulbright Program: A History;* The University of Chicago Press, 1965

Ker-Lindsay, James; *The Cyprus Problem: What Everyone Needs to Know;* Oxford University Press, 2011

Konold, Kristine; *Backstage at the Big War;* Brunswick Publishing Company, Lawrenceville, Virginia, 1991

Koumoulides, John T.A., (Editor); *Cyprus in Transition 1960-1985;* Trigraph, London, 1986

Lavender, David; *The Story of the Cyprus Mines Corporation;* The Huntington Library, San Marino, California, 1962

Lund, Michael and McDonald, Steve, (Editors): *Across Lines of Conflict: Facilitating Cooperation to Build Peace;* Woodrow Wilson Center Press and Columbia University Press, 2015

MacMillan, Harold; *Riding the Storm 1956-1959;* Harper and Row, New York, 1971

Markides, Kyriacos; *The Rise and Fall of the Cyprus Republic;* Yale University Press, 1977

Markides, Kyriacos C.; *The Accidental Immigrant: A Quest for Spirit in a Skeptical Age;* Hamilton Books, 2021

McFadden, Elizabeth; *The Glitter and the Gold;* The Dial Press, New York, 1971

Michael, Michális Stavrou; *Resolving the Cyprus Conflict: Negotiating History;* Palgrave MacMillen, New York, 2009

Miller, G. Wayne; *An Uncommon Man: The Life and Times of Senator Claiborne Pell;* University Press of New England, Lebanon, New Hampshire, 2011

Palley, Claire; *An International Relations Debacle: The UN Secretary General's Mission of Good Offices in Cyprus 1999-2004;* Hart Publishers, 2005

Powell, Lee Riley; *J. William Fulbright and His Time;* Guild Bindery Press, Memphis, Tennessee, 1996

Rutkoff, Peter: *Cyprus Portraits 2005-2013;* XOXOX Press, Gambier, Ohio, 2013

Sandole, Dennis J.D. and van der Merwe, Hugo (Editors); *Conflict Resolution Theory and Practice: Integration and Application;* Manchester University Press, 1993

Smith, Jean Edward, FDR, Random House, New York, 2007

Vestal, Theodore M.; *International Education: Its History and Promise for Today;* Praeger, Westport, Connecticut/London, 1994

Woods, Randall Bennett; *Fulbright: A Biography*; Cambridge University Press, 1995

Data Bases

Board Meeting Notes of the Cyprus Fulbright Commission; 253 Meeting Notes; March 5, 1962 to April 11, 2014

CIA Reading Room: cia.gov/readingroom

Commission for Educational Exchange between the United States and Cyprus; Cypriot Fulbright Scholars 1962-2014

Commission for Educational Exchange between the United States and Cyprus; Cyprus American Scholarship Grantees, 1981-2011

Commission for Educational Exchange between the United States and Cyprus; American Fulbright Scholars 1962-2014

Commission for Educational Exchange between the United States and Cyprus; CASP Short-Term Training Grantees, 1984-2014

Congressional Record: Law Library, Library of Congress, Washington, D.C. (Transcripts of various budget hearings including testimony by members of the Greek lobby)

Foreign Relations of the United States: Office of the Historian, Department of State. President Dwight D. Eisenhower, Documents 230-381; President John F. Kennedy, Documents 1-397; President Lyndon B. Johnson, Documents 1-375; President Richard Nixon, Documents 72-194; President Gerald R. Ford, Documents 72-194; President Jimmy Carter, documents 31-83. (Note: Documents beyond the Carter presidency have not yet been prepared, but no separate section on Cyprus is listed for the presidency of Ronald Reagan)

National Center for Educational Statistics; Table 330.10. Average undergraduate tuition and fees and room and board rates charged for full-time students in degree-granting post-secondary institutions by level and control of institution; selected years 1963/64 through 2018/19

Program Plans, Financial Files, Cyprus American Scholarship Program, and Miscellaneous Files of the Cyprus Fulbright Commission; 223 Folders, 1962-2014

Special Collections

National Archives, College Park, Maryland, Various documents related to Embassy activities in Nicosia, the visit of Vice President Johnson to Cyprus in 1962, and the special archive related to the Central Intelligence Agency.

Congressional Record, Library of Congress Law Library, Washington, D.C.;

Particularly discussions of appropriations to Cyprus after 1974 and the founding of the CASP program in 1981.

Special Collections, University of Arkansas Library, Fayetteville, Arkansas; Fulbright Collection, including documents related to the operation of the Fulbright program at the United States Information Agency and the Department of State.

Special Collections, George Mason University, Fairfax, Virginia; The papers of Dr. Louise Diamond, Box Two, Folders 2/3 and Box Five, Folder Two.

William J. Clinton Presidential Library and Museum, National Archives and Records Administration, Little Rock, Arkansas.

Journal/Newspaper Articles

Aslim, Ilksoy; *The Soviet Union and Cyprus in 1974 Events*; Athens Journal of History, Volume 2, Issue 4 (2016), pp. 249-262

Baici, Tamer; *The Cyprus Crisis and the Southern Flank of NATO (1960-75)*, IRTS, Volume 2, Issue 3 (Fall 2012), pp. 30-54

Bovington, Briana; Kerr, Emma; and Wood, Sarah; *Twenty Years of Tuition Growth at U.S. Universities*; U.S. News and World Report, September 17, 2021; https://www.usnews.com/education/best-colleges/paying-for-college/articles/2017-09-20/see-20-years-of-tuition-growth-at-national-universities

Broome, Dr. Benjamin J.; *Designing a Collective Approach to Peace: Interactive Dialogue and Problem-Solving Workshop with Greek-Cypriot and Turkish-Cypriot Communities in Cyprus*; International Negotiation 2 (1997), pp. 381-407

Broome, Dr. Benjamin J.; *Participatory Planning and Design in a Protracted Conflict Situation: Application with Citizen Peace-Building Groups in Cyprus*, Systems Research and Behavioral Science Systems Research 19 (2002), pp. 313-321

Broome, Dr. Benjamin J.; *Reaching Across the Dividing Line: Building a Collective Vision for Peace in Cyprus;* Journal of Peace Research, Vol. 41, No. 2 (March 2004), pp. 191-209

Bucik, Marko; *The Cyprus Problem: the assessment of the 1997-2004 United Nations mediation and the rejection of the Annan Plan*; Academia.edu; George Washington University, April 2012, pp. 1-1

Bureau of Educational and Cultural Affairs, Department of State; *An Informal History of the Fulbright Program* (https://eca.state.gov/fulbright/about-fulbright/history/early-years)

Diamond, Dr. Louise; *The Healing Power of Systems Change in a Fragile World*, Practicing Social Change, Vol. 1(April 2010), pp. 4-8

Diamond, Dr. Louise; *Reflections on the Cyprus Peace Process: A Systems View*;

Private Papers from Special Collections at George Mason University; Undated, but probably 1999 or 2000

Castleberry, H. Paul; *Conflict Resolution and the Cyprus Problem*; The Western Political Quarterly, Vol. 17, No. 3 (September 1964), pp. 118-130

Diamond, Dr. Louise and Fisher, Ronald J.; *Integrating Conflict Resolution Training and Consultation: A Cyprus Example*, Negotiation Journal (July 1999), pp. 287-301

Goshko, John M,. *Little Greek Lobby Wields Big Clout in Hill Squabble;* The Washington Post, June 20, 1978

Fitchett, Joseph; *Cyprus to Arrest, Try Six Rightists in '74 Death of U.S. Ambassador*; The Washington Post; February 4, 1977

Friedman, Thomas L., *The Big Deal of the Day*; The New York Times, March 27, 1997, Section A, p. 29

Hadjipavlou, Dr. Maria and Kanol, Dr. Bülent; *Cumulative Impact Case Study: The Impact of Peacebuilding Work on the Cyprus Conflict*, Collaborative Learning Projects, February 2008

Hadjipavlou-Trigeorgis, Dr. Maria; *Unofficial Inter-Communal Contacts and Their Contribution to Peacebuilding in Conflict Societies: The Case of Cyprus*: The Cyprus Review, Vol. 5(2), pp. 68-87

Hadjipavlou, Dr. Maria and Michael, Michális S.; *Locating the Cyprus Problem within Conflict Resolution*, Working Paper 2021

Hadjipavlou, Dr. Maria; *Conflict Resolution Empathy Building and Reconciliation The Case of Turkish, Greek and Cypriot Youth*, Chapter 14; *Cyprus and the Roadmap for Peace: A Critical Interrogation of the Conflict*, edited by Edward Elgar (Michális S. Michael, La Trobe University, Australia and Yucel Vural, EMC North Cyprus)

Howe, Marvine; *Cyprus Needs a University, but Gets Talk*; New York Times, March 13, 1983, Section 1, Page 11

Johnson, Lonnie R.; *The Making of the Fulbright Program, 1946-1961: Architecture, Philosophy, and Narrative*; Paper presented at the Blair Center at the University of Arkansas, September 1-2 (2015), pp. 1-29

Peterson, Scott; *Common Folk Try to End Cyprus Rift*; The Christian Science Monitor, February 13, 1998

Stergiou, Andreas; *The Exceptional Case of the British Military Bases on Cyprus*; Middle Eastern Studies, Vol. 51, No. 2 (2015), pp. 285-300

Stergiou, Andreas; *Soviet Policy Toward Cyprus*; Academia.edu; University of Thessaly, Greece

Swiny, Stuart; *CAARI – the House of the Dancing Bird; A History of the Cyprus American Archaeological Research Institute, Nicosia Cyprus, 1978-2000*; In *An ASOR Mosaic, A Centennial History of the American Schools of Oriental Research 1900-2000*, edited by Joe D. Seger (Boston, Massachusetts)

Turk, Dr. A. Marco; *Cyprus Reunification is Long Overdue: The Time is Right for Track III Diplomacy as the Best Approach for Successful Negotiation of this Ethnic Conflict*; U. of Loyola – Los Angeles International and Comparative Law Review, Vol. 26:205 (2006), pp. 205-255

Turk, Dr. A. Marco; *Rethinking the Cyprus Problem: Are Frame-breaking Changes Still Possible Through Application of Intractable Conflict Intervention Approaches to This "Hurting Stalemate"*; University of Loyola – Los Angeles International and Comparative Law Review, Vol. 29:463 (2007), pp. 463-501

Turk, Dr. A. Marco; *The Negotiation Culture of Lengthy Peace Processes: Cyprus as an Example of Spoiling that Prevents a Final Solution*: University of Loyola – Los Angeles International and Comparative Law Review, Vol. 31:101 (2009), pp. 101-134

Turk, Dr. A. Marco and Ungerleider, Dr. John; *Experiential Activities in Mediation-Based Training: Cyprus 1997-2013*, Conflict Resolution Quarterly (2016), pp. 1-20

Ungerleider, Dr. John; *Structured Youth Dialogue to Empower Peacebuilding and Leadership*, Conflict Resolution Quarterly, Vol. 29, No. 4 (Summer 2012)

Ungerleider, Dr. John; *Bicommunal Youth Camps and Peacebuilding in Cyprus*, Peace Review, Volume 13, No. 4 (December 2001)

Ungerleider, Dr. John; *The Impact of Youth Peacebuilding Camps. Connectedness, Coping and Collaboration* (unpublished)

Wenske, Caroline and Lindley, Dan; *Dismantling the Cyprus Conspiracy: The U.S. Role in the Cypriot Crises of 1963, 1967, and 1974;* University of Notre Dame, Draft May 16, 2008, pp. 1-83

Wilkinson, M. James; *Moving Beyond Conflict Prevention to Reconciliation: Greeks and Turks: A Tense and Costly Peace;* in *Leadership and Conflict Resolution/The International Leadership Series* edited by Adel Safty (Universal Publishers, 2003)

Reports

Advanced Conflict Management Training on the Cyprus Problem; For Greek and Turkish Cypriot Student Scholars in the Cyprus American Scholarship Program; Coolfont Resort and Conference Center, Berkeley Springs, West Virginia, May 22-28, 2005

Amideast: Quarterly Reports for the Cyprus American Scholarship Program – First quarter 1982 to fourth quarter 2010

Angelica, Marion Peters; *Evaluation of the Conflict Resolution Training Efforts Sponsored by the Cyprus Fulbright Commission 1993-1998;* CASP Scholar in Residence, Nicosia, Cyprus, July 1999

Cyprus American Archaeological Research Institute; Director's Report for July 1, 1982 to June 30, 1983; submitted by Dr. Stuart Swiny

The Cyprus Consortium (Conflict Management Group, Institute for Multi-Track Diplomacy, NTL Institute); *Cyprus Conflict Management Program: Draft Trainer's Manual/Advanced Training of Trainers Workshop*, October 1995

General Accounting Office; *U.S. Assistance to Cyprus;* Report to the Subcommittee on Europe and the Middle East, House Committee on Foreign Affairs, November 30, 1981, pp. 1-50

Institute for International Education; *Open Doors; International Educational Exchange between the United States and Cyprus 1970/1972 and 2018/2019.*

National Security Council; Statement of U.S. Policy Toward Cyprus; Washington, D.C., February 9, 1960 (NSC 6003)

Report of Design Workshops held during Fall 1994 and Spring 1995 with Conflict Resolution Trainers and Project Leaders; *Designing the Future of Peacebuilding Efforts in Cyprus*, by Dr. Benjamin J. Broome, May 12, 1996

School for International Training; Confidence Building Workshop for Greek and Turkish Cypriot Student Scholars; Brattleboro, Vermont. August 12-19, 2000

School for International Training; Bicommunal Peacebuilding Programs for Greek- and Turkish-Cypriot High School Students, July 18-August 1, 2005.

The School for International Training; Advanced Conflict Management Training for Greek and Turkish Cypriot Student Scholars in the Cyprus American Scholarship Program (CASP/Amideast); Battleboro, Vermont. May 23-29, 2010

School for International Training/World Learning; *Bicommunal Summer Youth Program: A Bicommunal Peacebuilding and Leadership Program for Greek and Turkish Cypriot High School Students;* Battleboro, Vermont, July 10-27, 2011

The United States Department of State, Office of Inspector General; Report of Audit: Embassy Nicosia Interaction with the Cyprus Fulbright Commission 99-GC-020 (Sensitive but Unclassified-Noforn) September 1999

United States Information Agency, Office of the Inspector General - Audit Report USIA-99-CG-017 The Cyprus Fulbright Commission (Sensitive but Unclassified) September 1999

Documents

Agreement Between the Government of the Republic of Cyprus and the Government of the United States of America for financing certain educational exchange programs; signed January 18, 1962, Nicosia Cyprus

Basic 40-Hour Humanistic-Transformative Conflict Management Skills and Mediation Training Course; prepared by Dr. A. Marco Turk, U.S Fulbright Senior Scholar, Cyprus Fulbright Commission Peacebuilding Program, 1997-1999.

Cable from Congen Nicosia (L. Douglas Heck, Consul) to the Department of State; Subject: Annual Educational Exchange Report, August 3, 1959 (Unclassified)

Central Intelligence Agency, Office of National Estimates; Staff Memorandum No. 44-61; The Current Situation in Cyprus, August 10, 1961 (Secret/Declassified December 10, 2014)

Department of State, Bureau of Educational and Cultural Affairs; Analysis of CEE/Cyprus Program Proposal for Academic Year 1962/63 (approved by the Board of Foreign Scholarship)

Memorandum for the President, from R.W. Komer to President John F. Kennedy. Subject: The Makarios Visit, June 1, 1962 (Secret/Declassified March 2, 1997)

Memorandum. Subject: Conflict Resolution Workshop May 23-29, 1999 at Duquesne University. memo from Kate Archambault and B. Melvin (Amideast) to Daniel Hadjittofi (Cyprus Fulbright Commission), dated June 23, 1999

Letter of Appointment for Mr. Daniel Hadjittofi - Employment of the Executive Director of The Commission for Educational Exchange between the United States and Cyprus, dated October 1, 2001

Letter, from Kate Archambault (Amideast) to Betsy Fenhagen (Cyprus Fulbright Commission) October 18, 1982

Reflections on Turkish Cypriot and Greek Cypriot Students' Perceptions of the Cyprus Conflict: Implications for Peace Education; by Sibel Erduran; Presented at the annual meeting of the American Educational Research Association, New York N.Y., April 8-12-1996, 30 pages

Summer Youth Camp Applications; 1997-2006; Papers of Executive Director Daniel Hadjittofi

The Cyprus Fulbright Commission Rapproachment Efforts in Brief, undated; Papers of Executive Director Daniel Hadjittofi

Fulbright-Administered Bicommunal Programs, 1993-2011; Papers of Executive Director Daniel Hadjittofi

Seeds of Peace Program Book, December 2000

Report of Design Workshops held during Fall 1994 and Spring 1995

VIDEOS

Profile: Dr. Louise Diamond; Public Broadcasting Service, Season One, Episode 107 (Fran Stoddard interviews Louise Diamond); aired November 19, 2001

Fulbright: 50 Years, 1962-2012; A video prepared by the Cyprus Fulbright Commission to mark the 50th anniversary of the Commission

Aikido the Way of Harmony: Life in Three Easy Lessons; by Richard Moon; January 30, 2013; www.moonsensei.com
(https://www.youtube.com/watch?v=DxyMZtA452k)

SPEECHES

Akinci, Mustafa; "The Cyprus Problem: 40 Years On," remarks at the University of Cyprus, Nicosia, Cyprus, July 2014

Brademas, Dr. John; Address to the Cyprus-American Association, The American Center, Nicosia, Cyprus, May 28, 1990

ORAL HISTORIES

Transcript, Judith Baroody Oral History; Interviewed by Charles Stuart Kennedy, May 4, 2016; The Association for Diplomatic Studies and Training, Foreign Affairs Oral History Project, Department of State

Transcript, Ambassador Thomas D. Boyatt Oral History; Interviewed by Self, September 30, 1992; The Association for Diplomatic Studies and Training, Foreign Affairs Oral History Project, Department of State

Transcript, Ambassador Raymond C. Ewing Oral History; Interviewed by Charles Stuart Kennedy November 29, 1993; The Association for Diplomatic Studies and Training, Foreign Affairs Oral History Project, Department of State

Transcript, Dr. Herbert Kelman; *Beyond Intractability*; Interviewed by Julian Portilla, 2003 (https://www.beyondintractability.org/audiodisplay/kelman-h)

Transcript, Ambassador Nelson C. Ledsky Oral History; Interviewed by Thomas Stern, June 28, 2003; The Association for Diplomatic Studies and Training, Foreign Affairs Oral History Project, Department of State

Transcript, Ambassador John W. McDonald Oral History; Interviewed by John Stuart Kennedy, June 5, 1997; The Association for Diplomatic Studies and Training, Foreign Affairs Oral History Project, Department of State

Transcript John Nix Oral History; Interviewed by Raymond Ewing, February 18, 1997; The Association for Diplomatic Studies and Training, Foreign Affairs Oral History Project, Department of State

Transcript, Ambassador Galen L. Stone Oral History; Interviewed by Malcolm Thompson, April 15, 1988; The Association for Diplomatic Studies and Training, Foreign Affairs Oral History Project, Department of State

Transcript, Cyrus R. Vance Oral History; Interview II, 12/29/69, by Paige E. Mulhollan; Internet Copy, LBJ Library

Transcript Ambassador Thomas G. Weston Oral History; Interviewed by Charles Stuart Kennedy March 4, 2005; The Association for Diplomatic Studies and Training, Foreign Affairs Oral History Project, Department of State

Transcript, Ambassador Fraser Wilkins Oral History; Interviewed by Peter Jessup, July 21, 1988; The Association for Diplomatic Studies and Training, Foreign Affairs Oral History Project, Department of State

Transcript, Ambassador Fraser Wilkins Oral History; A Gift to the John F. Kennedy Library from the General Services Administration and Records Service, March 7, 1976

Transcript, Ambassador James Alan Williams Oral History Interviewed by Ray Ewing October 31, 2003; The Association for Diplomatic Studies and Training, Foreign Affairs Oral History Project, Department of State

INTERVIEWS BY THE AUTHOR

Akcal, Idil; December 23, 2020 (via Zoom), Nicosia, Cyprus

Albayrak, Dr. Eldem; email exchange with Author, May 11, 2022, Famagusta, Cyprus

Anastasiou, Dr. Harry and **Yesilada**, Dr. Birol; February 22, 2018, Portland, Oregon

Angelica, Marion; February 15, 2018, Minneapolis, Minnesota

Antoniou, Chloe and Andrea; November 14, 2019, Nicosia, Cyprus

Antoniades, Aris; November 7, 2019, Limassol, Cyprus

Argyrou, Anna; November 17, 2017; November 17, 2021 (via Zoom) Nicosia, Cyprus; September 27, 2022 (via Zoom), Nicosia, Cyprus

Austrian, Sheila; April 5, 2019 (by phone), Chestertown, Maryland

Azgin, Fatma; November 18, 2017, Nicosia, Cyprus; December 8, 2021 (via Zoom), Nicosia, Cyprus

Ballyntine, Kerri; August 28, 2020 (via Zoom), Raleigh, North Carolina

Balswick, Dr. Jack; December 12, 2017 (by phone), Pasadena, California

Barin, Burcu; November 21, 2017, Nicosia, Cyprus

Barlas, Ceren; May 25, 2020 (via Zoom), Nicosia, Cyprus

Barlas, Pinar; May 15, 2020 (by video), Kyrenia, Cyprus

Baroody, Dr. Judith; July 16, 2016, Arlington, Virginia; September 6, 2019 (by phone) Arlington, Virginia

Berk, Taksim; November 14, 2017, Kyrenia, Cyprus

Boucher, Ambassador Richard; January 26, 2017, Washington, D.C.

Brattain, Steven; July 18, 2018, Washington, D.C.

Brill, Ambassador Kenneth; February 18, 2020, Bethesda, Maryland

Broome, Dr. Benjamin; March 1, 2018, Tempe, Arizona

Chigas, Diana; September 26, 2017, Cambridge, Massachusetts

Clerides, Katie and **Shammas**, Costas; November 16, 2017, Nicosia, Cyprus; July 5, 2021 (via Zoom), Nicosia, Cyprus

Constantinides Bradley, Dr. Margarita; May 2, 2020, Berkeley, California

Constantinou, Loucia; November 12, 2019, Nicosia, Cyprus

Davis, Dr. Tom; November 25, 2019, San Diego, California

Delikurt, Pembe; February 1, 2021 (via Zoom), Kyrenia, Cyprus

Demetriades, Achilleas; November 11, 2019, Nicosia, Cyprus

Demetriades, Lellos; June 22, 2016, Nicosia, Cyprus

Demililer, Sonuc; November 14, 2019, Nicosia, Cyprus

Denktash, Serdar; November 14, 2019, Nicosia, Cyprus

Donahue, Michael; July 20, 2020 (via Zoom), Denver, Colorado

Douglas, Walter; January 23, 2017, Washington, D.C.

Economidou, Katie; December 7, 2021 (via Zoom), Nicosia, Cyprus

Ellickson-Brown, Jim; April 29, 2020 (by phone) Eureka, California

Erkman, Gunfer; November 18, 2019, Nicosia, Cyprus

Ewing, Ambassador Raymond; July 16, 2016, Washington, D.C.

Feissel, Gustave; August 24, 2018 (by phone) Petaluma, California

Felsot, Dr. Allan; November 23, 2020 (via Zoom), Seattle, Washington

Firincioguillari, Olcay; February 5, 2021 (via Zoom), Nicosia, Cyprus

Fisher, Dr. Ronald; May 30, 2018, Washington, D.C.

Floridou, Savina; November 7, 2019, Limassol, Cyprus

Gaber, Hannah; November 21, 2017, Nicosia, Cyprus

Gaber, Dr. Pamela; November 17, 2018, Denver, Colorado

Georgiades, Costas; August 13, 2020 (via Zoom), Maastricht, The Netherlands

Georghiou, Claire, November 15, 2017, Nicosia, Cyprus

Georgiou, Dr. Stellios; April 26, 2021 (via Zoom) Nicosia, Cyprus

Glover, Roy; July 19, 2020 (via Zoom), Christchurch, New Zealand

Graze, Deborah; August 31, 2019 (by phone) Arlington, Virginia

Gursan, Huseyin; November 17, 2017, Nicosia, Cyprus

Hadjiandreou, Eliana; February 25, 2020, State College, Pennsylvania

Hadjiparaskeva, Christina; November 10, 2019, Nicosia, Cyprus

Hadjipavlou, Dr. Maria; November 22, 2017, Nicosia, Cyprus

Hadjittofi, Daniel; November 2017, Nicosia, Cyprus; November 2017, Nicosia, Cyprus; November 2017, Nicosia, Cyprus; November 2017, Nicosia, Cyprus; August 29, 2020 (via Zoom), Nicosia, Cyrus; November 9, 2020 (via Zoom), Nicosia, Cyprus; December 18, 2020 (via Zoom) Nicosia, Cyprus; April 1, 2021 (via Zoom), Nicosia, Cyprus; June 18, 2021 (via Zoom), Nicosia, Cyprus; October 6, 2021 (via Zoom), Nicosia, Cyprus; November 17, 2021 (via Zoom) Nicosia, Cyprus; May 20, 2022 (via Zoom) Nicosia, Cyprus.

Hansen, Dr. Julie; January 16, 2021 (via Zoom), Atlanta, Georgia

Herscher, Dr. Ellen; June 8, 2016, Washington, D.C.

Hicks, Dr. Fred; February 19, 2021, Miami, Florida

Hilmi, Esat; June 2016, Nicosia, Cyprus

Howard, Dan; June 6, 2016, Washington, D.C.; Dan with Mary Howard May 4, 2018, Chantilly, Virginia

Ince, Sarper; November 8, 2017, Nicosia, Cyprus

Jacovides, Ambassador Andrew; January 2017, New York, New York

Joria, Jerry; November 2, 2020 (via Zoom), Washington, D.C.

Joseph, Dr. Lennox; July 13, 2021 (via Zoom), Sifnos, Greece

Josephides, Alexandros; November 7, 2019, Limassol, Cyprus

Jossif, Dr. Antonis; June 5-6, 2022 (email exchange with Author), Nicosia, Cyprus

Kamali, Orcun; November 18, 2019, Kyrenia/Girne, Cyprus

Kamenos, Dr. Andreas; December 6, 2019 (by phone), Nicosia, Cyprus

Kernan, Timothy; May 30, 2018 (by phone) Washington, D.C.

Kibben, Roxanne; August 27, 2017, Schaumburg, Illinois

Kinkead, Dr. Joyce; November 19, 2020 (via Zoom), Logan, Utah

Kirk, Mary; March 9, 2020, Washington, D.C.

Klosson, Ambassador Michael; June 21, 2017, Washington, D.C.

Koenig, Ambassador John; February 20, 2018, Seattle, Washington; April 17, 2020, (via Zoom), Bellingham, Washington

Kostrikis, Dr. Leondios; November 7, 2017, Nicosia, Cyprus

Kuehl, Craig; Spring 2017, New York, New York; June 26, 2020 (via Zoom), New York, New York

Kyriakidou, Kyproula; November 20, 2017, Nicosia Cyprus; June 10, 2020 (via Zoom), Nicosia, Cyprus

Kythreotou Ioli and **Payiata,** Revi; November 5, 2019, Nicosia, Cyprus

Kyza, Dr. Eleni A; November 10, 2021 (via Zoom), Limassol, Cyprus

Laragakis, Nick; April 2, 2019, Washington, D.C.

Larson, Ingrid; May 3, 2019 (by phone), Washington, D.C.

Lazarou, Lazaros; November 13, 2019, Nicosia, Cyprus

Manatos, Andy; May 9, 2018, Washington, D.C.

Markides, Dr. Kyriacos and Markides, Dr. Emily; August 10, 2021 (via Zoom), Orono, Maine

Matsi, Sofia; July 27, 2020 (via Zoom), Nicosia, Cyprus

McCarthy, Dr. Andrew; November 25, 2019, San Diego, California

Michaelides, Dr. Sophocles; November 6, 2019, Nicosia, Cyprus

Michail, Ioanna; November 12, 2019, Limassol, Cyprus

Miller, Tom; April 23, 2020 (by phone), Washington, D.C.

Mouschovias, Dr. Telemachos; August 10, 2020 (via Zoom), Champaign, Illinois.

Ungerleider, Dr. John; April 30, 2017, Brattleboro, Vermont; email exchange with Author, May 15-16, 2022

Uzun, Birkan; July 7, 2020 (via Zoom), Seattle, Washington

Uzunoglu, Doruk; May 4, 2020 (by video), London, U.K.

Uzunoglu, Ipek; November 7, 2019, Nicosia, Cyprus

Van Dusen, Michael; May 18, 2020 (by phone), Washington, D.C.

Van Hollen, Senator Chris; March 27, 2019, Washington, D.C.

Vlassides, Sofoklis; December 12, 2019 (by phone), Koloni, Cyprus

Wagg, Michael; October 25, 2019 (by phone), Grand Rapids, Michigan

Walker, Dr. Anita; March 20, 2020 (via Zoom), Boston, Massachusetts

Wahba, Ambassador Marcelle; July 8, 2016, Washington, D.C.

Williams, Ambassador James and **Ewing**, Ambassador Raymond; March 25, 2018, Washington, D.C.

Wingate, Effie; January 17, 2017, Woodbridge, Virginia

Yaratan; Dr. Hüseyin; November 8, 2019, Nicosia, Cyprus

Yavuz, Dogan; June 2016, Kyrenia, Cyprus; November 11, 2019, Kyrenia, Cyprus

Yiordamli, Ambssador Rea; November 11, 2019, Nicosia, Cyprus

Yukselen, Dr. Mehmet Ali; November 8, 2019, Lefke, Cyprus

Zacharia, Dr. Giorgos; April 2017, Boston, Massachusetts

Zavallis, Stella; November 4, 2017, Nicosia, Cyprus; November 6, 2019, Nicosia, Cyprus

Zoppos, Demetrios; March 21, 2019, (by phone), London, UK

LIST OF PHOTO CREDITS/SOURCES

In order with which they appear in the book

Senator J. William Fulbright | *distributed under a CC-BY 2.0 license*
Maps of Cyprus | *distributed under a CC-BY 2.0 license & Image by Freepik*
Archbishop Makarios of Cyprus | *World Telegram & Sun photo by O. Fernandez distributed under a CC-BY 2.0 license*
Rauf Denktash | *under a CC-BY 2.0 license*
Ambassador Fraser Wilkins | *National Archives – 59-N-VS-2737-57*
Renos Kamenos | *Fulbright Commission photo*
Stella Yiasemidou/Kamenos/Zavallis | *Fulbright Commission photo*
Dr. Sophocle Michaelides | *provided by subject*
Dr. Kenan Atakol | *provided by subject*
Dr. Michael Sarris | *provided by subject*
Mikis Sparsis | *provided by Sparsis family*
Mustafa Raif | *provided by Raif family*
Lellos Demetriades | *provided by subject*
Dr. Chrysotomos Sofianos | *Fulbright Commission photo*
Dr. Mehmet Tahiroglu | *Fulbright Commission photo*
Dr. Ellen Herscher | *provided by subject*
Dr. Stuart and Laina Swiny | *provided by subjects*
Dr. Pamela and Hannah Gaber | *provided by subjects*
Eugene Rossides with President Richard Nixon | *(The Richard Nixon Presidential Library and Museum, 37-whpo-3719-16-i-2020-js.tif)*
Senator Claiborne Pell | *distributed under a CC-BY 2.0 license*
Ambassador Galen Stone | *National Archives – 59-N-VS-217-78*
Dr. Leontios Kostrikis | *provided by subject*
Orcun Kamali | *provided by subject*
House | *Fulbright Commission photo*
Daniel Hadjittofi – at Hamilton College | *provided by subject*
Daniel Hadjittofi | *Fulbright Commission photo*
Achilleas Demetriades | *provided by subject*
Ozdil Nami | *provided by subject*
Dr. Constantinos Pitris | *photo by author*
Marcelle Wahba | *provided by subject*
Katie Clerides and Costas Shammas | *provided by subjects*
Fatma Azgin | *provided by subject*

Katie Economidou | *provided by subject*
Serder Denktash | *provided by subject*
Dr. Louie Diamond | *provided by the Institute for Multi-track Diplomacy*
Diana Chigas | *provided by subject*
Dr. Benjamin Broome | *provided by subject*
History walk photos (3) | *Fulbright Commission photos*
BoldLeaders photos (2) | *Provided by BoldLeaders*
John Ungerleider | *Fulbright Commission photo*
Marco Turk | *CSUDH News: California State University Dominguez*
Board meeting | *Fulbright Commission photo*
Dr. Philippos Patsalis | *provided by Cyprus Institute of Neurology and Genetics*
Harriett Fulbright with Ambassador Michael Bandler | *Fulbright Commission photo*
Evie Sophianou | *provided by the family*
Dr. Nektarios Paisios | *provided by subject*
Pinar Barlas | *provided by subject*
Doruk Uzunoglu | *provided by subject*
Aris Antoniades | *provided by subject*
Eliana Hadjiandreou | *provided by subject*
Gulsen Oztoprak | *provided by subject*
Kyproula Kyriakidou | *provided by subject*
Anna Argyrou | *Fulbright Commission photo*
Fulbright Staff | *photo provided by Anna Argyrou*
Keith Peterson | *Photo taken at the University of Nicosia in 2013. Provided by the author.*

INDEX

ABOUT THE AUTHOR

Keith Peterson served 30 years with the United States Information Agency and the Department of State as a press and cultural officer. He served twice in Cyprus, in 1989-90 as the Assistant Public Affairs Officer and in 2011-14 as Public Affairs Officer.   In both postings he served on the Board of the Cyprus Fulbright Commission, first as the alternate to Board Chairman Lane Cubstead and, in 2011-14, as Chairman of the Board.

Prior to joining the Foreign Service in 1986, he was a print journalist with the Mankato (Minnesota) Free Press and the Daily and Sunday Herald based in Arlington Heights, Illinois. In his last three years with the Herald he was its chief editorial writer.   Since his retirement from the Foreign Service in 2015, he regularly contributes opinion articles to The Herald on foreign policy and government topics.

He earned B.S. and M.A. degrees in journalism at Northern Illinois University, where he was an editor and columnist for the university's nationally recognized student newspaper.   He did graduate studies in comparative social structures and international politics at the University of Stockholm (Sweden) and earned an M.A. in national security studies at the National Defense University at Ft. McNair in Washington, D.C.

He lives in Lake Barrington, Illinois and Punta Gorda, Florida.